SCOTTISH CASTLES

SCOTTISH CASTLES

by

Stewart Ross

LINE ILLUSTRATIONS BY
David Simon

LOCHAR PUBLISHING,
MOFFAT

In affectionate memory of my father

Published by Lochar Publishing Ltd
MOFFAT DG10 9JU
British Library Cataloguing in Publication Data
Ross, Stewart
Scottish Castles
1. Scotland. Castles — Visitors' guides
I. Title
ISBN 0-948403-36-5
(ISBN 0-948403-37-3 pbk)
Typeset in in 10 on 12pt Palatino by Annandale Press Services, Moffat

CONTENTS

ACKNOWLEDGEMENTS

The author is most grateful to the Taylor and Swan households for the generous hospitality they gave him while he was driving about the country researching this book. He would also like to thank Jim Hutcheson and David Simon for their invaluable help with the illustrations. Many curators and guides gave generously of their time, and the book would be a good deal duller without their witty and knowledgeable contributions. The comments and criticisms of two indefatigable proof-readers, Graeme and Irma Stewart-Ross, have saved the author from countless blunders and obscurities; his debt to them is enormous. Once again, however, his especial thanks are reserved for four understanding children, and for Lucy, without whose patience and remarkable typing skills this book would never have appeared on time, if at all.

S P E C I A L   N O T E

Many sites offer reduced rates for different categories such as advance bookings and group tickets. Details of these and possible alterations in opening times are available from individual castles, the Scottish Development Department (Tel: 031-244-3086) and the National Trust for Scotland (Tel: 031-226-5922).

While every effort has been made to ensure that all information given in *Scottish Castles* is correct, the publishers hereby disclaim liability to any party for loss or damage caused by errors or omissions, whether they result from negligence, accident or any other cause.

PHOTOGRAPHS OF DUNROBIN (p.179)
by DAVID SIM, PHOTOGRAPHER,
GOLSPIE, SUTHERLAND.

PREFACE

Most books are attempts at communicating enthusiasms. This one is no exception. Ever since school holidays spent grinding round the Highlands in an underpowered old Austin, I have been fascinated by the majesty, romance and sheer profusion of Scotland's castles. Like windmills in Holland or parish churches in England, castles are such an essential part of the Scottish landscape that it is almost impossible to imagine it without them.

But admiring a grand or beautiful object is not the same as understanding it, and generally the more one knows about a work of art and its creator the more one can appreciate it. The purpose of this book, therefore, is to pass on the author's love of his subject and perhaps encourage those new to the field to examine it more closely, in the certain knowledge that they will not be disappointed.

One or two words of caution. The book is unavoidably subjective in its selection of material and in the way it is handled, and the reader is asked to bear in mind that no two people's reaction to a building can ever be precisely the same. Nevertheless, I have tried to be fair and give praise where it is clearly due. Secondly, those who pick up this book expecting to find an academic manual will be disappointed. This is not a work limited specifically to architecture, and technical terms have been kept to a minimum. It deals instead with each castle as a totality, as a building and as a glass through which we may glimpse the past. I have given as much attention to a castle's history, both real and legendary, as to the structure itself. The flavour of the resultant pot-pourri of description and story may not meet with the approval of purists; though I hope that it may inform, amuse and perhaps even inspire those who wish to know something more about Scotland's wonderful heritage.

SUMMITS OLD IN STORY

Scotland is justly famous for its castles. Most of the humble dwellings of the nation's peasantry vanished long ago; comparatively few monuments to the dignity of the commercial classes remain from before the eighteenth century; and only a handful of aristocrats were able to afford stately homes to equal those found in more prosperous countries. But at castle building the Scots excelled. It was a passion for them, and they constructed fortifications of spectacular grace and flamboyance even when they were no longer strictly necessary for purposes of security. The countryside was ideally suited to their task. It furnished ample supplies of agreeable materials and the coastline, glens and mountains provided excellent defensive sites. Furthermore, the natural grandeur of the landscape ensured that almost every stronghold was set against an attractive background. The result is a remarkable display of defensive architecture, without strategic or aesthetic parallel in the Western world.

Scotland's castles are essential sign posts on the road to the past, the footprints of former generations upon the landscape. No one who wishes to understand the country's vigorous heritage can afford to pass by such tangible links with history, whose capacity to translate us to another time is both powerful and, on occasion, surprisingly disconcerting. To round a bend on the highway beside Loch Duich and behold the island citadel of Eilean Donan, or to glimpse the bulk of Crichton through the trees beside the Tyne, is suddenly to be brought face to face with another culture.

Although castles tell us much about the time in which they were built, they are more than just archives in stone. They have architectural significance as well as historical importance. Together with abbeys and cathedrals, castles were the greatest creations of their time, erected at vast expense by the most skilled craftsmen of their generation. They were not only shelters but displays, built to impress those who saw them with their owner's magnificence and good taste. Defensive strength alone was insufficient to do this. Whether in ruins or standing much as they did when they were built, they retain a stirring combination of power, majesty and beauty.

From the late thirteenth century until the accession of William and Mary in 1689 Scotland's history was painfully turbulent. Periods of stability were punctuated with long years of strife, when central control broke down and power passed into the hands of local chiefs and magnates. In such conditions all prudent men of means constructed dwellings capable of protecting their families and goods from marauders. As a result, the country is peppered with castles of every size and description. Estimates of their number vary from about 1,200 to 2,000. The reason for the discrepancy is not connected with powers of observation or scholarship but with definition. The higher figure includes all defensive structures, from primitive hillforts to Hanoverian garrisons. To avoid

GURNESS BROCH
Though the history of brochs remains shrouded in uncertainty these unique
Scottish refuges retain a special fascination for the modern visitor.

confusion this book concentrates primarily on buildings which bear the title 'castle'. Thus Floors is included, though it has no defensive pretensions whatsoever, yet Falkland Palace, with its towers and turrets, is omitted. The distinction may be somewhat arbitrary, but at least it has the merit of simplicity.

Classification is also tricky. Historians and specialist architects prefer a chronological approach, guide books divide castles by region, and comprehensive catalogues usually list their entries in alphabetical order. Since none of these presentations are particularly suitable here, the reader will find castles distinguished by a combination of venue and style. For example, there is a section on lochside castles, not because such castles exhibit similar architectural characteristics, but because they are an identifiable feature of the Scottish scene.

Within each category the choice is unavoidably subjective. The castles which have been selected are good examples of the class in which they are placed, open to the public, reasonably accessible, and capable of firing the imagination of the amateur (so the interest in never purely archaeological). Above all, they appeal to the author — which means, of course, that their inclusion may rest on the simple fact that the sun was shining on the occasions when he visited them.

GRASSY MOUNDS

Although every form of home is in some senses a castle, providing shelter against the elements and some sort of protection for people and possessions against thieves and marauders, the Celts were the first people living in Scotland to construct structures for more than incidental defence. Celtic hillforts were built in the first millenium BC and some, like Traprain Law in East Lothian, were inhabited for over a thousand years. They were sometimes of a gigantic size, more like fortified towns than castles. Eildon Hill North (Melrose) covered more than sixteen hectares and held a population of up to 2,000 people, housed in some 300 wooden huts. The degree of sophistication achieved by the Selgovae who lived there was considerable, for in order to provision their capital they must have engaged in complex patterns of trade and maintained a strict control over local agriculture. The excellent positioning of the settlement, which dominates the fords of the upper Tweed and offers clear views over the Cheviots to the south, was confirmed by the Romans, who raised a tall signal tower on the hill in the first century AD.

Given the primitive nature of Celtic weaponry, a well-manned hillfort must have been almost impregnable. Castle Law (Abernethy) was surrounded by a stone wall six metres thick, before which in some places an extra rampart was thrown up. The inhabitants also hewed out a large basin from the rock on which the fort stands, to serve as a cistern for drinking water at time of siege. No doubt in settled times it doubled as a fish tank. The fort on Eildon Hill was protected by three concentric earthen ramparts, each well over a kilometre in length. The engineers of Traprain Law faced their outer wall with stone, rendering virtually unassailable the craggy volcanic mound which lies like a recumbent beast guarding the lower reaches of the River Tyne.

The Romans were professional fort builders. Although they were ultimately unable to subdue Scotland and had to be content with Hadrian's Wall as their northern frontier in the British Isles, they moved further north in strength on several occasions. Fearful of the capacity of the local tribes to strike with sudden and devastating ferocity, they marked their progress with a series of fortified camps, watch-towers and armed signal posts. They arrived in Scotland as conquerors but their presence there was never secure enough for Roman civilisation to take root. There are no remains of villas, baths, theatres or similar manifestations of peaceful colonisation.

The Romans employed two principal routes into Scotland. The westerly one ran north from Carlisle, up Annandale towards the Clyde; that in the east (known in medieval times as Dere Street) led from York, through Redesdale, over the Tweed at Newstead and thence by way of Lauderdale to Lothian and the Forth. They approximate to the present-day paths of the A7 and A68. The sites of Roman camps have been identified along both these highways, although the casual tourist needs fair weather and a healthy imagination to make much of the grassy undulations which indicate the passing presence of Europe's mightiest empire. The most spectacular remains of Roman military occupation in Scotland are the Antonine Wall, built between the Clyde and the Forth, and Ardoch Fort, the site of which can be seen to the left of the A822 north of Bracco. But neither of these two monuments are as exciting as the brochs, contemporary strongholds built by the indigenous population.

THE BROCHS

The sites of about 500 brochs have been identified. Most are in the north and west of the country but they also occur as far south as Galloway. They are deeply mysterious structures. Clearly each one was carefully sited and meticulously crafted; and yet we know little about who built them and even less about the reasons for their construction.

Most brochs are now in ruins. The best surviving example stands on the western shore of the tiny Shetland island of Mousa, guarding the passage of Mousa Sound. It looks like a quaint cooling tower, tapering from a diameter of fifteen metres at the base to twelve metres at the wall head, some thirteen metres above the ground. Although the walls are solid at the bottom, where they are five metres thick, for most of their height they are double skinned, with tie stones placed at intervals to form galleries. Only by employing such a sophisticated design could stone walls be raised so high without the use of mortar. The cavity also houses a stairway. Huge slices of stone partitioned the inner courtyard and the tapering interior was once divided by wooden floors. The whole structure was presumably covered with some form of timber roof. Originally there may also have been a fighting platform around the summit. By the Middle Ages the original wooden partitions and roofing had rotted away, for when the doughty Donald Cam MacAulay cornered a party of Morrison cattle rustlers in Dun Carloway Broch (Lewis), he managed to scale the outer wall using his skean and smoke out the caterans by casting burning heather upon them.

The brochs were not built by a dominant aristocracy to overawe the local populace, as was the case with Norman castles in England. If this had been their purpose, the brochs would have been built inland, not on the coast. The towers had only one narrow doorway, leading through a dark tunnel in the wall to the interior, and most were served by internal wells. These observations suggest that they were not just impressive dwellings but places of refuge. Furthermore, though they are of remarkably similar design, they were not put up as part of some Celtic Maginot Line, master-minded by a single government. One expert has argued that they were keeps in which the Picts sheltered from the raids of slaving parties organised by the Romans or their henchmen. It is more likely, however, that they were not built with one such specific purpose in mind or even at roughly the same time, but that they evolved over hundreds of years. If this were the case, of course, there is no reason why those dwelling within the shadow of a broch should not have sheltered in it when threatened by slavers or any other marauders.

Brochs usually appear in clusters on fertile land. In the first century AD they were surrounded by dwellings and protected by outer earthworks. We do not know whether they were permanently inhabited or simply held ready for use when danger threatened, like air-raid shelters. Nevertheless, for all their mystery, the brochs of Scotland — the country's earliest form of castle — are a unique contribution to European architecture. A visit to Mousa or Dun Carloway takes the visitor directly back to the Dark Ages and beyond, to the very beginnings of the nation's recorded history.

K E E P S   O F   T H E   N O R S E M E N

Rothesay Castle on the Isle of Bute is a magnificent medieval fortress, complete with water-filled moat, curtain-walled keep (unique in Scotland) and an impressively restored great tower. Begun in the twelfth century, it was the first in a new generation of castles, the mighty stone fortresses of the Middle Ages, distinguished by their elaborate arrangement of tower, wall, ditch and battlement. However, there is little continuity in early Scottish castle building: between Mousa Broch and Rothesay Castle there is something of a lacuna. Kenneth MacAlpin and his successors obviously had fortified bases and palaces, yet next to nothing of them remains. In fact, it was not Scots but

Edinburgh Castle, one of the most famous urban landmarks in the world.

Eildon Hill North, whose broad summit supported a large sophisticated settlement in pre-Roman times.

The eleventh-century round tower at Abernethy. It probably served as a look-out post as well as a place of refuge.

Norsemen who were responsible for the erection of the oldest surviving stone castles on Scottish soil. Three fine examples remain: Cubbie Roo's Castle at Wyre on Orkney, Old Wick in Caithness and Castle Sween in Argyll.

Kolbein Hruga, known in the neighbourhood simply as 'Kobbie', was a prosperous twelfth-century Orkney landowner. To protect his family and household from marauders he built a stone tower, a form of medieval broch, about fifteen metres tall, eight metres across, with dense, mortared walls two metres thick. Access was through a doorway on the first floor, and a carved stone tank ensured that the occupants had sufficient drinking water to survive a lengthy siege. The keep was surrounded by a ditch and bank, topped with a stone wall. Kobbie's durable stronghold, albeit somewhat truncated, remains overlooking the Wyre Sound to this day.

The castle at Old Wick was built at about the same time as Cubbie Roo's and is of similar layout. Steep, sea-friezed cliffs afford protection on three sides. A ditch, rampart and some form of gatehouse closed the approach on the landward side. The base of the tower, which was originally somewhat taller than its Orkney counterpart, still stands four square and solid, jutting into the North Sea. Mariners know it as the Old Man of Wick. It has been noted that it is similar to some early Provencal castles, suggesting that the design may have been imported into Scotland by twelfth-century Norse crusaders.

Castle Sween is located on the east side of sea Loch Sween, which bites into western Argyll's Knapdale peninsular. It excites the interest of archaeologists and historians more than any other early castle, for not only is it ancient (the oldest castle in Scotland), but it is large and very well preserved. No one knows who built it. It may have been Suibhne, an eleventh-century magnate of the west, or Godred II King of Man, or even a Danish prince, Sueno. Whoever it was, he raised a fine fortress, approximately square in shape, with towering buttressed walls almost two metres thick, broadened around the ground floor entrance to afford increased protection. Towers were added later, the original accommodation being in wooden chambers within the enclosed courtyard, which also housed a well in the north-east corner. Stone steps lead to a walled parapet circling the wall head. The sophisticated design, quality of construction and aesthetic harmony of Sween were well ahead of their time. Although built in the eleventh or twelfth century, it saw active service at the time of Robert Bruce and was not finally rendered uninhabitable until the wars of the mid-seventeenth century. Fortunately the destruction was not extensive, and the father of Scottish castles remains a surprising monument to the skill and originality of its builders.

MOTTE AND BAILEY

The stone-built Viking keeps of the north and west were unusual for their time. A far more common form of castle in early medieval Scotland was the

Duffus Castle near Elgin. The fortress' man-made mound still towers menacingly over the surrounding farmland.

The motte of a twelfth-century castle was usually built to accommodate a light timber pallisade. When this was replaced at Duffus with a massive stone keep the result was disastrous, as this photograph illustrates.

motte and bailey. This was originally a Norman import, introduced by foreign aristocrats from the south, such as the Bruces and the Balliols, but soon copied by native Scots. Motte and bailey castles, which first appeared in the twelfth century, were the symbol and substance of Scottish feudalism, tangible reminders to those dwelling outside their embrace that now they had new and powerful masters.

The arrangement of a motte and bailey castle was simple. It consisted of two adjacent mounds, one steeper and taller than the other. A wooden keep was built on the higher of the two, protected by a palisade and ditch. The lower mound was similarly circumvallated, and the whole fortress was united by a further palisade and ditch enclosing both mounds. About 250 of these castles were raised in Scotland, mostly in traditionally troublesome areas such as Galloway, Moray and the Mearns. Since the buildings were of timber construction, the work of carpenters rather than stonemasons, nothing of them is left. This makes a visit to a motte and bailey castle somewhat unrewarding, for one is confronted with anonymous grassy mounds and undulations similar to those of a Roman or prehistoric site. They are best viewed from the air, a privilege afforded to few tourists. Nevertheless, three or four sites merit attention.

Urquhart is interesting because the builders used a natural mound of rock for their bailey and an impressive later castle still stands on the site. A motte can still be seen at Huntly, beside the bronze-coloured ruin of a lovely fifteenth and sixteenth-century castle. The Motte of Urr, north of Dalbeattie, is the site of the most extensive Anglo-Norman castle, probably put up by the de Berkeleys but soon taken over by the Balliols. Duffus Castle is also well worth a visit. It was built amid the swampy countryside north of Elgin in the mid-twelfth century, by the Flemish immigrant Freskin. Such flat terrain was ideal for the display of a timber-topped motte. But the gravely earth of the mound was wholly unsuited to bear the weight of the stone keep which was added about 150 years later: the new tower split, and the north-west corner, its masonry still intact, slipped gracefully downhill towards the inner moat. Duffus is best viewed from a distance, enabling one to appreciate the castle's domination over the farmland stretching away on every side.

CAERLAVEROCK CASTLE
An enchanting shield-shaped fortress on the banks of the Solway Firth.

Dirleton Castle in Lothian, a sophisticated medieval fortress whose ancient walls proved no match for the cannon of Cromwell's all-conquering New Model Army.

CITADELS IN STONE

This chapter concerns the medieval fortress at its most magnificent. In the later Middle Ages the three buildings outlined here, with their drawbridges, coned towers and lofty battlements, conformed very much to the idea of a castle favoured by illustrated children's history books and the film industry. But, as the reader will realise, the popular image is a static and simplistic one. Castles were not just bases for knights in unstained armour; they were living communities of soldiers, administrators, craftsmen and labourers. And the places in which they worked were continually updated in line with current military thinking and the domestic requirements of the demanding aristocrats who dwelt within their walls.

By the later thirteenth century dour keeps and combustible wooden towers had been replaced by sweeping curtain walls of smooth stone, protected at intervals by massive drum towers. These two developments enabled defenders to harass their assailants from either flank as well as from the wall head. An imposing gatehouse had taken the place of an inner defensive keep, reinforcing the castle where it was most vulnerable and daring the foe to venture an assault. The castle was now more a statement of power than a place of retreat. With this type of fortress European military architecture reached a spectacular peak. The glory was short-lived, however, for by the middle of the next century the cannon was emerging as a new and devastating weapon, capable of battering the stoutest wall to rubble and necessitating a revolution in defensive design.

Several castles mark the transition from the simple box shape to the sophisticated cycloid. Rothesay was originally a circle of curtain wall, sometimes known as a shell keep, to which four rounded towers were added later. The ground plans of Dunstaffnage and Inverlochy are basically square, with towers projecting at the corners. But it was through the doorways, not the uninterrupted stone walls or towers, that assailants stood the best chance of effecting an entrance, and consequently it was here that thirteenth-century engineers concentrated their defences. The idea for this development came from the Byzantine castles encountered by the crusaders, often to their cost. Concentric defence was another oriental import. This concept involved successive rings of defence, each inner circle higher than the one outside it, enabling defenders to fire upon assailants from every part of the castle. No truly concentric castle was built in Scotland, although Caerlaverock probably incorporated some features of the design.

Only a few really large castles were built in Scotland in the pre-gunpowder heyday. Nevertheless, those chosen here enable the visitor to imagine without too much difficulty how splendid this type of fortress must have appeared with all its walls and towers intact. Kildrummy, once the most powerful castle in northern Scotland, is the most difficult to interpret, for much of the upper walls have collapsed. Although smaller, Dirleton is today physically more impressive. Both castles boast proud histories. The same can be said of our third example, Caerlaverock, which is also one of the loveliest ancient monuments in Europe.

D I R L E T O N   C A S T L E

Dirleton, Lothian Region

Dirleton is a picturesque village lying just above a coastal loop off the Great North Road at the mouth of the Firth of Forth. Part of the hamlet's charm is its broad green, ringed on one side by neat seventeenth- and eighteenth-century houses and bordered on the other by the walled policies of Dirleton Castle. A pleasanter seat one could hardly imagine.

The castle surmounts an igneous outcrop that once dominated the prosperous barony of Dirleton, and is surrounded by broad flower beds and mature trees laid out in the former barmkin. The setting is unusually gentle for a country whose castles generally occupy more rugged positions, and before crossing the bridge to the monument itself the visitor is well advised to wander through the gardens in order to take in the civilised and compact beauty of the site. Dirleton's evocative southern aspect, furthest from the garden gates, is well preserved and affords an accurate impression of what the castle must have looked like in the later Middle Ages.

Three families were principally responsible for the construction and modification of Dirleton over the centuries. The first stone castle was built by the Anglo-Norman baron John de Vaux, seneschal to Alexander II's wife Marie de Coucy. Like Kildrummy, the design of Dirleton was influenced by the contemporary fortress erected by Marie's father at Chateau-le-Coucy in France, and when finished Dirleton was probably the most up-to-date castle in Scotland. In the fourteenth century the barony was acquired by the Halyburtons, who rebuilt much of the castle over a number of years, making provision for gun platforms and extending the accommodation. In 1515 the estate changed hands again, this time passing to the Ruthven family. Once again the castle's structure was modernised. New living quarters were added and formal gardens were planted at the foot of the stone steps descending from a door in the west wall. There were further changes in ownership before the current proprietors moved to a new house at Archesfield shortly after the Restoration of the Stuart monarchy in 1660, and the building was allowed to fall into disrepair.

Apart from its obvious aesthetic and architectural appeal, Dirleton is

The eastern side of Caerlaverock, showing the ruined south-eastern tower and the large windows punched in the curtain wall to allow light into the Earl of Nithsdale's new apartments.

famous for the part it played in the Wars of Independence and the seventeenth-century Civil Wars. It is also remembered for its association with the turbulent Ruthvens, who owned the castle between 1515 and 1600. Patrick, the 3rd Lord Ruthven, was a leading supporter of the Protestant Reformation and chief among the conspirators who in 1566 murdered David Rizzio, the unfortunate secretary of Mary Queen of Scots. Patrick's son William was created Earl of Gowrie in 1581. The following year, in an attempt to break the Catholic Earl of Arran's hold on the administration, he seized the young James VI and held him for a while at Ruthven House near Perth. The power of the Ruthvens was finally crushed in 1600, when the 3rd Earl and his brother were murdered for allegedly attempting to assassinate James VI.

In the summer of 1649 the castle featured in an even less glorious episode. The 'Dirleton Witches' were a group of wretched men and women upon whom local busybodies claimed to recognise the marks of the Devil. The victims were persuaded to make unlikely confessions, then incarcerated in Dirleton's cramped vaults. A while later they were brought out to face death by strangulation. Their bodies were burned.

THE CASTLE

Nothing remains of the castle which originally crowned Dirleton rock, though it was probably a motte and bailey fortress, built in timber and surrounded by a ditch. The mention of a 'castellum de Dyrlton' in 1225 probably refers to this structure, which was dismantled in the second quarter of the thirteenth century to make way for the de Vaux castle.

The best remaining example of de Vaux's work is perched on the southern edge of the rock. It consists of a massive round tower, splayed at the bottom to hamper undermining and rising to a formidable height above the surrounding ditch. The summit is now sadly vandalised, but originally it was probably crenellated and adorned with an overhanging wooden parapet. For many years the tower provided the castle's principal accommodation. The gloomy lower chamber, lit only by arrow slits, was considered fit only for soldiers and servants. The more comfortable room above was reserved for the lord and those close to him. It is an attractive polygonal shape, with a vaulted roof, four windows (three with built-in stone seats) which admit plenty of light, and a fine thirteenth-century fireplace. The room has easy access to a small private chamber in the adjoining square tower which was furnished with its own privy. (It is a pity that many guide books persist in calling a privy a 'garderobe'. The term may meet with academic approval, but the shorter word is equally accurate and far less confusing. The uninitiated, particularly children, all too readily assume overhanging 'garderobe' apertures to have been built for dispensing boiling pitch on the heads of assailants, when their real discharge was in fact a good deal more noxious, if not quite so dangerous.)

The de Vaux Tower was one of four built to defend the castle's vulnerable

For some inexplicable reason the eastern end of Kildrummy's chapel (visible behind the tower in the foreground) was permitted to project through the castle's curtain wall, thus producing a dangerously vulnerable point in the defences.

The drawbridge pit at Kildrummy. On the left is the small opening for the postern gate, which was secured with a wooden bar housed in the square hole behind the doorway.

southern wall, where the entrance was situated. A tower similar in size to the one already described once loomed to the east of the gate, but unfortunately it has been demolished and partly built over. The two remaining towers — one square, the other round — linked with that in the south to form a sort of keep or donjon. They are closely grouped around the entrance in a configuration unique in Scotland. This is the earliest example in the country of defences being clustered at the castle's weakest point, a trend which is most clearly illustrated by Caerlaverock. In the Middle Ages Dirleton was approached over a wooden bridge across the moat. The main entrance was defended by a drawbridge, set between two turreted stone walls known as jambs, and the passage beyond was protected by two portcullises, which retracted into the room above when not in use, and two double oak doors.

After the Wars of Independence the de Vaux castle was in a poor state of repair, probably as a result of Robert Bruce's policy of slighting the castles he recaptured from the English. Nevertheless the Halyburtons set about reconstruction with vigour. The present entrance and almost all the eastern side of the castle is their work. By filling in part of the ditch they built a spacious residence over and beyond the eastern curtain wall. The courtyard was crammed with a chapel, bakery, guardhouse and other smaller rooms. As the attractive but cramped accommodation in the south tower was no longer deemed large or grand enough, new kitchens and a Great Hall were constructed over the complex of service buildings. The lord and his immediate household were provided with a more spacious solar, or 'chamber of dais', which led off the northern end of the hall.

Though the Halyburton castle combined spacious accommodation with stout defence, it was still essentially a medieval building. This was not good enough for the Gowries, a go-ahead family who were close to the king and eager to display their patronage of the most up-to-date styles. At the back of the old de Vaux agglomeration of towers they constructed a comfortable three-storey residence, fashionable yet still rendered defensible by heavy grilles over the windows and several well-positioned gun ports. On the floor of the first storey they laid glazed tiles of the latest design, and below the castle walls they set out a formal garden. It was planted with holly and yew trees, and possibly incorporated the bowling green which is still in use to this day. Thus the wealth and good taste of the Ruthvens converted a centuries-old castle into what a contemporary described as 'the pleasantest dwelling in Scotland'.

THE MIGHT OF THE ENGLISH

After the death of the infant Queen Margaret in 1290, it fell to England's Edward I to settle the disputed succession to the Scottish throne. Edward willingly fulfilled his feudal obligation, and after extensive consultation nominated his vassal John Balliol as Margaret's successor. An astute and ambitious politician, Edward was not one to let slip such an excellent opportunity to extend his authority into Scotland, and before long his overbearing demands had forced King John to renounce his allegiance and rise in revolt.

In 1296 Edward marched north, overthrew Balliol, crushed Scottish resistance and returned south. Two years later he was back, this time to confront the nationalist uprising led by Sir William Wallace. Edward's army moved up the eastern side of the country towards the Forth, hoping to rendezvous there with supply ships from the south. In July a large detachment from Edward's army was ordered to take Dirleton Castle, a dangerous threat to Edward's right flank.

The siege was commanded by Anthony Bek, Bishop of Durham, one of Edward's principal advisors and reputed to be the wealthiest baron in the kingdom. Although in holy orders, he was a practical man of affairs, a politician and castle builder with an extensive knowledge of military matters. Even so, he found the towered citadel of Dirleton a difficult nut to crack. For several days his undernourished and lightly-armed soldiers tried in vain to break through the castle's defences, but each assault was bloodily repulsed by missiles and liquids hurled down upon the English from the battlements above. De Vaux and his masons had done their work well — Dirleton was proof against conventional assault.

Edward I was a general of distinction, with a passion for the latest military technology. Hearing of Bek's problems, he sent the bishop fresh supplies and, more importantly, giant siege engines.

In the days before gunpowder there were several methods of attacking a castle. Bek's original tactic of frontal assault with ladders and battering rams was swift and cheap, but ineffective against a fortress like Dirleton, with thick walls and a broad moat. Though mining could be tried on softer soils, on Dirleton's rock it was not even worth considering. That left treachery, starvation or the tactic favoured by Edward — bombardment. There were three principal types of assault machine: the ballista, a giant crossbow which fired immense iron darts; the mangonel, a stone-throwing catapult powered by twisted ropes; and the trebuchet, a form of giant see-saw which hurled a missile into the air when the massive counter-weight on the other end of the arm was allowed to fall. The largest trebuchets could hurl a 150 kg stone at least 100 m.

The morale of the Dirleton garrison plummeted as soon as the awesome machines sent by the English king lumbered into sight. Since there was no chance of their being relieved, the Scots knew that it would now be only a matter of days before they were forced to capitulate. And so it turned out. The walls were soon breached, and the dispirited garrison obliged to come to terms. They surrendered the castle to the English but were permitted to go free and keep their personal possessions.

Dirleton faced its last assault three and a half centuries later. Once again it was the English who stood outside its walls. Inside was a band of moss-troopers, Royalist irregulars who had been harassing the supply lines of Oliver Cromwell's republican army of occupation. The siege, if the minutes-long attack merits such a title, is a perfect example of how cannon had rendered the stone castle obsolete. The fourth mortar shot of Major General Lambert's artillery bombardment smashed the drawbridge and doorway, killing the officer responsible for that section of the defences. The garrison surrendered at once, handing over their weapons and the English prisoners they had taken. General Monk, who was in overall charge of the English operation, was a good deal less generous than Bishop Bek had been, and he executed three of the troopers' leaders on the spot.

INFORMATION

ACCESS   Via the A 198. The castle entrance is beside the village green.
Public transport

RESPONSIBILITY FOR THE SITE
        Scottish Development Department

TELEPHONE 0620-85330

OPENING HOURS
        April–September: 09.30–19.00
(Sun 14.00–19.00)

        October–March: 09.30–16.00
(Sun 14.00–16.00)

ADMISSION PRICE
        £1.00 (Senior citizens and children 50p)

FACILITIES   Disabled (limited)
Parking
Dogs (on lead)
Toilets (on village green)
Guided tours by special request

KILDRUMMY CASTLE

Kildrummy, Grampian Region

'Wherever you are in Gordon', announces the District's glossy tourist brochure, 'you are never far from a castle.' Although the same could probably be said of anywhere in the British Isles, Gordon does have a point, for the area is thick with castles of one sort or another. It has made the most of its heritage by organising a well-signposted Castle Trail leading for 150 miles around the District, taking in nine historic houses and castles. The reason for the area's abundance of fortified residences is not hard to find, for it straddles the vital east coast routes leading from Perth to the fertile north-eastern plain. In medieval times the region lay between the rebellious northern province of Moray, which harboured pretenders to the Scottish throne well into the thirteenth century, and the equally lawless Mearns to the south. Equidistant between the two, on the upper boundary of the ancient Earldom of Mar, stood the mighty Kildrummy Castle, dominating a strategically vital crossing of the River Don. It was the most powerful medieval castle in northern Scotland.

The ruins of Kildrummy Castle stand facing open fields on the crest of a ridge beside the A97, and to reach them the visitor must climb a narrow fenced path which leads from the car park. Although the convex hillside is not particularly steep, it is some while before the castle can be seen. This means that though siege machines could have been established here without too much difficulty, it would have been tricky for those manning them to find their range and ascertain the effectiveness of the bombardment. A more attractive view of the castle, and one which better demonstrates the strength of the site, is to be had from the Black Den of Kildrummy Gardens in the steep ravine to the north-west.

Kildrummy is not the most instantly rewarding of monuments to visit, for the castle is much devastated; the traveller needs time to become familiar with the site and allow the imagination slowly to reconstruct the noble towers and sweeping walls which once so impressed all who beheld them. Unfortunately this is rather difficult in summer months because the ruin is used as the backdrop for an exhibition of local sculpture. Striking though the images of the late twentieth century may be, livid metal frameworks and other obscure constructions sit awkwardly against the castle's weathered walls, distracting the eye and, even more infuriating, making photography almost impossible. Nevertheless, armed with Christopher Tabraham's first-class guide book (available at the entrance) and blessed with a fine day, the visitor with an hour or so to spare will find Kildrummy just as rewarding as any other major castle. Like a Scott novel, one must persevere to get the best out of it.

THE CASTLE

A stone castle was built at Kildrummy towards the end of the first half of the thirteenth century, probably following the rebellion of Moray in 1230. Those of a romantic disposition like to credit the design to Sir Gilbert, the multi-talented cleric from Duffus who was archdeacon of Moray (hence his title *de Moravia*) then Bishop of Caithness. It is more likely, however, that the castle was the work of William, Chamberlain of Scotland one of the Celtic Earls of Mar, who was related by marriage to the powerful Comyn family. The raising of a stout and loyal fortress at such a strategically vital point in the Highlands was almost certainly welcomed by the king, Alexander II (1198–1249).

The original plan was for a shield-shaped enceinte, with a massive keep at the rear. This structure, known as the Snow Tower, apparently bore a close resemblance to the donjon of Coucy-le-Chateau in France, erected by Duke Enguerrand, the father of Alexander II's second wife Marie. A similar continental influence has already been noticed at Dirleton and also exists at Bothwell, indicating how close thirteenth-century Scotland was to the mainstream of European military architecture.

Kildrummy's curtain walls were built of coursed rubble. Where the walls changed direction they were reinforced by projecting round towers, whose long arrow-slits are still a prominent feature of the castle's exterior. The northern

The windows of the first floor chapel at
Kildrummy. The small niche on the left was
probably used for storing the host and valuable
articles of silverware.

One of the neo-classical windows in the facade
of the courtyard block at Caerlaverock, erected
just before the outbreak of civil war in the
middle of the seventeenth century.

wall, facing the natural defence of the Black Den, was rebuilt later in more carefully shaped stone.

A great castle was not just a place of defence but a dwelling place for the lord, his family and their retainers. Indeed, the size of Kildrummy and the height of its fortifications seem to have been designed more to impress than offer first-rate defence. Thirteenth-century Scotland was an unusually settled realm, and as long as the castle could hold out against marauding parties from the north, equipped with little more than hand-held weapons, it served its military purpose well. This is apparent from the way the first-floor chapel, added after the original walls had been completed, was given an exact east-west orientation. This position defied all military good sense, for it left the east end of the building jutting through the curtain wall. To make matters worse, the projecting stonework was pierced with three attractive lancet windows, large enough for a man to squeeze through. When the Hammer of the Scots visited the castle in 1296 he must have smiled at the trusting naivety of those foe who had permitted such a bizarre weakening of the castle's defences: it was almost as if the lancets had been inserted as a target for siege catapults. One of Edward's first acts was to order the building of a new round tower to enclose the protruding chapel. The foundations of this structure can be seen in the grass below the window. We are told that Edward's tower was not completed and may never have shielded the vulnerable point above it. Nevertheless, owing to Edward's foresight or assailants' unwillingness to desecrate, the chapel window remains intact, a striking reminder that the medieval Scot feared God quite as much as his neighbour.

Accommodation was provided in Kildrummy by the round towers, a Great Hall along the north wall, with a more private chamber at its upper end, and later by a sixteenth-century tower house, built by the Elphinstones between the Great Hall and the Snow Tower. The Great Hall was clearly a fine building. Because its outer wall faced onto the ravine and was therefore safe from bombardment, the architect furnished it with four windows, each with stone seats which would no doubt have doubled as firing platforms. The lord's chamber at the western end of the hall was demolished to make way for the Elphinstone tower. It is often said that castles were cold and uncomfortable dwellings. Judged by modern standards they undoubtably were. Yet apparent among the ruins of Kildrummy are several fireplaces and many privies, suggesting that, compared with the rough and insanitary wooden dwellings of ordinary folk, this castle at least was a luxury residence, fitted with all mod cons.

Edward I was a military man. He recognised Kildrummy's strategic importance when he first visited the castle in 1296, but as evinced by his attitude towards the projecting chapel, he was displeased with the castle's defensive capabilities. Above all, he frowned upon the design of the gatehouse, isolated on the vulnerable south-eastern flank. Accordingly, when he visited the fortress a second time in October 1303 he took a personal interest in the massive new entrance complex which was then being built under the watchful eye of Master James of St George, the leading royal military mason-architect. Although little but the foundations of the Edwardian gatehouse remain, it seems to have been an almost exact replica of that raised by by Master James at Harlech in the 1280s. Kildrummy's narrow doorway was flanked by two tall towers fronting a rectangular building and dominating a wooden drawbridge which pivoted over a deep pit. The work was further reinforced a century later with a barbican in front of the entrance passage. Even when Edward had finished with it, Kildrummy was so strong that his men had to resort to treachery to repossess it in 1306.

T R E A S O N   A N D   F O R C E D   M A R R I A G E

Following the defeat and dethronement of John Balliol in 1296, Edward I of England ruled Scotland in his own right. As we have seen, he visited Kildrummy on two occasions, improving the castle's defences to make it one of the most impregnable in the land. Three years after his last visit he had cause to regret his efforts, for he found the castle held against him by the ambitious Bruce family. The Bruces had a double link with the Earls of Mar, owners of Kildrummy. Robert Bruce, who had seized the throne in 1306, took as his first wife Isabella, daughter of the Earl of Mar. King Robert's sister, Christian, furthered the ties and married Isabella's brother Gratney. Upon Gratney's death, Robert came into possession of Kildrummy, holding it for Gratney's son Donald of Mar.

In 1305 Edward had begun to doubt Bruce's loyalty and demanded that Kildrummy be put into the hands of someone whom he could trust. By the summer of 1306 Bruce's fortunes were running low, and he disappeared into the Highlands, leaving the ladies of his court to make their way to the security of Kildrummy under the protection of a number of powerful barons, among whom was the king's brother Neil. They were pursued by a powerful English force commanded by the Prince of Wales, the future Edward II. Unwilling to trust everything to the doughty walls of Kildrummy, the Scots divided their forces. The ladies continued to make their way north while Neil settled down to defend Kildrummy against all comers.

The siege of Kildrummy was a great medieval military set-piece. One of the mightiest castles in the land was held by men who could be certain of execution for treason should they succumb. Arrayed against them was an experienced professional army, equipped with the latest siege machinery. Though the Scots were unlikely to receive military support, time was on their side for the assault began in September and Edward knew that Kildrummy had to be taken swiftly lest his army be left in the Highlands at the mercy of the closing weather and the hostile local population. In vain were great boulders lobbed at the walls and arrows showered down upon the garrison by day and night. The castle held fast. On occasion Neil's men made the task of the assailants even more difficult by raiding their lines, burning tents, slaughtering the surprised soldiery and smashing their machinery.

Prince Edward grew desperate. He was not a military man at heart, and he longed for the settled comforts of court life. Moreover, the Scottish resistance was a considerable embarrassment to him. In the end, therefore, he decided that what he could not achieve by force, he would manage by guile. Every man has his price, and it did not take the English long to find a member of the garrison who was prepared to betray his fellows for a handsome reward. The traitor was no soldier, but the castle's blacksmith, a man named Osbourne. The Prince promised him as much gold as he could carry if he would deliver the castle into English hands. The blacksmith agreed to see what he could do.

A short while later the castle's grain store, temporarily housed in the Great Hall, burst into flames. The conflagration spread rapidly to other buildings, melting the great gate and killing and injuring many of the garrison. Neil had no choice but to surrender, and he was led away to execution at Berwick. 'Hang him on a gallows thirty feet higher than the rest!' muttered King Edward, no doubt piqued that any castle should have resisted his armies for so long and forced his son to resort to treachery.

Meanwhile, Osbourne had not been forgotten. It is said that the English gave him his gold alright, not in minted coins but in molten metal tipped down his throat. The punishment was cruel, but to the medieval mind it was apt for one who had sinned with the tongue. And it was certainly a less unpleasant fate than that meted out twenty-one years later to Edward II for his particular brand of sin.

Needless to say, the story of Kildrummy did not end in 1306. Although the fire-damaged castle was further slighted by English soldiers to prevent its use against them, within a few years it had been repaired. In 1336 it witnessed another siege, this time conducted by a pro-English Scottish faction. The successful defence was handled by King Robert's sister Christian, fighting for the exiled David II.

Early in the next century Kildrummy saw fresh turmoil, involving a combination of murder and forced marriage reminiscent of *Richard III*. The Earldom of Mar was held in her own right by Countess Isabel, who was married to Sir Malcolm Drummond. In 1402 Sir Malcolm was brutally murdered by a party of assassins who descended on Kildrummy. The gang was almost certainly in the hire of Alexander Stewart, an illegitimate son of the notorious Wolf of Badenoch, brother of King Robert III. Two years later the Stewart bastard came to Kildrummy himself to pursue his ambitions further. He stormed the castle and got to work on the terrified countess, several years his senior. Though we can only guess at the tactics he used, they certainly achieved the end he desired: in a macabre trumped-up ceremony held on the grass beside the towering gatehouse the castle keys were presented to the cowed Countess, with instructions that she was free to present them to whomsoever she wished. Isabel promptly proffered them to Alexander, who gratefully received the castle, the earldom — and the countess as his wife. The miserable lady Isabel died shortly afterwards, childless. When her husband followed her to the grave in 1435 the earldom of Mar and its estates, including the castle, reverted to the crown.

In the seventeenth century Kildrummy reverted to the Erskines, who had owned it in the late Middle Ages. It succumbed swiftly to Cromwellian artillery in 1654 and was further damaged by Jacobites in 1690. The last time the name of Kildrummy appears upon the screen of the nation's history is at the time of the 1715 Jacobite rebellion. 'Bobbing John' Erskine, Earl of Mar, raised the standard of James VIII at Braemar. From here he wrote to 'Black Jock' Forbes, his bailie at Kildrummy, informing him that if he did not present himself with four times as many men as he had already sent to fight for the Old Pretender, then Mar would devastate his own estates. This was not the way to inspire devotion. The Jacobites were defeated, their cause crumbled and the earl fled abroad. Kildrummy was slighted and became a handy source of good quality stone for local builders. The Snow Tower collapsed in 1805. Only at the very end of the nineteenth century was a serious effort begun to halt the decay of one of the nation's most historic monuments.

INFORMATION

ACCESS   Just south of Kildrummy village on the A97
Public transport (infrequent)

RESPONSIBILITY FOR THE SITE
Scottish Development Department

TELEPHONE 09755-71331

OPENING HOURS
April – September: 9.30 – 19.00 (Sun 14.00–19.00)

October–March: Sat 9.30–17.00, Sun 14.00–17.00)

ADMISSION PRICE
60p (senior citizens and children 30p)

FACILITIES   Disabled (limited)
Parking
Dogs (on lead)
Toilets
Guided tours by special request

C A E R L A V E R O C K   C A S T L E

Seven miles south of Dumfries, Dumfries and Galloway

Region

A pleasant but unexceptional country lane leads south from Dumfries along the eastern bank of the River Nith. For a few miles it winds beside the muddy waste of Blackshow Bank on the Solway Firth before running north again, towards the bridge over Locmar Water at Bankend. There is nothing remarkable in the flat, arable farmland on either hand, nothing even to suggest that it would make a site suitable for a castle. But turn left down a narrow track towards the distant firth and, suddenly, there it is. Caerlaverock. The castle of birdsong. The most lovely ancient monument in the British Isles.

Although the flat damp banks of the Solway Firth at the mouth of the Nith offer few naturally defensive positions, the strategic importance of the area has been widely recognised since at least Roman times. The countryside to the north is dotted with ancient forts, and a number of regular mounds betray the presence of a Roman camp. To the south, even nearer the sea than Caerlaverock, lie the remains of an earlier thirteenth-century castle, which was probably dismantled to make way for the present structure. Tradition has it that there was a Roman port in the area, for Caerlaverock not only makes a convenient point from which to harass north-south traffic passing through Annandale or Nithsdale, but it also guards the sea route from Cumberland and more southerly ports to south-west Scotland. This approach was strongly favoured in times when land travel was slow and dangerous.

The complex beauty of Caerlaverock unfolds as one approaches. The moss-dappled red sandstone of the castle rises majestically from the lush green of the surrounding sward, mown smooth as a fairway. Drawing nearer, the visitor comes across the reeded moat, with its reflections of tower, bank and sky. There are obvious comparisons with the English castles at Bodiam in Sussex and Kent's lovely moated stronghold at Leeds. But Caerlaverock's colouring surpasses both. There are two further surprises in store. The castle is triangular, tapering from its broad southern wall to a twin-towered gatehouse at the northern tip. It is also a castle of curves, not angles, for the sharpness of the groundplan is softened by drum towers at the corners. Finally, like an architectural Faberge Egg, the delightful stone shell encloses a gem. The southern curtain has been conveniently dismantled, giving the impression of a cut-away drawing. The opening reveals the ruins of a fine Renaissance mansion, fashioned from the same warm sandstone as the medieval fortress. The effect is quite enchanting.

THE CASTLE

Part of Caerlaverock's attraction is its simplicity. Though the castle is the product of several different periods of construction, each modification was obliged by the constraints of the site to adhere to the same basic design. The original castle was accurately described in verse by a French observer present at Edward I's siege of 1300:

It was shield-shaped, the three walls reinforced by towers at each corner. One of these was a tall double tower, wide enough to accommodate a strong gate beneath it. The entrance was further protected by a drawbridge and other defences. Ditches, brim-full of

Caerlaverock Castle: the jewel of Dumfries and arguably the most attractive castle in Scotland.

The delightful and surprising neo-classical facade of accommodation built within Caerlaverock's walls by Robert Maxwell, first Earl of Nithsdale.

water, surrounded the stout walls. I don't think that one could imagine a better situated castle...

The fortress thus described had been constructed in the 1270s by Sir Herbert de Maxwell. It owes its position to a rocky outcrop jutting from the sandstone shelf which underlies the region. Unlike earlier castles, which had separate gatehouses and keeps, at Caerlaverock the gatehouse and keep are combined in a challenging complex around the entrance, focusing the defence at the structure's weakest point. The castle's triangular shape emphasises this aggressive gesture: instead of appearing to sit back, waiting for assault, the castle threatens like a spear head, pointing at the foe.

Before reaching the walls assailants had to cross one or two water-filled moats. These were not very deep, but they were sufficient to deter any lengthy occupation of the ground immediately beneath the walls. In times of peace the ditches were spanned by bridges which were burned or pulled down when danger threatened. The original pathway into the castle probably ended in a pivoting swing bridge rather than in a drawbridge. The entrance passage, closed by iron-bound doors and a portcullis, was much as it is today, although in the fifteenth century the outer doorway was moved forward and stone infilling inserted between the towers to the height of the parapet. The walls which confronted Edward I in 1300 were topped with overhanging wooden hourds. During an attack these were covered in wet hides to prevent their being set alight by fire arrows. Since timber was easily smashed by heavy missiles, the galleries were later replaced by the present decorative stone machiolation, which helps give the structure its story-book appearance. The thirteenth-century masonry, neatly cut ashlar in even, mortared courses, is remarkable for the quality of its workmanship. Accommodation was originally provided in the gatehouse and towers, although no doubt there was some sort of stabling and storage capacity within the courtyard.

Caerlaverock was rapidly repaired by the English after the 1300 siege, and used as a garrison stronghold for the next twelve years. It was then partly demolished by the Scots to prevent its further use by occupying forces. In the early fourteenth century the castle underwent further siege, demolition and reconstruction, though by about 1320 it seems once more to have been in a good state of repair, and much of the building which faces us today dates from this time, including the noble Murdoch tower at the western corner.

The castle's accommodation was considerably expanded in the fifteenth century. The gatehouse was extended into a form of tower house, the fashionable style of residence for prosperous landlords at that time. We have already seen a similar development at Kildrummy. Within the courtyard an imposing range of rooms was put up along the west wall. Behind an attractive front of uneven stonework a number of comfortable rooms were laid out, each with a fireplace and partly-glazed window. (It was then the Scottish custom to close the lower half of a window with wooden shutters, leaving only the upper portion glazed. The arrangement was cheaper and warmer than full glazing, and facilitated the introduction of a breeze when the room became stuffy.)

There was little alteration to Caerlaverock in the sixteenth century, apart from the addition of gunports to the gatehouse, while seventeenth-century improvements ignored the building's military function altogether. During the 1630s (we can date the work exactly from a clear '1634' carved upon the tympanum of a surviving window) Robert Maxwell, 1st Earl of Nithsdale, constructed an L-shaped block of domestic accommodation inside the south and east walls, so transforming the castle from a fortress into a highly-fashionable country residence. We do not know what the southern wall looked like, but judging by the apertures remaining in the eastern curtain, it was probably punched through in several places to allow warm sunlight and fresh air to flood into the spacious hall and solar which the earl placed there. Tragically, these buildings were destroyed when the castle was slighted after a siege in 1640. Civil war ensured that the earl, whose good taste matched that of his royal master, enjoyed the splendour of his new apartments for only six short years.

A grand stairway, happily restored, leads from the southern range to the rooms on the eastern flank. Much of the delightful facade of this building still stands. It is remarkable for the cordial colouring of the stonework and the Renaissance decoration around the doors and windows. The tympana of the larger windows on the first and second floors are carved with scenes from classical mythology, and, interestingly but probably coincidentally, the mould-ings above the larger ground floor windows, decorated with heraldic designs, resemble the outline of the castle itself. The building's front has a somewhat top-heavy appearance, as the architect made the upper windows larger than those at ground level. Such imbalance would not have been acceptable later in the century, when the rules of classical proportion were better understood. Internally the rooms are well-appointed, although somewhat inconveniently arranged in order to give all the fireplaces access to a single chimney-stack. The balanced facade, shielding a less harmonious reality, is an interesting metaphor of the conformist state sought by Charles I and also no doubt by the Earl of Nithsdale. It is sad but rather appropriate that the turmoil which destroyed the Stuart polity should also have devastated its architectural counterpart at Caerlaverock.

SIEGE, TREACHERY AND TREASON

Caerlaverock was besieged and captured at least five times during three and a half centuries of active service. In 1300 it fell to the masterly tactics and giant war engines of Edward I. English artillery under the command of the Earl of Sussex achieved the same end in 1570. In the mean time the Scots managed to recapture the border stronghold from two of their most doughty foes,

Edward III (1356) and Henry VIII (1545). The final siege, which ended the castle's life as a habitable residence, occurred in 1640. Strangely, given the enormous improvement in artillery which had taken place over the previous centuries, this assault turned out to be the longest the fortress had to endure. It may be that the Earl of Nithsdale had been given plenty of time to put himself and his garrison of 200 soldiers into a state of sharp preparedness, matching the guns of the covenanters with well-positioned artillery of their own. As it was, the earl held out for thirteen weeks before accepting generous terms of capitulation. How he must have sorrowed to see his beautiful new building smashed by enemy cannon fire. And although his heart-broken reaction to the subsequent demolition is not recorded, it may readily be guessed at.

If a castle needs ghosts to complete its touristic attraction, then Caerlaverock must harbour at least two. The first is the spirit of Roger Kirkpatrick, a valiant soldier who had recaptured Caerlaverock and the surrounding area from the English in 1356. The following year he was murdered by his guest James Lindsay, within the very castle which Roger had striven so hard to master. Lacking the sang-froid exhibited by Shakespeare's Macbeth after a similar breach of hospitality, Lindsay fled over the drawbridge into the security of the night.

During the early part of his reign James I was a captive in England. During this enforced absence his uncle Robert Duke of Albany acted as Governor of the Realm, a position inherited in 1420 by his son Murdoch. These powerful 'Albany Stewarts' stood next in line to the throne. One of the first acts of James I after his return to Scotland in 1424 was to get the dangerous Duke Murdoch out of the way. He was arrested in March 1424 and confined at Caerlaverock, in the tower which bears his name.

For several weeks the baron gazed gloomily from his narrow window at the surrounding marshes, listening to the cries of the larks and watching as spring gradually brought colour and new life to the drab landscape. Perhaps Scotland too would experience a similar rejuvenation under her capable young king? The view from his prison did little to lift Murdoch's spirits. He had played his hand and lost. Now he could only wait on events.

Murdoch was not kept in suspense for long. When news came that the Duke's younger son had foolishly burned Dumbarton and slain the Red Stewart of Dundonald, James I's natural uncle, Murdoch was dragged from his tower and hauled off to confront the furious king. This time clemency was out of the question, and before the gates of Stirling castle on May 24th the Albany threat was finally ended with one swift blow from an axe.

INFORMATION

ACCESS   The castle is signposted from Dumfries. Take the B725 south and turn right about 12 miles from the town centre.

RESPONSIBILITY FOR THE SITE
Scottish Development Department

TELEPHONE 038-777-244

OPENING HOURS
April–September: 9.30–19.00 (Sun 14.00–19.00). October–March: 9.30–16.00 (Sun 14.00–16.00)

ADMISSION PRICE
60p (Senior citizens & children 30p)

FACILITIES   Disabled
Parking
Dogs
Toilets
Guided tours by special request
Small shop

LOCHSIDE CASTLES

A castle set at a lochside has a unique aesthetic appeal. There is a serene timelessness about Scotland's long stretches of mountain-sheltered water, beside which most common constructions appear paltry and out of place. The castle, however, is different. It alone sits easily in such a landscape, matching its permanence and blending into the foreshore like some powerfully sculptured rockfall. Fortifications thus situated are not, of course, architecturally all of a piece. Eilean Donan is a twentieth-century reconstruction, while Dunstaffnage is one of the country's oldest medieval fortresses. But neither is of the present. Like the Highlands themselves, they demand a longer perspective; they were when we were not, and they will be when we are no more. One cannot ponder Urquhart's shattered ruins, lapped by the peat-black waters of Loch Ness, without reflecting upon the vanity of human ambition. And yet, at the southern end of the same glen, Dunstaffnage still stands, an enduring example to man's indomitable spirit. It is as if these two great stone monuments have been established to remind us of our own noble frailty.

A loch is not a lake. Some are enclosed, others are open to the sea. Though two of the three castles chosen here stand beside tidal waters, their setting is altogether different from those of Tantallon and Dunnottar, where the waves of the ocean break against the very walls themselves. The castles of this section lie beside sheltered waters. Surprisingly, given the military and commercial importance of the lochs in Scottish history, there are not that many castles built on their banks which merit a lengthy visit. Some, such as Castle Stalker, Carrick, Kilcoy and Dundarave are in private hands. The castle of Loch Doon has not been included because neither it nor the loch remain as they were in previous centuries: the loch was flooded as part of a hydro-electricity scheme and the castle moved, stone by stone, to higher ground. Craig, Dryhope Tower, and Tioram are ruinous. Kilchurn and Inverlochy, although in the hands of the state and striking spectacles, are not open to the public. For convenience Dunvegan has been included in a different chapter — although it may be argued with some justification that it sits as easily here as Dunstaffnage. This leaves the pretty little ruin on an island in Loch Leven, closely associated with several Scottish monarchs. However, it is precisely because of its association with Mary Queen of Scots that Loch Leven Castle, albeit somewhat perversely, has been omitted. There is so much more to Scottish history than the romantic chaos of the reign of the half-French queen, and it is irritating to find her name bandied about at almost every historical site, however far-fetched and half-baked the association.

Eilean Donan, Urquhart and Dunstaffnage are three rich slices from a fascinating heritage. They have been selected for the variety of their history, the intrinsic interest of their architecture and the unsurpassed beauty of their

URQUHART CASTLE
Once one of the largest castles in Scotland this fortress commanded a vital site
beside the dark waters of Loch Ness.

The picturesque ruins of Kilchurn Castle at the head of Loch Awe. Unfortunately the building is closed to the public.

Dunstaffnage's dark and haunted walls served as a temporary prison for the Jacobite heroine Flora Macdonald in 1746.

settings. No work on Scottish castles would be complete without them.

DUNSTAFFNAGE CASTLE

At Dunbeg, Strathclyde Region

Dunstaffnage castle is built on a huge dark pudding of rock, known to geologists as Old Red Conglomerate, on a promontory jutting out into Ardmucknish Bay. To the south-west the Firth of Lorn expands like a trumpet into the Irish Sea. The Great Glen narrows to the north-east, leading straight into the Highlands and eventually to Inverness and the North Sea. The Grampians form the eastern backdrop, entered along Loch Etive and the main road over the Pass of Brander. From here the way leads through Glen Lochy and Glen Dochart and so on to Perth and the east coast. To the west the castle looks out over the water to Lismore, Mull and the Inner Hebrides.

The Dunstaffnage peninsular provides a sheltered anchorage where bright boats are moored on calm waters, protected from the prevailing south-westerly gales. A naval repair base was established here during the Second World War, giving rise to the modern village of Dunbeg. Throughout history the vital importance of this superb site has impressed itself upon those seeking to command western Scotland. King Robert Bruce, Oliver Cromwell and the Hanoverian red-coats were all quick to recognise Dunstaffnage's strategic significance.

Robert I made a point of slighting the castles he had seized from the English, regarding them as symbols and instruments of foreign repression. But in Dunstaffnage he made an exception, repairing it and installing a garrison loyal to himself. He needed the stronghold to overawe the Western Isles and to act as a base for operations against English naval incursions. We are indebted to this stroke of good fortune and military insight for the present excellent state of the original castle.

The approach to Dunstaffnage is unprepossessing as philistine planners have permitted the village of Dunbeg to sprawl westwards towards the neck of the peninsular. Motorists following signs to the castle for the first time will probably fear that contemporary buildings extend right up to the walls of the fortress itself. Fortunately, however, wisdom and good taste prevail at last, and a car park has been provided on the outskirts of the village several hundred metres from the castle, leaving the last part of the pilgrimage to be made on foot. The promontory on which the castle is built is sheltered on the far side by tall deciduous trees, leaving the grassy landward approach open. To the right is the curator's house, to the left the ruins of the ancient Gothic chapel which served the castle's inhabitants for centuries. Directly ahead is the castle itself, whose massive curtain walls have stood thus upon their rocky foundation for 750 years.

The dark rubble walls of Dunstaffnage tower above their elevated foundation of Conglomerate rock.

Dunstaffnage's four-storey Western Tower, the base of which contained the castle's prison.

THE CASTLE

It is very probable that Dunstaffnage has been used as a stronghold since man first appeared in the area. Even without walls the natural citadel could be defended by simply bombarding assailants with missiles and pushing the more venturesome off the rock face. There is a plausible tradition that Dunstaffnage was Dun Monaidh, the seventh century capital of the kings of Dalriada, and the early home of that much-travelled talisman, the Stone of Destiny. Most of the present castle is the work of Ewen MacDougall, Lord of Lorn. Lorn corresponds roughly to northern Argyll and once included the islands of Lismore, Mull, Coll and Tiree. The MacDougalls were direct descendants of Dugald, a son of the great Somerled (d.1164), the chief who led the people of the Hebrides against the Vikings. Ewen's building was an early enceinte, a straightforward wall of stone corresponding roughly to the quadrangular shape of the plateau which it crowned, with massive walls doubling the height of their natural platform. The soldiers patrolling the parapet walk commanded fine views in all directions, and when danger threatened they manned with bows and arrows the deep, slitted recesses (known as embrasures) which were built into the thickness of the walls.

Dunstaffnage was constructed before it became customary to concentrate defences over the castle gate, so at first the ruined Northern Tower acted as both keep and principal residence. The Great Hall extended from here to the gatehouse and communicated with the key defensive positions at either end. There was also a range of buildings along the north-west wall, although all that can be seen here today is the dilapidated remnants of an eighteenth-century house, erected by the 11th Captain of Dunstaffnage for the greater comfort of himself and his household. The Western Tower, which is still standing, housed a windowless prison and further accommodation. The remaining corner has no tower at all but is strengthened by a bulbous thickening of the wall.

The original entrance to Lord Ewen's castle was placed directly above a sloping fissure, which probably served as a path to the summit of the rock. From a military point of view this was perhaps not the best place to site the gateway, and the entrance fortifications were the only part of the castle to be extensively remodelled by later generations. To enter the castle visitors have to climb a buttressed stone stairway built against the rock face and the lower gatehouse wall. The present steps, only about a century old, were constructed in the same place as those they replaced. They come to an abrupt halt before reaching the castle gate, which stands at a right angle to the stair head. The clever design meant that an assailant who reached the top of the stairs found the door to his left, separated by a precipitous drop. The awkward turn is now made on a wooden platform, serving the same purpose as the original bridge, which was either pivoted in the middle or raised on chains suspended from beams jutting out of the wall above the entrance. The attractive gatehouse dates largely from the late sixteenth century, although it incorporates three pretty dormer windows from the eleventh Captain's house. An arch of the original gatehouse can still be seen in the western wall on the ground floor.

Dunstaffnage's straightforward design and medieval completeness lend it an awesome aspect, which is heightened in wet weather when the walls and the base rock turn grey-black. Apart from the rather fine gatehouse, it is not a castle of aesthetic architectural appeal. It was not the intention of those who built it to provide the area with an ornament, but with a defensive stronghold. And in that they succeeded admirably.

FROM THE ELL-MAID TO FLORA MACDONALD

Dunstaffnage is doubly haunted. A sprite, known as the Ell-maid of Dunstaffnage', stalks the ruins with the clanging footfalls of armoured feet. She comes to foretell happiness or woe to the family who own the castle, announcing her prophesy with dolorous shrieks or cries of laughter. Even when this supernatural harbinger is at rest there is an eerie sense of history about the place, as if past events have been absorbed by the thick walls. In the shadowy courtyard the boundary between past and present is mysteriously dissolved.

A full story of Dunstaffnage would be virtually a brief history of Scotland. Little is known of events surrounding the castle's early life, when it served as the seat of the mighty MacDougall Lords of Lorn. There was little love lost between this ancient Celtic clan and the Anglo-Norman aristocracy, the de Brus, de Comyn, Balliol and FitzAlan (Stewart) families who acquired lands in Scotland in the early medieval period. So when Robert Bruce claimed the throne in 1306 it was not surprising to find the Lords of Lorn ranged against him, although out of personal rivalry rather than any desire to serve under an English master. The showdown between the two came in August 1308 when King Robert met the forces of John of Lorn in the Pass of Brander, the narrow road leading from the east to Loch Etive and Dunstaffnage. The battle-hardened and disciplined royal army was too much for John's levies, who broke and fled into the mountains. The castle fell the next year. From this time onwards, apart from two brief episodes, the stronghold remained in the hands of those loyal to the government, whether it were Stewart, Covenanting, Cromwellian or Hanoverian.

Dunstaffnage is famous as a Campbell castle. The clan began their long association with the place in 1322, when Robert I raised his loyal henchman Arthur Campbell to the position of Constable of Dunstaffnage. For a while, however, the Crown kept proprietorship of the vital fortress in family hands, conferring the Lordship of Lorn upon John Stewart. It was during the period of Stewart ownership that the castle saw one of the most blackguardly incidents in its history. In the winter of 1363 the Stewart Lord of Lorn planned to marry his Maclean mistress and thereby take advantage of lenient Scottish law to legitimise his son and heir. Disarmed and in jovial mood he left the castle, passed down the stone steps and started to walk over damp grass towards the chapel, some 150 metres away. He never completed the journey. In the open space, in full sight of the soldiers on the walls and horrified onlookers standing at the chapel door, he was struck down by a band of MacDougalls, the origins of whose grudge lay deep in the past. For a few months the castle was held once more by the family who had built it. But their triumph was short-lived. A royal expedition retook the stronghold and in 1470 it was given to Colin Campbell, 1st Earl of Argyll, with whose family it has remained ever since.

Garrisoned by the loyal Campbells, who threw in their lot firmly with the Stewarts and their successors, Dunstaffnage was frequently used as a base for subjugating the troublesome western region of the kingdom. It served as a barracks, a rallying point and, on several occasions, as a place of execution for rebels. John Cameron of Lochiel was beheaded there in 1585, and in 1647 the elderly father of Montrose's second-in-command was strung up on a gibbet beneath the castle's grey walls. The Campbells were fortunate to maintain their possession of Dunstaffnage later in the century. Archibald the 9th Earl, who had fallen out with the Catholic James VII, landed here in 1685 and raised the standard of Protestant rebellion. The gamble failed and the castle was partly destroyed as a result. Campbell fortunes were restored by William III, and the family did not again risk its position by challenging the government in London. 'James VIII' (the Old Pretender) considered landing at Dunstaffnage in 1715 but found the castle's loyalty to the Hanoverians unshakeable. Similarly, when his son Bonnie Prince Charlie tried for the last time to seize the Scottish throne for the House of Stuart the stronghold held fast to its paymasters. No safer place than Dunstaffnage could be found for the temporary incarceration of that romantic Jacobite heroine, Flora Macdonald. After her arrest in the summer of 1746 she was held in the castle for a day or two, before being taken south to the Tower of London.

The stone steps into Dunstaffnage lead the traveller with unerring certainty into a vivid and evocative past. Unfortunately, but not surprisingly, it is mostly cruel deeds which are remembered. The innumerable happy gatherings, feasts, dances and uninterrupted marriages have passed by without comment, although they too have their rightful place in the monument's long, eventful story.

ACCESS	The castle is signposted from the village of Dunbeg, three miles north of Oban. Public transport	ADMISSION PRICE	60p (Senior citizens and children 30p)
RESPONSIBILITY FOR THE SITE	Scottish Development Department	FACILITIES	Parking Dogs (on lead) Toilets (in village) Guided tours by special request
TELEPHONE	0631-624-65		
OPENING HOURS	April–September: 9.30–19.00 (Sun 14.00–19.00)		

EILEAN DONAN

By Dornie village, Highland Region

There is only one major road from the east to the Skye ferry at Kyle of Lochalsh. After leaving the Great Glen it runs beside Loch Cluanie for a while, then threads its way through the awesome Glenshiel before descending to the head of Loch Duish. Although the waters here are tidal, there is no glimpse yet of the sea. The road follows the right bank of the loch until it meets with Loch Long, stretching away to the north-east. Ahead the Atlantic funnels into Loch Alsh, and the mountains of Skye are visible in the far distance, framed between the wooded hills of the mainland. It was here, on a small island a short distance from the shore of Loch Duish, that Donan, an early Celtic saint, decided to settle and live as a hermit. He may have built himself a hut from the remains of an earlier Pictish fort on the island. No doubt he was visited from time to time by disciples bringing him food or asking about the revolutionary new gospel he proclaimed, but most of the time he spent in that lovely and remote spot was devoted to quiet prayer. Though the island was subsequently named after the holy man, rarely since his time has it witnessed such blessed tranquillity.

Only those fortunate enough to see Eilean Donan in fair weather are able to appreciate fully the beauty of the castle's situation. All too often the views up Loch Duish and westwards over Loch Alsh are obscured by rain and mist; the waters of the lochs are grey, the hills reduced to colourless shapes and the horizons lost in cloud. But on a bright day, particularly in autumn when the colours are so warm and varied, Scotland can boast of no more picturesque castle. It appears a photographer's dream, yet each year more disappointing pictures must be taken of this site than any other in the country, for no photograph can begin to capture the totality of the scene. However, those wishing to disprove that statement may like to start by climbing the old road to the isles, running through the trees above the A87.

Purists are disappointed to find that Eilean Donan is a twentieth century construction. It is no mere Disney fantasy, however, for it was put together in an attempt to recreate the original castle. The only blatantly unhistorical part of the modern stronghold is the bridge linking it to the mainland. The present owners wished for more frequent intercourse with the outside world than St Donan, and their sturdy means of egress also provides thousands of lucrative tourists with a more comfortable and rapid means of access than the boat which once served the island. On the other hand, the bridge ensures that at the height of summer the confined site is transformed into something more akin to a multinational rabbit warren or Tower of Babel than a citadel.

THE CASTLE

It is said that at some time early in this century Farquhar MacRae had vision. He saw the castle of Eilean Donan, then in ruins, rebuilt to its former glory and restored as the headquarters of the Clan MacRae. The work was eventually undertaken at considerable expense by Lt. Col. John MacRae-Gilstrap. The workmen were instructed to stick as closely as possible to the original methods of construction, shaping the stone and timber by hand. Their labours were supervised by George Mackie Watson and the eventual outcome, although apparently not accurate in every detail, is a fair replica of the fortress which once stood on the island. The dream had come true.

The first medieval castle on Eilean Donan was a simple enceinte of curtain wall, no doubt entered through some sort of gatehouse and protected by an overhanging platform and arrow slits. The fortifications need not have been very elaborate in the days before artillery, for any attack could be foiled by setting fire to hostile vessels with flaming arrows launched from the wallhead. The keep was built in the late fourteenth century, when the castle was in the hands of the Earl of Ross. It served as a look-out, a final point of refuge and a secure and comfortable lodging within the walls. In the original tower the stone-vaulted basement (now dubbed the 'Billeting Room') had no access from the outside and was entered from above by a wooden stairway. It was used for storage. The present vaulting is largely the handiwork of the visionary Farquhar MacRae.

The room known as the 'Banqueting Hall' is where the Great Hall of the Ross keep once stood. It is now full of historical knick-knacks and fine furniture. A splendid wrought iron yett, recovered from the well at the time of the restoration, serves as a reminder of less settled times. The main entrance to the castle was on this floor and was reached by means of timber stairs ascending from the courtyard. Although Eilean Donan hardly compares with the mighty castles built at about the same time, such as Kildrummy or Tantallon, it was a secure seat, proof against such small-scale and lightly-armed raids as were to be expected in the remote north-west. Since it was safe against a shore-based attack, the only real threat had to come by sea. And that, as we shall see, was precisely from where it came.

THE FINAL ARROW

Much of the early history of northern and western Scotland is concerned with the struggle between the native Scottish kings and the Norse invaders. Gradually the Scandinavians were driven from the mainland, but it was not until the thirteenth century that the Western Isles were finally absorbed into the Kingdom of Scotland. The crucial battle was fought on the beach at Largs on 2 October 1263. It resulted in the retreat and subsequent death of Norway's King Haakon, and the cession of the Hebrides and Man to Scotland three years later.

As a gesture of thanks for support in the crucial fight Alexander III gave the isle of St Donan and the lands about it to Colin Fitzgerald, a son of the Irish Earl of Desmond and Kildare. At this time the castle was a plain walled enclosure. Tradition has it that early in the next century Robert Bruce sheltered here when fleeing from the English. His host was John MacKenzie, Chief of Kintail. It seems as if the Bruces thought less of the standard of law and order in the area than they did of its hospitality, for when in 1331 Robert's nephew Randolph Earl of Moray visited Kintail in his capacity as Warden of Scotland, he executed a number of wrongdoers and spiked their heads on the battlements 'pour encourager les autres'. The gory sight must have been hardly visible from the mainland and probably sobered the garrison as much as the surrounding peasantry.

During the next two centuries Eilean Donan passed from the crown to the Mackenzies, and for some time it was one of several strongholds of the MacDonald Earls of Ross, Lords of the Isles. The powerful Earl of Huntly deprived the MacDonalds of their island fortress in 1504, although we do not know precisely how he managed to overcome the stronghold. Two years later we find the MacRaes first installed as Constables of the castle, a title they still hold to this day. The remaining history of the fortress is largely concerned with two famous sieges.

The roots of the trouble of 1539 can be traced far back into clan rivalry and vendetta, the details of which hardly concern us here. Suffice it to say that in the year in question the powerful Donald Gorm of Sleat, who was in open rebellion against the authority of the crown, sailed down Loch Alsh with a number of galleys, intending to take the key position of Eilean Donan. The seriously under-manned castle looked an easy target for the doughty Gorm. But in the nick of time the garrison was reinforced by a passing band of clansmen led by Duncan MacRae, who nursed a bitter hatred of the Lord of Sleat for the murder of his uncle. As the galleys approached, Constable John Dubh ordered his men to take up positions on the water's edge where they were able to strike down a number of Gorm's men as they struggled ashore. But the defenders were soon outnumbered and compelled to withdraw into the castle. Since there were not enough of them to man every battlement, it was not long before Gorm's soldiers had scaled the outer walls and forced the garrison to retreat once more, this time to the keep.

The situation was getting desperate. The Constable lay dying, pierced in the chest by a chance arrow fired from one of the ships. Ammunition was running low — Donald MacRae himself, now in charge of the defence, had only one arrow left. And, worst of all, Gorm's men were hewing down their vessels' masts to make battering rams capable of reaching the elevated doorway. There was no hope of relief. Within minutes the keep would be breached and Gorm's enraged warriors storming through the open doorway. Donald realised that only one chance remained, and a slim one it was too. Sheltering behind the battlements he strung his bow with his last arrow. He

The spectacular castle of Eilean Donan occupies a powerful position on the island of St Donan in Loch Duish. It is said that the stronghold's twentieth- century rebuilding was undertaken according to plans seen in a vision by Farquhar MacRae.

then stood up and, holding his breath to steady his arm, he took aim and fired.

Gorm was directing operations from the ships below and the range from the battlements was considerable. Although Donald's aim was true, it looked as if his arrow would fall short. Nevertheless, though it missed the man's chest where it had been aimed, it did not pass the target altogether. With a cry of pain the great Lord of Sleat fell forward, clutching at his foot where the barbed arrow had entered. It had severed an artery.

A faint cheer arose from the battlements as, despite the ministrations of his men, a pool of blood spread around the stricken Gorm, staining the deck dark crimson. The man was bleeding to death. The news of the tragedy spread swiftly among the men of Sleat, causing them to lose heart. Gathering together their weapons and carrying their wounded with them, they withdrew to their ships, cast off, and sailed back to the west whence they had come. The castle was saved.

There was no such fortunate ending to Eilean Donan's last siege. Apart from the Robin Hood-like accuracy of Donald MacRae's archery, the most remarkable point about the assault of 1539 was the apparent absence of fire-arms on either side. This was certainly not the case when the Royal Navy attacked the castle in 1719.

After the failure of the 1715 Jacobite rebellion the French were unwilling to risk further money and men in a similar venture, so James the Old Pretender turned for assistance to the Spanish court. In the event, however, only forty-eight Spanish soldiers managed to make their way to Scotland. Here they made contact with William Mackenzie, the 5th Earl of Seaforth, and settled down in Eilean Donan to see what happened. They did not have long to wait. On the morning of 10 May three British frigates appeared in Loch Alsh. The *Worcester*, *Enterprise* and *Flamborough*, commanded by Captain Boyle, were furnished with the very latest naval weaponry, cannons capable of reducing to rubble in a matter of minutes a medieval fortress such as that which lay before them. The first few broadsides made it clear to the garrison that resistance was pointless. The white flag was hoisted above the broken battlements and the vanquished were taken aboard the warships in irons. The ancient castle was left at the mercy of the elements and local crofters searching for ready-made building stone. So it remained, an overgrown ruin, until two centuries later Farquhar MacRae started dreaming...

INFORMATION

ACCESS   The castle can be seen from the   ADMISSION PRICE
                A87 by the village of Dornie   £1.00
                Public transport (infrequent)
RESPONSIBILITY FOR SITE   TELEPHONE   059-985-202
                Private

OPENING HOURS

    April–September 10.00–12.30,
    14.00–18.00

FACILITIES   Disabled (limited)
    Parking
    Toilets in village
    Guided tours available
    Shop

URQUHART CASTLE

By Strone village on the west shore of Loch Ness, Highland Region

The best way to appreciate the importance of the position occupied by Urquhart Castle is to open a physical map of the Highlands. The long scar of the Great Glen cuts the region in two, serving not only as a frontier but also as an important communications route, running north-east from Fort William to Inverness and linking the provinces of Argyll and Moray. For much of its sixty-mile length the glen is filled with the deep and mysterious waters of Loch Ness. Urquhart occupies a sandstone promontory on the western shore, about one third of the way down from the loch's northern tip. It commands sweeping views up and down the loch and is a popular vantage point for monster-spotters.

Urquhart Castle is not just a convenient look-out post. It also guards the entrance to the broad and fertile Glen Urquhart, which sprawls westwards towards Glencannich Forest. In the days before the construction of metalled highways in the Highlands this also marked the starting point of a track to Loch Alsh, Skye and the Hebrides, passing either up Glen Affric or beside Loch Mullardoch to Carnach. The motorist travelling westwards from Inverness must regret that this path was never exploited by the road-builders, for it cuts many miles off the present circuitous journey.

Tourists accustomed to craning their necks upwards to get a glimpse of a well-sited castle receive something of a surprise when first coming across Urquhart, for the ruins of the stronghold occupy a site well below the level of the main road. The approach to the castle from the large car park is downhill. The immediate observation about such a position is that it makes bombardment from the landward flank a rather simple task. Archers, catapult operators or artillerymen had only to position themselves carefully on the hillside to have the stronghold almost entirely at their mercy. On the other hand, it may be argued that the principal danger to the fortress was to be expected from the loch, and on this side the defences were excellent. The water was two metres lower before the construction of the Caledonian Canal, so that the cliffs rose a formidable twelve metres above the shore. The outcrop to the south of the site

Urquhart Castle, holding a vital position on the shores of Loch Ness, was besieged and captured on many occasions during its long and troubled history.

The proud remains of Urquhart Castle, seen against the glittering cold waters of Loch Ness.

was another sixteen metres above the clifftop. Moreover, the stronghold was not built to withstand sophisticated, mechanised assault. It was a highland outpost, designed to counter the raids of land-pirates and offer some security to the farming folk of Glen Urquhart, tasks for which its high walls and towers were thought to be sufficient. Nevertheless, as we shall see when looking at the castle's history, it was captured almost as often as it was seriously besieged, suggesting that by the fourteenth century the vulnerable site was already out of date.

THE CASTLE

Many of the tourists mooching about the ruins of Urquhart have a somewhat bewildered air. The fortress's glorious position on the loch side is easily and warmly appreciated. The ruined tower at the northern end of the promontory can still be climbed and conforms to the customary image of what an ancient castle should be. But little beside remains, apart from obscure stumps of walls and half-shattered masonry hulks. What is more, the outline of these remnants does not appear to conform to the customary arrangement of a castle. In some ways the scattered stones are more reminiscent of an abandoned village than a fortress.

The reasons why Urquhart is not an easy monument with which to come to terms are the advanced state of dilapidation of the structure and the unusual design of the original castle. The curtain walls were built in the shape of a letter B, with the straight side against a dry ditch to landward, roughly parallel with the road. A modern timber crossing replaces the original drawbridge. The northernmost dwelling, on the left as one approaches the castle over the bridge, is the larger of the two and features the standing tower at its tip. The keep stood on the taller hill, overlooking the ditch.

There was a castle at Urquhart in the twelfth century, at the time of King William the Lion. We know next to nothing about it, apart from the fact that it was almost certainly of the motte and bailey variety, and was unusual in having two baileys and a natural rocky outcrop as its motte. The remains we now see are those of a castle begun by Alan Durward, who came into possession of the site in 1229. The southern or upper bailey was dominated by a massive shell keep with very thick walls, which formed the residence for the lord and his family. Some time later a hall and solar were built on the lower bailey, along the lochside wall. They have been so seriously dismantled that only their outlines remain. The mound to their west was once surmounted by a chapel.

The two structures which retain most of their original appearance are the gatehouse and the sixteenth century residential tower. Some say the gatehouse was put up on the orders of Edward I after he had taken the castle in 1296. Others suggest that it was of a much later construction, not being anywhere near grand enough to merit an Edwardian hallmark. It consisted of two drum-fronted towers backing onto a square blockhouse. The entrance passage was defended by the usual arrangement of iron-bound doors, portcullis and murder holes in the ceiling, through which the garrison could inconvenience assailants who had managed to advance that far. The tower on the left looks as if it has been thrown down by a giant. In fact it was deliberately destroyed with gunpowder by a garrison retiring after the Jacobite troubles in the early 1690s.

The partially-collapsed tower at the northern end of the castle reflects the Scots' preference for vertically constructed residences in the early modern period. The base of what was once a most stylish building is the oldest part of the structure, dating from the thirteenth century. The bulk of the tower, including the fireplaces, privies and stairways, is sixteenth-century work. What little remains of the parapet and turrets suggests that they are later still — perhaps early seventeenth century. The small square corner turrets projecting over the walls were like miniature residences, each furnished with fireplace, window, gunloop and personal privy. They must have been rather comfortable little look-outs.

A WELL-NIGH UNTENABLE FORTRESS

The story of Urquhart is a sorry one. Time and again it was besieged, captured and destroyed, only to be rebuilt for the unhappy cycle to begin again. Recognising the intrinsic weakness of the place, Cromwell's soldiers did not consider it worth garrisoning. Eventually it was mortally wounded with the explosion of 1691, and finished off in the great storm of February 1715, which blew the south side of the tower house into the deep waters of the loch.

The man whose name is first associated with Urquhart is Alan Durward, Justiciar of Scotland and in the middle of the thirteenth century one of the most powerful men in the country. His family name, like that of the Stewarts, comes from the position he held at court — 'door-ward' or door-keeper. His wide-ranging estates included not only the area around Urquhart but also land in Atholl, the Mearns and Mar. Through marriage he claimed the title of Earl of Atholl. If a rather strange story we have of him is to be believed, he was a hard and ruthless baron who exploited to the full the wealth available to him. Shortly after taking over a piece of property, Durward approached one of his new tenants with a demand for an increase in rent. The man objected, but when offered his superior's right hand on a pledge that this increase would be the last, he agreed to accept the deal. To his intense irritation, however, he found Durward making the same demands the following year, and offering to guarantee the bond in the same friendly manner. Once again the tenant was bullied into submission and shook hands on the bargain. When the trick was tried a third time, the frustrated tenant demanded his master's left hand, commenting wryly that it might be less perfidious than the right. Durward was accused of treason in 1252 and fled to England, where he also had prosperous estates, and Urquhart was taken over by the equally powerful Comyn family.

All that remains of Urquhart's gatehouse after it had been blown up by a retiring garrison at the end of the seventeenth century.

When Edward I swept into Scotland in 1296, intent on reducing the country to submission, castle after castle fell to his awesome siege machinery. Some, such as Dirleton, put up a stiff resistance. Other less well-appointed strongholds, including Urquhart, succumbed easily to the English onslaught.

The details of how Edward's men effected the capture of Urquhart are not known. No doubt they shipped men and machinery down Loch Ness from their base at Elgin. Then, blockading the castle with heavily-armed barges on the loch, they assembled catapults on the slopes above it and battered the terrified garrison of ill-trained Highlanders into submission.

The locals watching the English operations from a safe distance obviously learned something of the art of attacking a castle, for when Edward returned to the Highlands in 1303 he found Urquhart once more in the hands of nationalist forces. A fierce fight followed and the English established themselves for a second time in the commanding base on the shores of the Great Glen. The issue of the nationality of the castle's owner was settled once and for all five years later when soldiers loyal to Robert I won it back for their king. The fortress was then extensively repaired and strengthened. In the reign of David II (1329-1371) Edward III attempted to emulate the exploits of his grandfather, but he had neither the time nor the means to besiege Urquhart effectively. It remained one of only five Scottish castles which never fell to the invader.

In the later fourteenth century Urquhart was once again in the front line, this time as a principal royal fortress for containing the destructive ambitions of the MacDonalds and their allies in the north-west. From time to time these restless people, led by a chief who styled himself (often with little legality) 'Lord of the Isles', swept east in an orgy of destruction. Four times they pillaged Glen Urquhart and seized the castle. On each occasion they were driven back and the walls painstakingly patched up again. Clearly, though, the castle was becoming less and less effective as a place of refuge. A passing band of Covenanters ravaged it in 1644 and, as we have seen, Cromwell did not bother to man it. He relied instead on a frigate patrolling the waters of the loch to keep an eye on the area.

The castle last saw action in 1689, when it managed to drive off a feeble Jacobite force. Thereafter, like so many other fine ruins, it served only as a quarry for local builders until in Victorian times it was finally secured for posterity.

INFORMATION

ACCESS — Urquhart is visible from the A82, near the hamlet of Strone, 17 miles from Inverness. Public transport (infrequent)

RESPONSIBILITY FOR THE SITE — Scottish Development Department

TELEPHONE 04562-551

OPENING HOURS — October–March: 9.30–16.00 (Sundays 14.00–1600) April–September: 9.30–19.00 (Sundays 14.00–19.00)

PRICE OF ADMISSION — £1.00 (Senior citizens and children 50p)

FACILITIES — Parking, Dogs, Toilets, Guided tours by special request

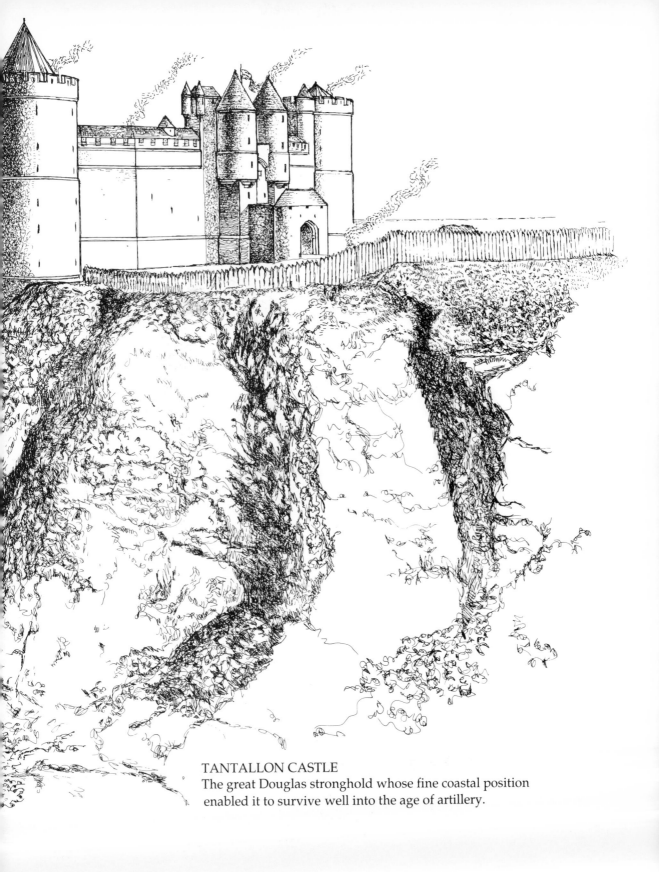

TANTALLON CASTLE
The great Douglas stronghold whose fine coastal position
enabled it to survive well into the age of artillery.

Dunnottar Castle, without doubt the most impregnable fortress in Scotland.

FORTRESSES BY THE SEA

Ronald Macgregor has produced a splendid map of Scotland on which are marked all the country's known castles. The result is a startling cartographic attack of measles, remarkable for its completeness but highly confusing for someone wishing to plan a tour of the country's fortresses. There are over 1,300 black symbols, each representing a site of some significance. Understandably they are clustered around the major centres of population which, given the inhospitable nature of much of Scotland's inland terrain, are generally near the coast. So in trying to boil down the large number of castles for inclusion in this chapter to only three, one is presented with an almost insurmountable problem. Whatever the choice, someone's favourite seaside stronghold is going to be omitted.

Some castles have already been mentioned. Cubbie Roo's, Sween and Old Wick, for example, were touched upon in the brief introduction to the medieval period. Dunstaffnage, with a little licence, has been included in the chapter on lochside castles. Culzean and Dunrobin will be described later. If we exclude the fortresses which are not actually on the sea itself, such as Rothesay or Muness (the most northerly castle in the British Isles), then we are still spoilt for choice. Some, Blackness and Dumbarton for example, have been rather distorted by modern military occupation, as have Stirling and Edinburgh. Others are too ruinous or small to merit more than a passing reference. This rules out monuments such as Scalloway, Keiss, Knock and Girnigoe-with-Sinclair (a Siamese twins castle).

We are now left with some dozen exciting structures, all powerfully evocative of the nation's past, and all well worth a visit. Ravenscraig on the Firth of Forth was one of the first castles in Scotland to be built in the age of artillery. Further north, at St Andrews, are the sad ruins of a fortress which was once one of the finest in the kingdom. The original stronghold was built by a bishop, the second was the grand palace of archbishops in the age of conspicuous ecclesiastical consumption which preceded the Reformation.

At the other side of the country, on the western shore and the islands it overlooks, there is a cluster of shoreline fortresses. Skipness on Kintyre is an ancient enceinte enclosing a sixteenth-century hall or tower house. Mingary, standing guard over the northern entrance to the Sound of Mull, is another medieval enceinte, although it was still strong enough to be garrisoned as late as 1745. At the other end of the sound, on the island itself, Duart castle is positioned on one of the west coast's most striking locations. The ruin was tastefully and tactfully restored by Sir Fitzroy MacLean during the course of this century. Two further island citadels complete the picture. Lochranza, on the northern tip of Arran, is a sixteenth-century castle that started life as a Stewart hunting lodge. The romantic and remote Kisimul, for centuries the seat of the MacNeils of Barra, also owes its present condition to careful restoration. It is the most westerly castle in Britain.

Three mighty fortresses on the sea have yet to be mentioned: Dunvegan, Tantallon and Dunnottar. Their resonant names alone make them worthy of consideration, and each has featured time and again in the country's history. Though they were built on sites chosen because the sea afforded protection on three of their four flanks, they are very different in appearance. For many reasons, therefore, they are simply too memorable to be omitted.

DUNNOTTAR CASTLE

South of Stonehaven, Grampian Region

Following the execution of his father early in the previous year, in June 1650 Charles II landed in Scotland in a desperate attempt to win back his throne. On his progress south he was received at Dunnottar Castle by William Keith, the 7th Earl Marischal, and served plentiful fresh salmon. About a year later, now the crowned King of Scots but still no nearer the English throne, Charles graced the stronghold with his presence a second time. On this occasion seven fine lambs were prepared for his consumption.

No doubt the king was impressed by the Marischal's hospitality. Charles was equally approving of his host's castle, for when he moved into England a short while later he left for safekeeping in Dunnottar's vaults not only the royal regalia of Scotland (which it was the Marischal's hereditary right to safeguard) but also his papers, plate and other valuables. It was generally agreed that there was no more secure place in all Scotland.

Charles' bid for the throne ended at the battle of Worcester on 3 September 1651, after which he was once more forced into exile. Cromwell's troops pushed into Scotland. Soon a single fortress stood out against them — Dunnottar. The siege lasted eight months, and despite the ferocious bombardment of the republican cannon it was starvation which eventually compelled the garrison to surrender.

English troops poured eagerly into the shattered fortress and ransacked it for the treasure which had been denied them for so long. They found little. The papers and regalia had been smuggled out during the siege and safely hidden beneath the floor of nearby Kinneff parish church, where they remained hidden for the next eight years. The regalia are now on view in Edinburgh Castle.

The story of the regalia and the siege of 1652 is a splendid testimony to Scotland's most perfect natural defensive site. No other medieval castle moved so comfortably from the age of slings and arrows to that of gunpowder. The reason for this is immediately clear as soon as one sees the rock upon which the stronghold is founded. Approach has to be made on foot, down a fenced path through the fields on the cliff tops south of Stonehaven. At first it is not apparent that there is a castle before one at all, for the slope hides the shore beneath it. Then, gradually, the fortress is revealed. First the keep, then the outbuildings, until finally the whole position stands before one, as impregnable a situation as one could imagine. The sea does not just enclose three sides, it surrounds almost entirely the gigantic mass of conglomerate which rises vertically from it.

The way to the castle leads down a cliff path and across a narrow tongue of land to the tiny doorway, half hidden by the sheer crag rising on its right hand side. A tall wall, as daunting as the cliffs themselves, blocks the only scalable fissure in the rock. General Overton, who commanded the English forces besieging the castle in 1652, reckoned that so puissant a position could never be taken by storm. He was probably correct.

The ruined buildings of Dunnottar do not match the grandeur of the castle's position. The gatehouse and donjon are stout, and the residential accommodation is attractive. But neither can equal the majesty of the promontory itself. The broad and lofty plateau, which covers an area of 3.5 acres, is unusual for its lack of curtain wall. In some places it has collapsed, in others it simply never existed, forty metres of cliff face being thought defence enough. The sense of space thus created, and the quaint juxtaposition of military and domestic architecture, combine to give the airy and open summit a feeling of confidence quite unlike that of any other castle. The visitor emerges from the dark labyrinthine ways of the gatehouse onto a spacious plain set about with the remains of an English country house, a pleasant cottage with its garden, workshops, a bowling green and a well. There is a battered keep, of course, but the overall impression is one of the peaceful domesticity of a self-contained hamlet. Dunnottar is more eyrie than fortress.

THE CASTLE

Dunnottar has three major structures which were primarily military in purpose: the gatehouse, the keep, and a small sentry box overlooking Old Hall Bay in the south-west corner. There is also a wall and a redoubt on the extreme westerly point of the site. The spur of rock that juts out towards the mainland here is known as the Fiddlehead because an observer once reckoned it to be shaped like a violin. In fact, lacking a waist, it is more akin to a lute or even a short-handled cooking pot. At the end of the handle the rock has been cut away to prevent it being used as a means of ingress. It is not clear when this was done but there is a gate in the pan handle's defences known as 'Wallace's Postern'. It is possible, therefore, that in 1297 the daring patriot made his successful assault on the stronghold by advancing along the sharp ridge, which was later severed so that this approach could never be used again.

The formidable gatehouse does not tower above the surrounding terrain in the normal manner. Rather, it is built onto the rock and even, in places, cut into it. On the right as we approach is a five-storey sixteenth-century building, known as Benholm's Lodging. It protects the entrance with three tiers of awesome-looking but rather ill-positioned gun-ports and loopholes. The small doorway had no need of a drawbridge. It was secured with a yett, a thick wooden door and a portcullis. An assailant managing to break through this menacing assortment then faced an impossible climb up a series of narrow stairways, sloping paths and tunnels — all murderously overlooked — before reaching the main body of the castle. There is stabling on the summit, which must tell us something about the size of the horses in Stewart Scotland as well as the skill of the grooms who had to lead them to their stalls. A number of gloomy vaulted rooms lead off the entrance passage. These include a guardroom, barrack room and magazine. At the far end of the basement of Benholm's Lodging is a horrible little prison, cut from the living rock.

The keep was built at the south-west corner of the plateau before the erection of the present gatehouse. It remains the dominant architectural feature of the castle, overlooking the entrance and the cliffs on the landward side. It is an L-shaped building of the late fourteenth or early fifteenth century, whose walls once rose fifteen metres above the ground. The masonry is rubble, except at the corners where more carefully-cut blocks are employed. It was four storeys high, with a store and prison in the basement, and a Great Hall on the first floor. The internal arrangements were reorganised when the Keiths found their small first-floor kitchen overwhelmed by the hospitality expected of an Earl Marischal. A spiral staircase leads to a corbelled parapet walk on the wallhead. The stairs end in a neat little stone hut, known as a cap-house.

The overall impression of the keep is one of simple solidity. As accommodation for one of the country's leading magnates, however, it must have been out-of-date shortly after it was finished. Not surprisingly, there are more commodious dwellings in the close vicinity.

William, the 4th Earl, was something of a curmudgeon. He spent many of his later years in anti-social solitude, shuffling about the keep, grumbling at the servants and peering out over the grey waters of the North Sea. To the locals he became 'William o' the Tower'. His was not the sort of grim household in which his son William and his bride Elizabeth Hay wished to spend the jolliest years of their lives. Either before their marriage or shortly after it, no doubt as a result of mounting family tension, a new house was built for them outside the keep. The young couple chose a site to the right of the keep's iron-yetted front door, near the middle of the castle. It is sheltered from south-westerly gales by the stables and other outbuildings overlooking the cliffs in that corner, and gives onto a sunny, low-walled little garden at the rear. Known now as the Priest's House or Waterton's Lodging, it must have been a delightful residence and a pleasant contrast to the military starkness around it.

If the Priest's House is a surprise for a castle site, the Quadrangle

The Earl of Atholl's lodging at Balvenie Castle. The unassailable security of Dunnottar enabled the architect of the castle's sixteenth-century buildings to reject completely this traditional tower design.

buildings at the opposite corner of the plateau are even more unexpected. While their contemporaries were still building upwards, in the form of noble towerhouses, the Earls Marischal preferred to expand horizontally, in the current English style. First to come was the westerly range of guest rooms, surmounted by a long gallery, probably put up by William o' the Tower to keep his visitors as far away as possible from his own apartments. He certainly would not have had any trouble paying for the new building, for it is said that he could make a leisurely progress from one end of the country to the other, staying on his own estates at every stage of the journey. Other sides of the Quadrangle followed, largely the seventeenth-century work of George the 5th Earl Marischal, although the chapel is somewhat earlier. George was a sophisticated man of the Renaissance, equally at home with his books as he was undertaking a diplomatic mission on behalf of the king. Aberdeen's Marischal College owes its existence to his munificent patronage. The whole Quadrangle complex is unashamedly domestic, reminding us how sharply the needs and tastes of the aristocracy had changed over the preceding century or so. There is no longer a hall, but a dining room and drawing room. The Countess's suite in the eastern block has its own bedroom and dressing room, and the infamous

Whigs' Vault, though there is a prison beneath it (the castle's third) has a fine private bedroom suite above, known as 'The King's Chamber' after its use by Charles II. Though the Vault itself was built as a storeroom, it later served a much more grizzly purpose.

THE BLACK HOLE OF DUNNOTTAR

For many centuries Dunnottar rock was topped with little more than an earth and timber palisade. Given the site's virtual impregnability anything further was undoubtably considered superfluous. Nevertheless, from time to time it did fall to intrepid assailants, although we do not know whether through strategy or treachery. The awe-inspiring promontory was also regarded as an especially holy place, giving rise to a curious incident in the late fourteenth century when Sir William Keith built the first stone castle there. He was promptly excommunicated by the Bishop of St Andrews for desecrating sacred ground. Only after an appeal to the pope and the payment of substantial compensation was the sentence lifted.

Despite its religious associations Dunnottar has seen innumerable manifestations of human cruelty. There always seems to have been some unfortunate or other in one of its several prisons, condemned to reside in dark, cold misery. Tradition has it that the Danes slew King Donald II at Dunnottar, and when Wallace seized the summit in 1297 he burned alive some of the defeated garrison in the citadel's church. On roughly the same spot a witch was similarly dealt with 300 years later.

A number of monarchs have visited Dunnottar over the centuries. Athelstan of Wessex marched this far north in 934. Edward III called in while trying in vain to hammer the Scots as his grandfather had done. Mary Queen of Scots brightened the place with her gay presence, and her son James VI held a meeting of his Privy Council there.

In 1645 Dunnottar withstood the forces of Montrose, although the seventh Earl Marischal, who had been a comrade in arms of the doughty Royalist a year or so previously, had to watch in impotent anguish as his rich estates were put to fire and the sword by the frustrated enemy. He received cold comfort from a bystander who observed with tactless piety that the reek of burning 'will be a sweet-smelling savour in the nostrils of the Lord!'

There has been space here to touch upon only a few of the stories which surround this celebrated monument. Yet there is one tale without which no guide to the castle, however brief, would be complete. It concerns the wretched Covenanters imprisoned within the Whigs' Vault in 1685.

The Catholic James VII came to the thrones of England and Scotland in 1685. He already had an unsavoury reputation in the northern kingdom, owing to his behaviour there during his brother's reign, and at his accession there was an uprising of the hotter sort of Protestants, known generally as Covenanters. It was led by the Earl of Argyll, who returned from exile and gathered his forces at Dunstaffnage. The revolt was soon crushed, however, and on 24 May 167 Covenanters were placed in Dunstaffnage for safe keeping.

What happened next has been the subject of much exaggeration, rather like the story of the Black Hole of Calcutta. The bare facts are these: 122 men and 45 women were incarcerated in the Whigs' Vault and given only such food and water as they could pay for. The conditions rapidly became extremely squalid. Almost all the prisoners were struck down with illness, and several died. After a time, to relieve the overcrowding some of the men were transferred to the cell below the Vault, where conditions were scarcely more comfortable. The Governor's wife was so smitten with the parlous state of the internees that she persuaded her husband to transfer all the women and a dozen of the men to more spacious surroundings. Even so, some of the inmates determined to escape. They did so at night by climbing out of one of the Vault's windows and scaling down the precipice. Twenty-five managed to get away by this route before some washerwomen raised the alarm. Fifteen prisoners were recaptured and imprisoned in the gatehouse. Here they were subjected to torture by burning. A number of them had their fingers reduced to ashes and one or two died of their injuries. Those who survived the ordeal of the prison house and the torment of their captors were transferred elsewhere at the end of July.

Later accounts spoke of the Whigs' Vault as being windowless, and of the guards deliberately spilling drinking water on to the floor in front of the parched prisoners. The torture by lighted taper, which was practised upon those who were recaptured, was described in bloodthirsty detail. The immorality of confining men and women at close quarters for a long period of time impressed itself forcibly upon the imaginations of puritanical writers. The general insanitary condition of the cell, awash with refuse and excrement, lost nothing in depiction. Even allowing for indignant embellishment, the whole episode was a shameful disgrace, and a pointed example of the cruelty which can be perpetrated in the name of religion.

Thirty years later an Earl Marischal was again involved in anti-government action, this time on the side of the rebels. As a consequence of his participation in the ill-fated 1715 Jacobite rebellion his castle at Dunnottar was forfeited, sold and dismantled. Its ruins remain for us to contemplate. We can scarcely imagine the extraordinary events they have witnessed.

INFORMATION

ACCESS The castle lies 2 miles south of Stonehaven, on the A 92

RESPONSIBILITY FOR THE SITE Private

TELEPHONE 0569-62173

OPENING HOURS April-October: 9.00-18.00 (Sundays 14.00-17.00) November-March: Mon-Fri 9.00-about 16.00, depending on the weather

ADMISSION PRICE £1.00 (Children 50p)

FACILITIES Parking Dogs

TANTALLON CASTLE
Near Canty village, Lothian Region

A huge block of igneous rock rises from the rough waters at the mouth of the Firth of Forth, where its shore slopes south towards Berwick and the English border. It is a bleak spot, favoured by gulls and hermits but avoided by all who care for human company and comforts. One cold February, however, a rowing boat struck out from North Berwick and made for the Rock. A young lad sat huddled in the stern among the stores. From the solicitous attention paid to him by other members of the small but distinguished-looking party of fellow travellers it was clear that he was a person of some standing. The anxious looks on their faces betrayed the importance of their mission.

The year was 1406. The twelve-year-old boy for whom so much concern was being shown was Prince James, the second son of King Robert III and, since the murder of his brother four years earlier, heir to the throne of Scotland. His father was a weak and unfortunate man, crippled by the kick of an unruly horse before he came to the throne, and quite unequal to the task of governing his troubled realm. James was taken to Bass Rock on the first stage of a proposed journey to France, where he would be safe from the machinations of his ambitious uncle Robert, Duke of Albany. It was strongly rumoured that Albany lay behind the death from starvation of James' elder brother. Now only the feeble Robert III and the young prince lay between Albany and the throne. The boy hoped to remain among the gannets of Bass Rock for only a day or two before a friendly vessel carried him to safety. But no ship came.

During his enforced captivity James no doubt wondered whether his flight was really necessary. When the weather cleared he could see on the mainland the awesome sand-red towers of Tantallon, one of the newest and probably the most secure fortress in Scotland. Could he not be transferred there? Surely it was proof against attack by his enemies, and at least he would be more comfortable in the castle. Even the guards huddled round their fires enjoyed greater luxury than their future king on his gull-infested rock.

As it turned out the boy had to wait four weeks in the uninspiring company of the Earl of Orkney and a Welsh bishop before he was picked up by a merchantman from Danzig, by which time the English had been alerted to the escape. The *Maryenknight* was intercepted off Flamborough Head and James led off to the Tower of London. When news of what had befallen reached the ears of Robert III, it broke his heart. He refused food and died a few days later.

James did not forget Tantallon. One of his first acts upon returning to Scotland after eighteen years of exile was to break the power of his uncle's family. Duke Robert was now dead, but his son Murdoch had taken over his father's position as Governor of the Realm. He was arrested, imprisoned in Caerlaverock for a while, then executed. Now the king had to find somewhere

Tantallon, one of the few medieval castles which made a successful transition into the age of gunpowder.

The Macleods have been masters of Dunvegan Castle since the early Middle Ages and the castle contains a wonderful collection of clan memorabilia, including the miraculous 'Fairy Flag'.

to detain the traitor's widow. He knew of just the place. She was sent to Tantallon and locked in the eastern tower, upon which the prince had gazed so longingly many years before.

There was some sense in James' childhood musings. Had he remained in Scotland, he would have been as safe in Tantallon as anywhere in the kingdom. The castle stands on a rocky promontory, surrounded on three sides by vertical cliffs thirty metres high. The neck of the peninsular is closed by a gigantic curtain of stone, reinforced by three massive towers, before which runs a formidable rock-cut ditch. It was the last major castle of enceinte to be built in Scotland. The curtain walls on the cliff tops were in fact never completed, so the site has the appearance of a cardboard box lying on its side with one of the opening flaps raised vertically into the air.

Like the goddess Diana, Tantallon is as celebrated for its beauty as it is for its strength. From a distance it resembles an Indian temple as much as a castle, for much of the masonry is fashioned from a delightful red sandstone which the wind and rain has weathered into smooth and beautiful shapes. On a sunny evening the great curtain wall glows like an ember. Against a backdrop of ocean cliffs, with grassy mounds and ditches before it, the fortress displays a combination of shape and colour unique among British castles.

THE CASTLE

The design of Tantallon is the simplest imaginable. Nature has done most of the architect's work for him. All that he was left to do to make the site secure was block the approach from the south-west. The original castle was built in about 1350 for William, the 1st Earl of Douglas. It is likely that the outer line of defence was a ditch and rampart, although those we see today are largely the work of later improvements. Behind this earthen wall is a broad green, known as the Outer Ward, featuring a pretty stone dovecot. A wide ditch has been cut into the hard ground of the peninsular where it narrows to a defensible width. Behind this rises the curtain wall, fifteen metres high and more than three-and-a-half metres thick. At its eastern end is a D-shaped tower five storeys high. It was on the third floor of this building that the Duchess of Albany was imprisoned. Cramped though her quarters may have been, they were a great deal more comfortable than those afforded to petty criminals. They were held in the damp fastness of a pit prison below the circular tower at the western end of the wall, known as the Douglas Tower after the family who built it. This structure originally provided the castle's principal accommodation.

Unfortunately both of Tantallon's great towers were badly knocked about in the siege of 1651. The outstanding feature of the remaining fortification is the massive gatehouse in the centre of the curtain wall. It was built long after the revolution in castle building which had concentrated defences away from the keep, and is a good example of the new style. However, because of the excellence of its position Tantallon continued in use as a fortress longer than most medieval castles, and in order to bring the defences up to date the keep-gatehouse was extensively re-modelled. This makes it quite difficult nowadays to see how it has developed.

A visitor to the fourteenth-century castle passed over a drawbridge, beneath a portcullis and then through no less than three double-leaved yetts. Above rose the gatehouse, over twenty metres high, with four storeys of spacious accommodation above a portcullis chamber. From the front the entrance had a most elegant appearance, the two projecting jambs on either side of the door expanding some ten metres from the ground into corbelled round turrets in the shape of firework rockets. Openings were left where the square form budded into the turret. These machiolations, which can be seen behind the present entrance facade, enabled the soldiers within to cover the base of the walls.

In the early fifteenth century a barbican was constructed in front of the original gateway, but this entrance was either destroyed in the siege of 1528 or deliberately pulled down to make way for the third reconstruction, which took place in the 1530s. For some reason the sixteenth-century builders used a greenish coloured stone, employing the original sandstone only in horizontal bands across the new Fore Tower. The gateway was extended forward and reduced in size to offer a smaller target for artillery. The rounded Fore Tower was fitted with gunholes to enable the defenders to return the fire of their assailants. While this work was being carried out the curtain was strengthened by filling in some of its internal chambers and crenellation was added to the wall head. The site was further modernised by digging extensive earthworks in front of the vulnerable masonry. In this way a castle built to resist flying stones and battering rams was converted into one capable of withstanding the onslaught of heavy guns.

Within the castle there was a range of domestic buildings, which was extended and adapted over the years to meet the changing needs of the inhabitants. A hall ran eastwards from the Douglas Tower, and later a bakehouse, kitchen and brewhouse were added to occupy the whole of the clifftop overlooking the haven. Opposite the curtain wall and facing the Bass Rock a sea gate was begun but never finished, probably because it was thought that no one would ever be foolhardy enough to attempt an assault on the fortress from this flank.

There is an ancient Scottish proverb linking Tantallon and the Bass Rock: 'Ding doon Tantallon — mak a brig to the Bass'. In other words, an attempt to capture Tantallon is about as foolish as trying to build a bridge to the Bass Rock. Had he heard it, the saying would have brought a wry smile to the lips of James I.

DING DOON TANTALLON

Tantallon was built not as a national stronghold but as a family seat. Fifteenth-century Scotland was a country of strife. Time and again the monarchs of the House of Stewart battled to assert their authority against the power of overmighty subjects, only for their work to be undone during the minorities of their successors. James I was twelve when his father died; James II inherited the crown at the age of six, James III was eight, James IV fifteen and James V but a one-year-old baby. The ill-luck of the Stewarts played into the hands of an ambitious aristocracy, foremost among whom were the Red Earls of Douglas. From the strength of its towers to the appropriate hue of its masonry, their mighty sea-girt fortress at Tantallon was a living symbol of resistance to the crown.

Douglas fortunes rose on the broad blade of 'the Good Sir James', who fought alongside Wallace and Robert Bruce during the Wars of Independence and who died in Spain while carrying Bruce's heart on crusade against the infidel. The 1st Earl Douglas, a nephew of this doughty warrior, took as his mistress his brother-in-law's widow Margaret Stewart, Countess of Angus. They had a son George, who acquired the Angus title. Upon the death of the 2nd Earl the Douglas family divided between the 'Black' and 'Red'. It is with the latter, the Douglas Earls of Angus, that Tantallon is most closely associated.

The first four earls were more concerned with outwitting the rival Black Douglases than challenging the power of the crown. Their loyalty was rewarded with the trust of James I who, as we have seen, used Tantallon as a prison for the Countess of Albany and later for a recalcitrant Lord of the Isles. However, with Archibald the 5th Earl the Red Douglases began to tread more dangerous paths.

James III (1460-1488) was a cultured, capable but somewhat tactless young king. In trying to rid himself of baronial tutelage he sought the advice of less well-born but more loyal advisors. Aristocratic resentment boiled over in 1482 when, led by the devious Archibald Douglas, they murdered some of the king's favourites. For his part in trying to circumscribe the actions of the leading player on the political stage, Archibald was henceforth known as 'Bell the Cat'.

Bell the Cat's restless duplicity continued into the next reign. In 1491 James IV ordered him to retire to Tantallon and cease meddling in affairs that did not concern him. Archibald's response was to prepare his fortress for siege. The eighteen-year-old king appeared before the castle in October, bringing with him from Edinburgh the whole of the royal siege train. While his vessels blockaded the castle on the seaward side, his artillery pounded the walls from the south-west. But Tantallon was no medieval relic, likely to collapse when the first cannon ball smashed against its crumbling stonework. Furthermore, the season was late for campaigning, and the royal army cold and disgruntled in its makeshift accommodation. An action which at first looked as if it might be over in a matter of days, soon gave every indication of lasting for weeks or even months.

James was an impetuous man, a quality which twenty-two years later would eventually lead to his undoing on Flodden Field. Painstaking siege warfare was not to his liking. Bored with the lack of action, he passed long hours playing cards, at which he lost a good deal of money. Still no breach appeared in Tantallon's defences, and there was certainly no sign that the garrison wished to consider terms. So in the end the king came to an agreement with Bell and Cat, packed up his guns and went home.

In 1528 a similar scene was re-enacted. It involved another teenage King James (V) and another treacherous Earl Archibald (6th). Once more the royal artillery was wheeled out from its arsenals. It included two gigantic pieces, known with macabre affection as 'Deaf Meg' and 'Crooked Mouth'. As the soldiers marched to the fray they chanted confidently 'ding doon Tantalloun, ding doon Tantalloun', in time with their step. But, as in 1491, the weather was closing in. And Tantallon had been strengthened with earthen ramparts to enable it better to withstand the fiery utterances of Meg, Mouth and their hellish children.

In the end it was not boredom which brought the siege to a close but bad management. After about two-and-a-half weeks of fruitless bombardment the royal army ran out of ammunition. Though fresh supplies could be obtained from France, that meant further expense and a long wait into the winter. Irritated and frustrated, the king ordered a withdrawal. His soldiers were undoubtably relieved at the prospect of going home, but they were also annoyed at having risked their lives for no apparent purpose. In a desultory manner they began to pack up their tents and prepare the heavy guns for the long haul back to Edinburgh. Discipline grew slack.

Earl Archibald determined to teach the young king a lesson in warfare. Seeing the disarray in the lines before him, he gathered 160 of the garrison about him and ordered a surprise counter-attack. The little band of hand-picked men sallied forth with remarkable alacrity. The royal forces were thrown into such confusion that, almost before they knew what was happening, the Douglas troops had made themselves masters of a goodly part of the royal artillery. Ding doon Tantalloun? It was much easier said than done.

James V was quick to learn. The following year he achieved through negotiation what he had failed to do by force and for a while Tantallon became a royal castle. Over the next hundred years the fortress continued to feature from time to time in the nation's history. But really the days of the stone-built castle were over. The grand old fortress put up one last heroic show of resistance in 1651, when it withstood the guns of General Monk for seventeen days. At the end of this prolonged and skilfully executed bombardment, however, the flanking towers were in ruins and the accommodation uninhabitable. Three hundred years after its construction, Tantallon had finally fallen.

INFORMATION

ACCESS   The castle is signposted off the A198 2 1/2 miles east of North Berwick. Public transport nearby

RESPONSIBILITY FOR THE SITE
Scottish Development Department

OPENING HOURS April-September: 9.30-19.00 (Sun   FACILITIES   Disabled (limited)
              14.00-19.00) October-March:9.30-   Parking
              16.00 (Sun 14.00-16.00)   Dogs
ADMISSION PRICE   Toilets
              £1.00 (Senior citizens and   Guided tours by special request
              children 50p)

DUNVEGAN CASTLE

Dunvegan, Isle of Skye

The great stone-throwing machines of Edward I, the cannon of the Stewarts and the artillery of the New Model Army managed between them to reduce to ruins most of Scotland's ancient castles. Dunvegan, however, was spared. The seat of the MacLeods was too remote to be accessible to cumbersome engines of destruction. Only a sea-borne attack, such as that which destroyed Eilean Donan, would have proved feasible, and fortunately it was never deemed necessary. Moreover, in the days when civil political conflict was settled by force of arms rather than by the ballot box or in the law courts, the MacLeods did not usually become closely involved in national affairs. They had enough on their hands defending their widespread estates from the depredations of neighbouring clans. Nevertheless, the Victorians did their best to succeed where others had failed, and those visiting Dunvegan in the hope of finding much that remains from the Middle Ages will be sadly disappointed. The castle of today owes as much to the restrained imagination of Robert Brown of Edinburgh as to any medieval master mason.

This does not mean, of course, that Dunvegan is unattractive or unworthy of a visit. Far from it. It is one of the most romantic and celebrated of Scottish castles, steeped in the history of the MacLeods and their rivals, and containing a number of relics, both quirky and interesting. The fortress is built upon an isolated clump of rock, the shape of a twisted heart. Behind rises Beinn Bhreac, before lies Loch Dunvegan and the flat-topped mountain known with proprietorial pride as MacLeod's Tables.

The slopes around the castle were bleak and unadorned until the MacLeods planted them with trees in the nineteenth century to lend their ancestral sea a softer, more homely appearance. This has made the sheltered approach from the car park and tourist complex rather dull, particularly as the appearance of the castle from this side is, to put it politely, uninspiring. A visitor has the feeling of being admitted through the tradesman's entrance which, in fact, is almost correct. For hundreds of years the only way into the castle was through the sea gate on the other flank, overlooking the loch. This western facade is altogether more imposing. It is a considerable shame, therefore, that it is never seen by the majority of tourists. The best views are to be had from the scattered farm buildings on the opposite side of the loch, or from the rocks projecting into the seal-rippled waters a little further up the coast. Dunvegan displays herself at her finest in the evening, when the setting sun adds colour to otherwise anaemic-looking walls.

THE CASTLE

As it stands today Dunvegan is the product of at least nine separate rebuildings. On each occasion the existing structure was normally left intact, so that we are presented with a living exhibition of Scottish architectural development. The problem of distinguishing the separate styles was given a final twist under the twenty-fifth MacLeod chief when much of the hotch-potch of buildings was unified behind a battlemented romantic facade, complete with corbelled turrets and an imposing new tower.

Dunvegan Rock was in all probability a defensive site long before recorded history. In the Middle Ages the position passed into the hands of a Norse prince named Leod, a younger son of Olaf King of Man and the Northern Isles. Leod built a simple but sturdy castle of enceinte (probably like those at Kisimul and Mingarry) by throwing a thick curtain wall about the rock. It was entered by a heavily defended sea-gate and protected on the landward side by a steep gorge.

In the fourteenth century a solid keep was added at the northern end of the site. Although remains of this structure can be seen at basement level, it was in such a poor state of repair that extensive rebuilding was needed during the last century to prevent its collapse. The third development came in about 1500 with the erection of the Fairy Tower at the other end of the site. The work was ordered by the 8th chief, Alasdair 'Crotach', or hunchback. He emulated many of his contemporaries by putting up a fashionable tower house amid the ruins of a medieval castle — we have already seen how this was done by the Grants at Urquhart and the Elphinstones in Kildrummy. A century later Rory Mor built a long hall from the Fairy Tower along the ridge above the gully, no doubt to improve the domestic accommodation now that the keep was becoming unserviceable.

Towards the end of the seventeenth century Rory Mor's hall was rebuilt and a Piper's Gallery added to its eastern wall. At the same time a new block was put up on the south-western face of the Fairy Tower, making the occupied part of the castle into an L-shape. The only development over the next hundred years was the construction of a large door to the landward, approached from the ravine by a long flight of stone steps up which Dr Johnson puffed when he visited the castle in 1773.

The present shape of the castle is largely the work of two architects, Walter Boak and Robert Brown the Younger. The former united existing buildings by extending Rory Mor's hall to a refurbished keep. Then, appropriately, Chief Norman (known as the General from the rank he

In 1406 the future James I spent four unhappy weeks marooned on the Bass Rock while on his way to France. The ship which eventually rescued him was captured by the English, and it was another eighteen years before James returned to Scotland.

purchased while on service in India) arranged for his architect to construct a Barrack Block north-west of the keep. Now, for the first time since the medieval walls had crumbled away, the castle extended the full length of its imposing site. The General's son added the mock gatehouse in 1814-15. It remained for Brown and the 25th Chief to pull the whole structure together and turn it into a Victorian stately home. The result is not to everyone's taste, but at least it avoids the more ostentatious 'Gothick' fantasy of Dunrobin. Moreover, whatever one may feel about the outside of the castle, the interior is a delight to behold. Laden with treasures and mementoes, it has a comfortable, lived-in feel. The presentation is not slick, but the feeling of aristocratic amateurishness only adds to the castle's friendly charm.

LEGEND AND CLARET DRINKING

As befits a castle with so civilised an air as Dunvegan, stories associated with the place are more mystical than military. True, the MacLeods were involved in their fair share of dirty dealing. In the time of Alasdair Crotach, for example, they smoked to death the entire MacDonald population of Eigg who had taken refuge in a cave. This was in revenge for the murder by exposure in an open boat of a young MacLeod lad who had been unwisely chasing after a MacDonald lass. Smoking or burning people to death was clearly not all that uncommon in the Highlands, where most houses had thatched roofs. The MacLeod population of Waternish died this way when the MacDonalds fired the church into which they were crowded one Sunday morning. Only one woman managed to escape, by squeezing through a very narrow window behind the altar. But in her struggle to get out she tore off her breasts on the rough stonework and subsequently bled to death.

THE GREEN LADY

Across the waters of Loch Dunvegan the sounds of revelry waft with the evening breeze. There are great celebrations in the Chief's hall tonight, for his young wife has just given birth to a son Iain, who one day will be the sixth chief. Dressed in their finery for the occasion, MacLeods are gathered in from all around to drink their lord's French wine and share in his happiness. The light from the broad log fire plays on their weather-beaten faces; there will be dancing later and some of the Highlanders are already singing. Their ballads tell of the might of their clan and the prowess of its great Chiefs.

Some distance away, in the fastness of the new tower at the castle's southern tip, the young Iain MacLeod is asleep, watched over by his nurse. Roused by the sound of distant music and seeing her charge so peaceful, the woman tiptoes to the door, opens it quietly and slips away to join the celebrations in the keep. For just a second or so, she tells herself. But the minutes pass. Carried away by the merriment she loses all sense of time as she is whirled about the floor in reel and strathspey.

The Chief's wife is seated by the blazing fire, watching the celebrations and smiling calmly to herself. Then, suddenly, her hands tighten and a look of disbelief comes into her eyes. Is that the nurse dancing? How long has she been here? And where is the baby? Muttering a hasty word of explanation to those around her, she stands and walks quickly from the room. Once outside in the cool air of the courtyard she breaks into a run, her quick steps echoing on the cobbles, her dress billowing behind her. Soon she is at the tower, throws open the door and starts up the steps towards the baby's chamber on the first floor. Then she pauses, amazed.

The sound of gentle singing can be heard from inside Iain's bedroom. The words and tune are those of a lullaby of especial sweetness. Quietly, she goes to the door and peeps in.

A little woman in green is sitting beside the cradle, holding the baby boy in her arms and singing softly to him. She has wrapped the child in a banner of silk which shimmers in the candle-light. Half angry, half frightened, the mother approaches and her shadow falls across the scene. Slowly the fairy looks round and, seeing the mother, stands, holding out the child still wound in the mysterious flag. 'He was crying,' she explains, 'and I came to comfort him. Here, he is yours. Keep the flag, for the night is chill. Besides, it is a fairy banner. As long as your clan keeps it, they will come to no harm.'

With these words, the lady vanishes, leaving the astonished mother holding her doubly precious charge. Still bewildered but relieved to find her son well, she makes her way back to the hubbub of the hall. A hush falls on the company as she enters. Then they let forth a great cheer, for she holds the future of all of them safe in her arms.

*   *   *   *   *

Later that night the lady told her husband what had befallen. From that time forth no nurse was employed at Dunvegan who could not sing the fairy lullaby. And whenever the Fairy Flag was waved in battle victory fell to the MacLeods. The banner is preserved to this day, threadbare but intact, secure from souvenir hunters behind protective glass. In the last war MacLeod airmen wore replicas of it beneath their flying jackets to keep them safe. The Fairy Room in the Fairy tower is open for all to inspect.

The version of the origin of the Fairy Flag given above is certainly untrue. But then so are the legion of other Gilbertian tales which tell of it being brought back from a crusade, found in a box, or even given to a heart-broken MacLeod Chief by his fairy wife as she slipped back to Fairyland. However, we are not concerned here with history, but with mystery. And they both have their place in the rich culture of the Highlands.

Within the same room as the Fairy Flag is Rory Mor's Horn, a relic with rather more macho associations. It was torn from the head of a bull by the mighty Chief Malcolm. The enraged animal had been set upon a young Campbell who had offended his chief. Upset at the iniquity of such a cruel punishment, Malcolm had leapt into the ring, thrown the bull to the ground and broken its neck. 'Hold fast!' the crowd had yelled during the frantic wrestling match between man and beast. Their cry was adopted as the motto of the MacLeods. To this day, to mark his coming of age, the Chief's heir is expected to down a horn-full of claret at one draught. The vessel holds well over a litre. The men of Skye can drink as well as tell stories.

INFORMATION

ACCESS   The castle is just north of
          Dunvegan on the A850
          Public transport to Dunvegan

RESPONSIBILITY FOR THE SITE
          Scottish Development
          Department

TELEPHONE   047-022-206

OPENING HOURS
          26th March-31 October: Mon-Sat
          10.00-17.30

ADMISSION PRICE
          £3.00 (Senior citizens £2.50;
          children £1.50)

FACILITIES   Disabled
          Parking
          Dogs (in grounds only)
          Toilets
          Shop
          Restaurant

Craigievar Castle: a near-perfect example of the tower house, Scotland's most distinctive contribution to European architecture.

TOWERS OF STRENGTH AND BEAUTY

The tower house is Scotland's best-known contribution to European architecture. It first appeared in the fourteenth century as an unadorned block, a secure dwelling for the wealthy. Defensive needs initially overrode domestic considerations; in some early towers, for example, even the kitchens were not included in the main structure. Gradually, however, as society became more settled and the Stewarts strengthened their grip on the machinery of government at both the national and local level, greater attention could be paid to comfort and and aesthetics. Windows were enlarged, entrances constructed at ground level and, on occasion, a kind of service-tower was placed alongside the main tower to form an L-shape. Later still, three towers were sometimes built as a single unit in a Z-plan, and the upper storeys became increasingly elaborate. These buildings were really only half-castles.

The genre reached a glorious apogee of vertical construction in the early seventeenth century. External walls remained unadorned and embellishment of openings for doors and lower windows restrained. However, as if to compensate for the austerity below, the architects gave full rein to their creativity in a blossom of corbelled turreting at the wall-head, the like of which can not be found outside Scotland. The whole design, seen in its full glory at Craigievar, is a lovely combination of clean line and controlled extravagance, enhanced by the contrast between the pastels of the building and the natural colours of the surrounding gardens.

There are several reasons for the Scots' unique penchant for building tower houses. By the later fourteenth century the castle of enceinte was rapidly becoming obsolete. It was very expensive to construct, maintain and defend, and at time of siege required a large garrison to man the extensive walls and towers. Moreover, as the highly efficient campaigns of Edward I had shown, given time an attacking army equipped with the latest offensive weapons could be certain to secure the investment of almost any castle. Defence against a determined and well-funded aggressor was even more difficult by the end of the fourteenth century, when siege cannon had become part of the customary stock-in-trade of a well-equipped army.

The response of the Scottish nobility to this situation was to withdraw into simple towers, easy and relatively cheap to build, yet perfectly capable of providing security against incidental assault. Even if landowners had been able to afford it, there was little point in building another Kildrummy, or even a Tantallon, when artillery could threaten it so effectively. Besides, siege guns were almost exclusively a royal province, so constructing a stronghold capable of withstanding them was implicitly to challenge the authority of the ambitious Stewart monarchs — a step which few wished to take. Finally, with the decline of the feudal system the castle no longer had to serve as a barracks for the

SMAILHOLM TOWER
A border refuge which evokes most powerfully the region's troubled past.

lord's host.

The tower house, therefore, was not a throw-back to the Norman keep. It originated as a purely practical response by the native aristocracy to the problems of the later medieval period, and in all its various manifestations over the following two and a half centuries it remained almost exclusively Scottish in inspiration. In particular, the baronial exuberance of the later examples was no mere French import. Furthermore, however grandiose a tower's superstructure might become, the need for defence was never entirely forgotten and it was still called a castle. Even during the long years of peace following the majority of James VI, when tower houses were put up by the score all over the country, it was considered necessary to make some allowances for defence. Only when the troubles following the accession of William and Mary had subsided did the Scots finally come down to earth, so to speak, and build on the horizontal plane.

Though Drum, Thirlestane and several other mansions started life as tower houses, the original buildings have subsequently been subsumed beneath later extensions and alterations. The six examples of tower house chosen for this chapter, with the exception of Glamis, stand largely as they did when first built, and so provide the reader with a relatively straightforward history of this singular but fascinating permutation of the Scottish castle.

THREAVE CASTLE

West of Castle Douglas, Dumfries and Galloway Region

A visit to Threave castle is a small adventure. Clear notices direct vehicles from the A75, up a farm track and into a car park. But there is no sign of the castle yet, and tourists are faced with a long walk and a boat trip before they reach their destination. A narrow fenced footpath, interrupted with innumerable gates, slopes down to the River Dee through the fields, then follows the bank for about a hundred metres before ending up at a small landing stage.

Threave's stark tower is now visible on the edge of a low grassy island in the stream, and by ringing a bell a ferry can be summoned to carry one to it. Until recently passengers were rowed across the river, but now a less romantic outboard motor ensures a quicker passage. Once safely ashore (and disembarkation is not always easy when the river is in flood), the monument lies only a few steps away across neat and level lawns. The difficulty of reaching the castle, even in the late twentieth century, emphasises just how secure a defensive position it occupies.

Threave was a Black Douglas castle, built in about 1370 by Archibald the 3rd Earl of Douglas to control Galloway for King David II. The well-chosen

Threave Tower, showing clearly the putholes at the wall head which once housed the wooden joists of the overhanging gallery or bretach.

The tiny doorway at Smailholm. It was clearly designed for defence rather than ostentation.

island site had probably been used as a place of defence for centuries. According to tradition it was the headquarters of the ancient Lords of Galloway, and Archibald may well have selected it with this in mind, for the region was notoriously unstable and he was keen to establish any link, however tenuous, with traditional loyalties. The fortress was also important because of its proximity to the border with England. Though the surrounding farmland is unexceptional and the tower itself is rather bleak, the presence of the gentle waters of the Dee softens the setting. This, together with the castle's historical and architectural importance (and the novel experiences involved in getting there), afford the site a pleasant memorability, especially in fine weather.

THE CASTLE

The man who built Threave was known to his contemporaries as 'the Grim', and it has often been remarked that the castle he raised on the island in the Dee did little to help his sinister reputation. In fact, like a successful sheriff in a Western, being considered mean and unyielding was probably no handicap when it came to imposing his will on a lawless region. Therefore it may have been with a perverse practicality that he commanded those responsible for the construction of Threave to eschew luxury and adornment, and concentrate instead on the erection of a building which would prove stubborn in defence and awesome of aspect. Respecting their master's wishes, the craftsmen did as they were bid, and produced a tower as grim as its master.

The walls of the five-storey tower are more than two metres thick. With the exception of the stone-vaulted third floor, where the Great Hall was situated, the levels were divided by timber joists and floorboards. The basement was used for storage, though later a dismal pit prison was constructed in one corner. Given the damp nature of the site, neither prisoners nor supplies can have lasted long down there. Overlooked by a stone gallery, which also acted as a fighting platform and a gruesomely didactic gibbet, the wooden drawbridge admitted visitors to a ground floor entry hall and kitchen area. The doorway was altered slightly in the last century when the castle was rearranged to house French prisoners taken in the Napoleonic wars. The Great Hall occupied the whole of the third floor, but all that remains of it now are the broad fireplaces staring incongruously into the void. The two remaining floors contained bedrooms and a bare barrack room. The lack of privies in the latter suggests that it was intended for prolonged occupation only at times of siege, particularly as it was directly above the Douglas bed chamber. For most of the time it probably served as a small arsenal.

An elaborate overhanging wooden hoarding crested the walls on the three sides nearest the river. This enabled the defenders to overlook the base of the tower and drop missiles upon assailants. The holes into which the joists of the hoarding fitted can still be seen, giving the top of the tower the appearance of a gigantic dovecot. Another interesting defensive device is the positioning of the spiral or wheel stair. It was built in the corner furthest from the entrance, so that a raiding party who managed to break through the gates and the yett still had to cross an enfiladed open space before they could have access to the upper floors and wall head. The whole tower was surrounded by a ditch which filled with water in all but the driest seasons, and a small harbour on the river side of the castle was the most likely entrance for provisions.

The fortress built by Earl Archibald was one of the most sophisticated early tower houses in Scotland. Yet in one respect it was strangely lacking. The earl had made no provision for defence against gunfire, though twenty-five years before the castle's completion soldiers from the British Isles had met with cannon at the battle of Crecy and strategists were already discussing the revolutionary potential of the new weapon. The omission was made good about eighty years later, when Earl William built a low masonry wall around the tower's landward side. It was furnished with ample bow slits and, more importantly, the three corner towers were pierced with cannon ports — the first example of such a defensive capacity in any Scottish castle.

THE FALL OF THE BLACK DOUGLASES

The history of Threave is closely linked with the story of the Black Douglas Lords of Galloway. Archibald the Grim died on Christmas Eve 1400. He had successfully won control over Galloway and his family's power was already causing the government concern. Over the ensuing half century a prolonged and bitter struggle took place between the Stewarts and a handful of overmighty families, among the most powerful of whom were the Earls of Douglas. The drama came to a stirring climax before the defences of Threave, when the crown was finally triumphant and the power of the Black Douglases was broken forever.

In 1440 the young James II (1437-1460) had witnessed the judicial murder of the 6th Earl of Douglas at the celebrated 'Black Dinner' held at Edinburgh castle. The Douglases were a resilient family however, and when in 1444 the 8th Earl married the 'Fair Maid of Galloway', his second cousin and heiress to the Galloway title, the family seemed as puissant as ever. The king resorted to subterfuge, sending Earl William on a mission to Rome and trying to seize the Douglas estates in his absence. When this failed the earl was granted a safe pass to dine with the king at Stirling castle. Twelve years had passed since the last ill-fated Douglas dinner engagement, but if William had forgotten the incident, his master had not, and what occurred may well have been preplanned. Before long the conversation between the monarch and his subject grew heated, and a quarrel broke out. Drawing a knife, James stabbed William in the throat. Courtiers sprang forward to assist the king, and before anyone knew what was really happening one of them had split open the earl's head with an axe.

If James thought that this bloody deed would break the family he so

Threave, showing the surrounding wall which contained provision for cannon. It was one of the first castles to be built in the form of a tower house.

The gaunt outline of Smailholm Tower, a border stronghold much admired by Walter Scott.

despised, he had miscalculated. His namesake, James the 9th Earl, married his brother's widow and resumed the vendetta with the Stewarts. Fighting broke out in 1455. One by one the Douglas strongholds succumbed to the firepower of the royal artillery, so carefully collected and prepared by the gun-loving monarch. Earl James fled to England. By July of all his castles only Threave remained outside the king's grasp, and the siege there had already begun.

It soon became clear to James from the reports he was receiving that Threave was putting up far stiffer resistance than he had expected. Not only was the place very difficult to get at, but recent improvements in the defences had markedly improved its ability to withstand cannon fire. So the king decided to put in a personal appearance. He set up his headquarters in Tongland Abbey and directed operations by day from a tent beside the river. With the arrival from Linlithgow Palace of heavy siege guns, known as bombards, the weight of material being hurled at Threave increased considerably. Before long the castle's outbuildings lay in ruins, though the main defences appear to have remained intact. Then, suddenly, the siege ended.

We do not know why Threave surrendered. Perhaps the garrison would have continued their resistance longer if their master had been there to lead them. But Earl James was safe in England, and when rumours of what the king was prepared to offer reached the beleaguered Douglas soldiers, they opted for terms which were both honourable and (if unexplained payments from the royal coffers are interpreted correctly) lucrative.

Later Earl James invaded Scotland twice to try to get his lands back. He was captured on his second expedition and imprisoned in Lindores Abbey, where he died in 1488. King James, on the other hand, was blown to bits by one of his own cannon while attempting to recapture Roxburgh from the English in 1460. From his old adversary's point of view, there was a certain justice in the unfortunate manner in which he died.

Threave was inhabited until the middle of the seventeenth century; but after the Covenanters had slighted the castle following a lengthy siege no one considered it worth restoring. By that time the days of such fortifications were over anyway. Access by boat was all very well in lawless times, but it was more of a nuisance than a boon when security was of only incidental importance. Besides, the stronghold's cramped and rheumatic accommodation was not popular with a generation accustomed to more comfortable living. By the time of Charles II there were many more congenial dwellings to be found elsewhere.

INFORMATION

ACCESS   The castle is signposted from the A75 south-west of Castle Douglas

RESPONSIBILITY FOR THE SITE
Scottish Development Department

OPENING HOURS
April-September: 9.30-19.00 (Sun 14.00-19.00)

ADMISSION PRICE
60p (Senior citizens and children 30p)

FACILITIES   Parking
Guided tours by special request

SMAILHOLM TOWER

By Smailholm Village, Border Region

The present border between Scotland and England was arrived at only after centuries of conflict. From the time of the Wars of Independence to the accession of James VI to the English throne in 1603 the governments on either side of the disputed divide were unable to do much about the raids and counter-raids which were endemic to that rugged and lawless region. Indeed, both administrations were usually prepared to turn a blind eye to acts of piracy perpetrated by their own nationals. Although the fighting could flare into large-scale conflict when it involved a major border family, such as Percy or Douglas, for most of the time the protagonists were small bands of raiders, known in Scotland as 'reivers'. Thieves and rustlers would gather at a pre-arranged spot, then sweep over the border in an orgy of pillage, burning and murder before retiring whence they came, laden with all the booty they could carry and driving stolen cattle before them.

The Pringles were a typical family of well-to-do border farmers. They owned estates around the village of Smailholm (meaning small 'holm' or settlement) and were continually struggling to defend their persons and possessions against the reivers. Towards the end of the fifteenth century, perhaps after some particularly devastating raid, they decided to build themselves an imposing new residence. The result was Smailholm Tower. Though the building is not really a castle, it is an excellent example of a tower house. Its site and history illustrate well just why such defensible strongholds were needed at a time when further south military architecture was rapidly going out of fashion.

There is nothing aggressive about Smailholm. It was built to serve as a watch-tower and a place of refuge. It could not withstand a siege, for it contained neither well nor kitchen. But when reivers appeared on the horizon the Pringles could lock themselves in their tower and watch from its fastness the unhappy scenes unfolding beneath them. From the top of the tower, some seventeen metres above its rocky base, there are fine views in all directions — to the Cheviots, the Lammermuirs, the Eildon Hills and into the low-lying Merse. A watchman at the tower-head could spot daylight raiders while they were still far off, and so enable local defence forces to be mustered.

The purposes of the tower are apparent as soon as one sees it. The citadel perches on Sandy Knowe Crags, above the farm which bears the same name. The pastoral nature of the setting is pointedly brought home to the visitor who arrives at milking time, when the gate between the farmyard and the track leading to the Crag is closed to prevent cattle wandering off onto the open heath. It is a still and remote place, where in the early evening mists rise and the sombre rocks around the tower glower with dark menace.

THE TOWER

Like Threave, the keynote of Smailholm is practicality. Its walls of local granite are about two metres thick, roughly fashioned, with blocks of red sandstone at the corners to tie them together. The few windows, originally protected with iron grilles, are small and situated well above the ground. There is a single narrow door on the south side, reinforced by a wrought iron yett and overlooked by a sinister gunport. A similar aperture can be found high in the west wall from where it was possible to command the barmkin gate. The upper storey was rebuilt in the seventeenth century to provide parapets along the north and south sides and a snug shelter beside the chimney for the look-out.

The inside of the tower was scarcely less stark than the outside. The exception was the hall, situated above the vaulted basement. It must be imagined with a log fire blazing in the attractively moulded fireplace, rich hangings decorating the walls, a painted ceiling, matting or carpets on the floor and soft cushions on the stone window seats. Even on a stormy night both rain and reiver must have seemed far away to those comfortably ensconced in such a chamber. The top two storeys were reserved for the family's private chambers. Quite recently the interior of the tower has been brightened considerably with a new reception area, informative displays and a delightful exhibition of tapestries and model figures. The restrained good taste of the refurbishment is a hallmark of the excellent work of Historic Buildings and Monuments, a branch of the Scottish Development Department.

Although it stands alone today, Smailholm was obviously not designed to be complete in itself. A number of other buildings once stood in the area, the most important of which were constructed on the same rocky knoll as the tower and surrounded by a thick wall to form a barmkin. This comprised two courtyards, on the west and east flanks of the rectangular tower. The smaller of the two was just an open space, while the larger one, at the west end, held a hall and a number of smaller rooms, one of which must have been the kitchen. In winter the chances of food remaining hot during the passage from the oven to the table must have been slight. In the later 1630s Smailholm was sold to the Scott family who moved from the tower into a new, more comfortable house on the site of the old hall. It was this family which gave Smailholm its most famous literary and historical association.

'B O N N Y ! B O N N Y !'

Because it played no part in the lives of kings or the magnates of the realm, little is recorded of Smailholm's history. We know that the stronghold was so pressed in the 1540s that John Pringle finally swallowed his pride and became an 'assured Scot' — meaning that he promised the English never to molest their lands nor to interfere with their reivers when they came over the border. In return, the marauders undertook not to touch his property. Apart from that, we can only guess at the sights and sounds which the tower witnessed during the hundreds of years of its occupation. Yet the lack of specific knowledge about Smailholm's past only added to the monument's romantic appeal in the eyes of the young Walter Scott, who in his youth came to stay with his uncle at Sandyknowe Farm.

It was while staying at Sandyknowe that Scott first heard the lays and legends of the region. He was later to present them to the public in his first successful publication, the *Minstrelsy of the Scottish Border*. Smailholm, 'the Old Grey Strength', remained firmly fixed in the poet's affections all his life. He refers to it in *Marmion*, and the year before his death he brought the painter Turner to view the 'mountain tower' and sketch it. There is a story that one day, when a tremendous thunderstorm was raging around the borders, the young Scott could not be found by his anxious uncle and aunt. Eventually they decided to look beside the tower. Here, lying on the grass in the pouring rain with the storm raging around him, they found their charge. He was staring up at the tower, clapping his hands and muttering 'Bonny! Bonny!'.

Smailholm Tower is not beautiful. But, as Scott discovered, it is able to evoke the turbulent history of the borders more readily than any other monument in the region.

I N F O R M A T I O N

ACCESS   The tower is signposted from the B6404 three miles north-east of St Boswells

RESPONSIBILITY FOR THE SITE
    Scottish Development Department

OPENING HOURS
    April-September: 9.30-19.00 (Sun 14.00-19.00)

ADMISSION PRICE
    60p (Senior citizens and children 30p)

FACILITIES   Parking
    Dogs (on lead)
    Guided tours by special request

ELCHO CASTLE

By Elcho hamlet, Tayside Region

Elcho is not one of Scotland's most well-known castles. It has little association with monarchs or other makers of the realm, and no famous author or artist has found inspiration from its form. Nevertheless, it is a charming building, excellently preserved amid the fields and orchards on the south bank of the River Tay, to which it was once connected by a private canal.

The castle, whose unusual name derives from the estate's original title of Elchock, is approached down a muddy little byway which branches left from the road to Kircaldy as it leaves Perth. The setting is quiet and pastoral — outside the month of August the castle's gravelled car park is normally empty on weekdays. As a consequence, a visitor is able to enjoy the rare pleasure of exploring a fine monument in solitude.

The ground in front of the building is open. The northern face is sheltered by tall trees, forming a horseshoe round the quarry from which the castle's building stone was dug at the end of the sixteenth century. Now an attractive garden, this hollow was once the quay at the end of the canal, and for many years it served as the chief means of access to the castle for stores and other heavy goods.

There was a fortification of some sort at Elcho long before the present castle was built, and Wallace is reported to have been in the area on several occasions during his guerrilla warfare with the English at the end of the thirteenth century. He once visited a lady friend in nearby Perth, then in the hands of the enemy, only to find when he arrived that she had undergone a change of heart and betrayed him. Exercising his celebrated charm, he persuaded her that he was not such a villain after all, and she helped him to escape disguised as a woman. While making his way out of the city he was challenged by two English soldiers, who had become suspicious of the brawny-looking crone striding towards them down the street. Wallace threw off his disguise, slew his assailants, and fled to join his men hiding on the banks of the Tay near Elcho.

Sensing a fine opportunity to trap Wallace at last, the English gathered together a large force and prepared to sweep the area. To make their task easier they commandeered a bloodhound and gave it Wallace's scent from the clothes he had discarded in the street brawl. As the search party drew near, stumbling to keep up with the straining animal at their head, Wallace lost his nerve. The hound had to be diverted, at any cost.

Singling out the least trustworthy member of his band, Wallace killed him and spread his fresh blood upon the ground in a false trail. The Scots then made off in the opposite direction. The ploy was successful, for the confused dog soon gave up the hunt for his human quarry and started chasing rabbits instead. Angry and frustrated, the English called off the search and made their way wearily back to Perth.

But for Wallace the incident was not yet closed. That night the ghost of the man he had murdered returned to haunt him. The sight was more than the conscience-stricken warrior could stand and he fled from the house, smashing down the front door in his hurry to get out. Recently a Canadian couple found a spectral shape on a photograph taken in Elcho's basement. The shadow was probably just bad workmanship on the part of the laboratory which developed the film… The site of Elcho castle may well be peaceful and the building's history relatively uneventful, but the surrounding area is not without interesting association.

THE CASTLE

At first it may seem rather strange to find Elcho in a chapter about tower houses, for compared with Threave or Smailholm the castle does not look much like a tower. It is, however, a good example of the way the basic tower design had developed by the last quarter of the sixteenth century. The castle is essentially a large rectangular block embellished with additional square and rounded towers. The largest of these is attached at the south-west corner to make an L-shape. Some commentators have suggested that the jamb was once a freestanding tower in its own right, erected in the fifteenth century. Although it is matched by a smaller version of itself on the north-west corner, the two are not directly aligned, and this haphazard arrangement is cited as evidence that the castle is not of a single construction. In fact, such uneven layout is very much in keeping with the rest of the structure (why, for example, place two round towers close together on the northern face but none on the south?), and may merely be the result of the patron changing his mind as the building was in progress. Whatever the explanation for it may be, Elcho's apparent lack of overall planning certainly enhances the castle's charm.

The doorway in the angle between the square tower and the main block leads into a ground floor taken up with storage rooms, a cellar and spacious kitchens dominated by a gigantic fireplace. The member of the Wemyss family who built the castle might have been eccentric, but he certainly knew how to live well too. The ascent to the first floor is made up a broad stone stairway of some grace. Passing through a small lobby, the visitor then enters the Great Hall. This, and the private room leading off it to the east, are light and well-proportioned chambers which in their day must have been most attractive. The remains of a stone frieze can still be seen in one corner of the hall. Whoever designed this part of the castle certainly had no intention of making it private. It would make an ideal set for a French farce, for there are no less than four separate entrances: the main stairway and three spiral staircases leading to the bedrooms above. Another rather eccentric feature of the castle is its inordinate number of privies — one en-suite in virtually every room. Unfortunately the reason for the designer's obvious obsession for convenience has not come down to us.

Elcho was clearly a residence of some comfort. But it was also a castle, a place capable of being held against any incidental assault. The main building was once surrounded by a strong wall, though all but a fragment of this has disappeared. There are also numerous gun loops in the castle's exterior, covering almost every approach, and the entrance is secured by a yett and overlooked by defences at the wallhead. Iron grilles still protect the windows. Though the Scots welcomed 'King James' Peace', they were obviously wary of its durability. The castle at Elcho reflects their guarded optimism.

THE WEMYSS FAMILY

Elcho is still owned by the family who built it, although the castle's fabric is now in the care of the state. The Earls of Wemyss, who trace their descent back to the Macduffs of Fife, were in possession of Elcho long before the Reformation. The present castle was probably raised by Sir John Wemyss, a soldier of renown who died in 1572. The family was elevated to the peerage some fifty-five years later. Although the Wemysses played their part in affairs of state, there is no record of the earl's seat at Elcho being involved in the civil conflicts of the middle years of the seventeenth century.

In fact, the name of Elcho appears in connection with matters of moment only twice. The first was in 1745, when the earl's eldest son joined the forces of Bonnie Prince Charlie, fought at Culloden and fled to France. The estate passed to his younger brother. In 1773, when the castle was no longer considered a suitable residence for a member of the aristocracy, it was used by local farmers as a grain store. There was a severe dearth that year, and troops had to be called out to prevent the castle being stormed by the starving citizens of Perth.

Although Elcho's story may not be exciting, had the castle been involved in more turbulent happenings it would almost certainly not have been preserved in its present condition. We owe a silent vote of thanks, therefore, for generations of Wemyss prudence.

INFORMATION

ACCESS	The castle is signposted from the A912 just south of Perth	ADMISSION PRICE	60p (Senior citizens and children 30p)
RESPONSIBILITY FOR THE SITE	Scottish Development Department	FACILITIES	Disabled (limited) Parking Dogs Toilets Guided tours by special request
TELEPHONE	0738-23437		
OPENING HOURS	April-September: 9.30-19.00 (Sun 14.00-19.00)		

Elcho Castle, which stands on the southern bank of the River Tay near Perth. It was linked to the river by a small private canal.

Claypotts, a delightful monument to Scottish eccentricity and architectural ingenuity.

CLAYPOTTS

Near Broughty Ferry, Tayside Region

Claypotts. The name is as delightful as the castle it describes. It is a great pity, therefore, that the suburbs of Dundee have been permitted to encroach almost to the very walls of this most unusual fortified house, so that it now stands amid an undistinguished twentieth-century housing development rather than against its original background of open farmland. The busy A930 roars by to the north, side roads run like tarmac moats to the east and south, and a well-kept but incongruous bungalow has been built on the remaining flank, only metres away from the castle's entrance. The developers have not even left enough room for a car park.

The ancient farm buildings which used to stand adjacent to the castle were demolished in the 1960s, when the area was turned over to housing; this enables us now to see Claypotts as it was intended, with the numerous gun ports on the ground floor commanding a clear 360 degree field of fire. The lawns and flower beds of the small policies remaining with the castle are beautifully kept and help to prevent the monument looking too much like a museum exhibit in its incongruous setting.

THE CASTLE

No one who sees Claypotts ever forgets the place. It looks like an imaginary exercise for students of architectural drawing, comprising as many improbable features and unusual angles as it is possible to put into one small building. There are windows and gun ports, round walls and flat, chimneys, corbelling, crow stepped gables, parapets — and a dormer window thrown in for good measure. Undoubtably the most unusual feature is the existence of two square watch rooms atop rounded towers at the northern and southern ends of the building. It is almost as if they had been constructed at ground level, then pushed into the air on their hydraulic stone foundations. This quaint design has tested the descriptive powers of all who try to put it into words, forcing them to resort to phrases as irregular as the building itself, such as 'corbelled-out' or 'squared-off'.

The Strachan family built Claypotts between 1569 and 1588, the south tower being added to the central block almost twenty years after its counterpart at the opposite corner. The building, which is one of the earliest examples of a Z-plan tower house, is composed of five towers: a traditional rectangle in the centre, D-shaped towers at the south-western and north-eastern corners, and much smaller segment towers for the stairways in two of the angles between the main building and its rounded projections. The new layout had both military and domestic advantages. The Z-shape (not, in fact, a very accurate description; a stretched figure 2 would be better) gave the architect much greater scope when he came to lay out the accommodation. In Claypotts, for example, he was able to place the kitchen in one of the towers, leaving the rest of the basement free for storage, while on the next floor he devoted the whole of the central rectangle to the hall and still had room for two further chambers on the same level. The benefit of the Z-plan from a defensive point of view was that it did away with most of the vulnerable projecting right angles found in a simple quadrilateral or L-shaped castle. Nevertheless, all-round cover was provided at Claypotts only by chopping away part of the eastern stair tower where it obscured the view from a flanking gun port, and by placing a loop-hole at the back of the kitchen fireplace. Obviously this would not have been of much use had the castle needed to be defended in a hurry!

Practical though the overall plan of Claypotts may be, there is no obvious reason, apart from sheer exuberance, for the eccentricity of the upper storey. With one exception, the rooms within the drum towers are roughly square, so despite their outward appearance the chambers on the top floor are different from those in the rest of the building only in that their external walls conform to the layout within. Another delightful peculiarity of the building is the positioning of the two watch rooms. The northern one, which was the first to be built, fits exactly over the barrel form beneath it. The overlapping corners are supported on moulded stone corbelling. At the southern end, however, the fit is not so close. The corbelling is there, but on either side the curve of the tower extends beyond the wall of the room above it and the gap has had to be filled with stonework.

The closer one looks at Claypotts, the more extraordinary it appears. Yet, for all its oddity, as a piece of architecture it works. The castle provided comfortable and spacious accommodation; it could be defended easily against small-scale attack; and it is a building of unmistakable charm.

A   Q U I E T   L I F E

As far as we know the gun ports of Claypotts never emitted anything more venomous than the stale air of the cellars which they ventilated. Violence passed by this most peaceful-looking of castles, for its owners either settled their conflicts without resorting to armed force or they conducted their campaigns elsewhere. In the seventeenth century the Claypott estates passed to the Grahams of Claverhouse. This was the family of 'Bloody Clavers', the John Graham of Claverhouse who threw in his lot so unequivocally with James V11, and who died in the hour of his victory at Killiecrankie. However fiction, not fact, links this man with his castle beside the Tay, for the scourge of the Covenanters rarely visited the place.

Another legend claims that the castle was built by Cardinal Beaton for his favourite mistress. Quite why the lady should have needed such a strongly fortified residence is not explained; besides, since the cardinal died in 1546 and the date of the castle's construction is plainly recorded on its stonework (1569 — the five is carved upside down), simple mathematics proves the impossibility of the story. Even the castle's obligatory ghost was benign: it was a domesticated brownie who at night performed routine household chores. Eventually it was chased away by a jealous servant who feared for her job.

INFORMATION

ACCESS	Follow the A930 east from Dundee. The castle is near Broughty Ferry, just south of the main road		April-September: 9.30-19.00 (Sun 14.00-19.00)
RESPONSIBILITY FOR THE SITE		ADMISSION PRICE	
	Scottish Development Department		60p (Senior citizens & children 30p)
TELEPHONE 031-244-3089		FACILITIES	Parking (in street) Dogs (on lead)
OPENING HOURS			Toilets Guided tours by special request

CRAIGIEVAR CASTLE

Craigievar, Grampian Region

If Threave marks the unimaginative beginning of the Scottish penchant for building towers, Craigievar is the movement's crowning glory, and it is regarded by many as the loveliest building in Scotland. Standing amid trees in a small park above Leochel Burn, it is overlooked in the west by the wooded slopes of Craigievar Hill, a steep outcrop of the Grampians, while to the east the rich farmland of the ancient earldom of Mar falls away to Aberdeen and the sea. The first views of the castle, from the main road running past the Mill of Kintocher, are unfortunately scarred (particularly for zoom lens photographers) by telegraph poles and their attendant wires, which follow the course of the burn. Not until visitors approach the castle on foot from the secluded car park can they begin to appreciate the building's masterly form. But no one is ever disappointed with what they behold.

In the late Middle Ages the Craigievar estate was owned by the Mortimer family. They began to build a castle on the present site in the early years of the seventeenth century, but they fell on hard times and were forced to sell their lands before the new residence had developed much beyond the planning stage.

The man who acquired the unfinished castle and its policies was a successful merchant named William Forbes, known in trading circles as 'Danzig Willie' or 'Willie the Merchant'. Although he had made his money in commerce, Willie was no bourgeois upstart. He had been raised in Corse castle,

Craigievar Castle, built in the early seventeenth century by 'Danzig Willie', a successful merchant of exquisite taste.

not far from Craigievar, and educated at Edinburgh University. He married well, choosing as his wife Marjorie, a daughter of Provost Woodward of Edinburgh. Willie's elder brother Patrick, a man of a stern and pious disposition, trained for the ministry then lived as a laird for a while before accepting the see of Aberdeen in 1618.

It is said that on several occasions, while trying to make his way in business, Willie borrowed money from Patrick, but each time he lost it on some venture or other and had to approach his brother for more. Eventually Patrick tired of subsidising the apparently hare-brained schemes of his younger brother, and he refused to make any further loans unless Willie could provide satisfactory collateral. Sure enough, after a while the improvident trader was back, pleading with his brother for just one more loan. 'And who,' demanded Patrick pompously, 'is your guarantor?'

Willie knew his brother well and, showing the sort of quick thinking and judgment of personality which were eventually to bring him commercial success, he replied unashamedly, 'God Almighty. I have none other to offer.'

Addressed in those terms, Patrick could make but one reply. He handed over the money and Willie went on to make the fortune which enabled him to build Craigievar. His business involved the export of fish and wool, frequently through Gdansk (Danzig as it was then, hence his nickname), and the import of Memel pine from Sweden. Appropriately enough, this is the wood which was used to panel his new home.

THE CASTLE

Craigievar is an architectural gem. It is a castle of two levels, growing like a giant peach-coloured mushroom among the trees. The lower two-thirds comprise a cluster of three harled towers, which taper almost imperceptibly as they rise from the ground. They are pierced by a single plain door and a minimum of windows. At tree-top level, however, the design suddenly alters. A stepped table of corbelling runs round the whole structure, upon which rests an elaborate display of coned and ogee-topped turrets, chimney stacks, crow-stepped gables and neo-classical balustrades. Surprisingly, such an array of artistry on the upper storeys does not make the castle appear top-heavy. The design exudes confidence and lightness, not ostentation, and the overall impression is one of assured balance.

Completed in 1626, Craigievar may be seen as an architectural represen-tation of the state of Scotland in the early part of the seventeenth century. The austerity and insecurity engendered by generations of lawlessness are still there, reflected in the defensive simplicity of the lower part of the castle and in the retention of the tower form. Yet this is contrasted, in the flamboyance of Craigievar's skyline, with the half-century of peace and mounting prosperity which the nation had enjoyed since the majority of James VI.

The ground plan of the castle-house (neither word alone describes the building satisfactorily) is of traditional L-plan design, with a lesser tower inserted in the right angle between two larger ones. However, unlike other examples of this format, the recessed tower does not house a stairway but a series of small rooms. The vaulted ground floor contained the kitchen, a number of storerooms and a chamber believed to have served as a prison. A wide granite stairway leads to the first floor and the grandest room in the castle, the hall. Architectural historians wax almost as lyrical over this chamber as over the building as a whole. It is an unusual but nevertheless harmonious blend of medieval form with Renaissance decoration. The vaulted roof, huge fireplace and carved wooden screen shielding the servants' entrance are features common among great halls throughout the land. What makes Craigievar different is the remarkable plasterwork on the ceiling and above the fireplace, and the oak panelling, carved with what local craftsmen considered to be classical motifs. The creamy plaster decoration was executed by itinerant English journeymen, using moulds whose form has been identified elsewhere, notably at Glamis and Muchalls. The room's most striking feature is the gigantic coat of arms over the mantelpiece. It is that of the king of Scotland, with the lion in the first and fourth quarters. The right to display this proud heraldic device was reserved to royal tenants-in-chief, lairds with the authority to administer justice — 'pit and gallows' — in local courts.

An attractive withdrawing room is situated on the opposite side of the main staircase from the hall. Its warm and homely feel comes largely from the Memel pine panelling on the walls, which conceals the door to a small secret room, known as the 'Prophet's Chamber', set into the smallest of the three towers. The religious connotations of the apartment's name are probably misleading, for the sanctum was more likely to have served as the laird's private study and strong-room. Other rooms of note are the Queen's Bedroom (so named because it was hoped that one day a queen might grace it with her presence) and the Long Gallery on the fifth floor, intended for recreation or display of family treasures.

The castle has nineteen rooms, linked above the first floor by no less than five stairways and adorned with a number of well-executed portraits and interesting pieces of furniture. The accommodation is maintained in an excellent state of repair and decoration by the National Trust for Scotland. Indeed, Craigievar has such a lived-in feel about it that some visitors drifting round the castle feel almost like trespassers, half-expecting to find Danzig Willie asleep in one of the beds or seated at a table pouring over his accounts.

CAREFUL LAIRDS

The history of Craigievar has been blessedly uneventful. The castle's defensive capabilities were needed only twice. The first time was shortly after its completion, when the area was threatened by a band of highland freebooters who swept in from the distant Grampians. They were led by one Gilderoy, a man notorious for his cruel rapacity. Craigievar was in the hands of Danzig Willie's son, also William Forbes, an MP and baronet of Nova Scotia. He managed to beat off the raiders, and in 1636 Gilderoy and his gang were brought to justice — they were executed in Edinburgh and their severed heads set up in various parts of the city as a warning to others who might be contemplating similar infringement of the king's peace. The next year, however, this peace faced a far more serious challenge in the form of the nationalist revolt of the Covenanters.

Sir William Forbes ignored his recent elevation to the peerage (a privilege for which, anyway, he probably had to pay) and placed loyalty to his conscience above that to his king. He raised a troop of horse to fight for the Covenanters and distinguished himself in battle on more than one occasion. Nevertheless, when in 1644 the all-conquering Royalist general Montrose was in the vicinity, the baronet found it convenient to withdraw into the security of Craigievar. At that time the castle was surrounded by a defensive wall, a picturesque section of which can still be seen in the grounds. It is doubtful though that the stronghold would have been able to withstand a strongly pressed attack for long, and therefore Sir William was lucky that Montrose's plans led him elsewhere. The outer wall would have detracted from the castle's appearance, as can be seen from a similar construction at Braemar, and fortunately in more peaceful times it was allowed to crumble away.

The rest of the story of Craigievar is largely one of domestic tranquillity and careful preservation of the building's celebrated fabric. There is a ghost, of course — an unfortunate Gordon who was shoved to his death from a fourth floor window. But he now seems more intent on making a less dramatic exit from the castle, through the front door, than with bringing harm to any of its inhabitants. The 7th Baronet undertook a faithful repair of the structure in the 1820s, at a cost of £680, and in 1963 a group of benefactors generously enabled the castle to be acquired by its present administrators.

INFORMATION

ACCESS — The castle is signposted from the A980 seven miles south of Alford

RESPONSIBILITY FOR THE SITE — National Trust for Scotland

TELEPHONE — 033-9839-635

OPENING HOURS — May-September: 11.00-18.00

ADMISSION PRICE — £2.10 (Children £1.10)

FACILITIES — Parking
Dogs (grounds only)
Toilets
Guided tours

GLAMIS CASTLE

Glamis Village, Tayside Region

Glamis is a palatial residence, approached down a broad avenue of spreading trees. The light, almost fairy-tale, look of the castle is not to everyone's taste and at least one writer has commented that it appears to come straight from Disneyland. This is, of course, a wholly unjust criticism, for Glamis has remained largely unaltered since the seventeenth century, hundreds of years before the fun parks of the USA were even dreamed of. Moreover, it is hardly the fault of the Lyons family, who have lived on the estate since they were given it by King Robert II in 1372, that their residence should inspire the romantic dreams of a culture deprived of an indigenous ancient architecture of its own.

Landscaped policies enable Glamis' graceful red towers to be seen to their best advantage. But here too there have been critics, notably Sir Walter Scott. He considered the eighteenth-century remodelling of the castle's grounds, which cleared away the remains of decayed earthworks and walls, to have been an 'atrocity'. Such an attitude is perhaps understandable in one who devoted much of his life to the preservation and popularisation of his country's heritage. But few of today's visitors would prefer to see the elegance of the structure compromised by a more cluttered surrounding. The best that can be said for Scott is that he never saw the landscaped grounds in their mature splendour. Had he done so, he might not have been so condemnatory. As with Craigievar, we are dealing here with an intact building of impressive beauty, whose appeal and interest are not primarily as a fortress but as a piece of architecture. Just as the ruined majesty of Tantallon is enhanced by the broken ramparts which lie before it, so the stately home at Glamis benefits from its appropriately cultured setting. The few pieces that remain from the seventeenth-century garden, two statues of monarchs and a baroque sundial, are not sufficiently obtrusive to spoil the view. A formal Dutch garden, very much on the lines of that done away with two centuries ago, was laid out to the east of the front entrance in the 1890s, but it is not open to the public. The neo-classical gates (the 'De'il Gates'), which once arched the drive in front of the castle, now mark the entrance to the estate from the main road between Dundee and Kirriemuir.

Visitors with an eye to things military may wonder at Glamis' rather poor defensive position. Two explanations for this have been put forward. The first, somewhat fanciful, tells that the builders of the original castle began to lay their foundations on a nearby hill. Unfortunately, this site was already occupied by a colony of fairies, who much resented the intended eviction. As fast as the masons raised their walls during the day, the little people threw them down by night. In the end the humans gave up the unequal struggle and built their castle on lower though less defensible ground. The story may owe something to the fact that the area around Glamis has always been regarded as holy. Long ago St Fergus lived here, preaching the Christian gospel to the heathen Picts.

The second explanation for the castle's weak siting is more practical. Glamis was not built as a castle at all, but as a royal hunting lodge. Although the marshy land beside Dean Water may have deterred casual aggressors, the place was selected because it made a convenient gathering point for horsemen. Later a more substantial stronghold was built there, but by that time considerations other than defensive potential were taken into account.

T H E   C A S T L E

It does not require a trained eye to see that Glamis, like many fine cathedrals, is the product of several periods of building. In late twentieth-century Britain, timidly obsessed with architectural restoration and reconstruction rather than creation, it is not fashionable to appreciate buildings compiled in this manner. However, Glamis is none the worse for being the work of many hands, a blend of several styles and tastes. It is still possible to distinguish the original tower house and the variety of subsequent additions is part of the castle's unique charm.

The structure is so large and complicated in detail that it is not possible here to do more than offer an outline of the different generations' work and point out a few of the more interesting features. Some hold that there was a stone tower on the site when it came into the possession of Sir John Lyon at the end of the fourteenth century. If this was the case then the building was swallowed up by the L-shaped tower house which lies at the heart of the present building, giving it its overall horizontal form. The tower's walls were two and a half metres thick and it was divided into four storeys, all but the uppermost of which were vaulted. The stark basement, now known as Duncan's Hall, is served by narrow stairs. Access to the upper floors was facilitated in the last century by the construction of a wider stone stairway. The first floor or Lower Hall (today called the Crypt) probably housed the original entrance, which was reached from the outside by a ladder or wooden stairs. The room must have been unpleasantly cold and draughty, for it had no fireplace. The inconsiderate laird reserved it for the use of his servants. The Great Hall has appropriately been re-christened the Drawing Room. With its fine plasterwork, beautiful furniture and array of family portraits it is difficult now to imagine it as a rush-strewn medieval chamber in which the head of the Lyon family held court. The large picture on the wall to the left of the fireplace, which captures the eye as soon as one enters the room, is of the 3rd Earl and his family, with the castle in the background. Apart from the obvious interest of a representation of Glamis in the late seventeenth century, the feature of the painting most remarked upon is the fleshy armour worn by the earl and his eldest son. It gives the rather daring impression of their being half-naked.

The first major reconstruction of the castle took place under the hand of Patrick Lyon (1575-1615), 9th Lord Glamis and 1st Earl of Kinghorne, a close favourite of King James VI. He raised the tower, embellished it with cone-capped turrets, and added a stair tower, interrupted with a ground-floor doorway, in the angle of the L. Apparently at this time the castle was surrounded by a courtyard or barmkin. The large rounded towers to the left and right of the central block are the only features remaining from this configuration, for the two sides opposite the entrance were pulled down by the 2nd and 3rd Earls to make the castle easier to manage and more attractive to look at. The 3rd Earl inherited what was virtually a ruin. He was an astute and meticulous man, however, and working on plans drawn up by his predecessors he left the castle much as we find it today. His finest bequest was the chapel, with ceiling panels painted by Jacob de Wet.

At one stage plans were prepared for a complete remodelling of the castle in a pseudo-Gothic style, but thankfully these were never implemented. Nevertheless, some changes have been made to the 3rd Earl's design. The west wing was destroyed by fire in the early part of the nineteenth century and was rebuilt with a flat roof and crenellations, according to a design by James Wyatt. The east wing was similarly altered to maintain the symmetry of the facade. The southern range was reconstructed about fifty years later. Since then the castle has been subject to only minor alterations.

The interior is stacked with treasures and souvenirs. Apart from the usual morbid display of weaponry, there are delightful tapestries, paintings (including the gigantic 'Fruit Market' by Rubens and Snyders) and intricate Meissen porcelain. However, the guides are usually pressed most closely not on questions of art or architecture but on the royal apartments, for Glamis is probably best known today as the childhood haunt of Lady Elizabeth Bowes Lyon, H.M. Queen Elizabeth the Queen Mother. Princess Margaret was born in the castle. The rooms used by the royal family, in particular that known as the Queen Mother's sitting room, display a charming combination of comfort and good taste. The copy of a portrait by de Laszlo of the Queen Mother, then Duchess of York, is one of the most arresting in the castle's collection.

'GREAT GLAMIS'

Glamis reeks with history. Its most widely-known association though is pure myth: Macbeth was not Thane of Glamis, he did not live in the castle (even if there was one at his time), and he did not murder a venerable king named Duncan here, or anywhere. The choice of Glamis as a title for the central figure in *Macbeth* was probably to flatter (or annoy?) the 1st Earl, who in 1603 had travelled south to London with James VI when he acquired the English throne. Shakespeare was quite capable of twisting history to suit his needs; he deliberately made his witches display Banquo's successors as far as King James

Glamis Castle. The building grew from a simple hunting lodge into one of the most majestic castles in Britain.

Though Glamis is rich in genuine historical association, the famous greeting which Shakespeare put into the mouths of the three witches - 'All hail, Macbeth! Hail to thee, thane of Glamis!' - is entirely fictional. The estates of the real Macbeth lay in the north-east of the country.

in order to please the court. The truth is that Duncan was slain by Macbeth, five years his senior, in a fair fight. To name a vault in the castle 'Duncan's Hall' is to employ Shakespearian license, albeit harmlessly. Similarly, the castle also has a 'King Malcolm's Room', in which it was once believed that Malcolm II, the grandfather of Duncan I, had died in 1034. Such a contention is clearly false, and is recognised as such. Nevertheless, the grand-sounding name is retained, for obvious reasons.

The real Thanes of Glamis, the Lyon family (Bowes Lyon since the eighteenth century), have a long history as bloody and dramatic as any theatrical fiction. Sir John Lyon was murdered in 1382; the wife of the 6th Lord Glamis was burned to death at the instigation of King James V; the 8th Lord was killed in a brawl by the gate to Stirling castle; his brother (Master of Glamis) played a major part in the Ruthven Raid to kidnap James VI; when Mary Queen of Scots visited the castle she was heard to say that she wished she were a man... The list of incidents and adventures is endless. Perhaps three might be singled out.

The 6th Lord Glamis married the attractive and accomplished Jane Douglas, sister of Archibald, the 6th Earl of Angus. Archibald married Margaret Tudor, widow of James IV and mother of the young James V, and used his position to exercise considerable influence over the king, particularly from 1525-1528. Eventually King James escaped from Archibald's clutches and the earl fled to England where James could not get at him. Unable to take revenge on his stepfather, the king grew suspicious of anyone associated with the refugee, even with Lady Glamis. In 1537 she was found guilty of plotting to kill the king and suffered the horrible fate usually reserved for witches and heretics. Castle guides will tell you that she haunts the chapel, in the form of a grey lady. Spectre there may be, but it is unlikely to be the spirit of Lady Jane Glamis. The chapel was not completed until more than a century and a half after her death. Moreover, the 6th Lord, her husband, died in the year Archibald Douglas crossed the border into England and she later remarried. At the time of her death, therefore, Jane was living far from Glamis. Yet perhaps she had happy memories of the place and so returns there in spirit? One can never tell with ghosts.

The first Lyon at Glamis was plain Sir John. His grandson became the 1st Lord Glamis and Patrick, the 9th Lord Glamis, also acquired the title Earl of Kinghorne. His namesake the 3rd Earl (the man who wore titivating armour) added the Earldom of Strathmore to the title. He was also one of the last men in the kingdom who maintained a jester to keep him amused and ensure that household squabbles did not get out of perspective. We are not told what he made of Earl Patrick's sartorial taste, but in the end the fool's ability to persuade his master to look on the lighter side of things failed him, and he was dismissed for paying court to one of the earl's daughters.

The 6th Earl had strong Jacobite sympathies, and in 1715 he permitted his castle to be used by the Old Pretender as a makeshift court. The uninspiring

'James VIII' rewarded Earl Charles by touching for the King's Evil (scrofula) in the chapel, declaring that on all his continental travels he had seen no house to match Glamis. When he absent-mindedly left his watch under his pillow and departed without it, a serving maid ran off with it and her family hung on to the souvenir for several generations before returning it to the castle. (Perhaps the timepiece had been intended as a reward for services rendered — the Stuarts were notoriously lascivious.) Thirty years later Thomas the 8th Earl, who at the age of ten must have witnessed the invasion of his house by the Pretender and his extensive entourage, entertained the Duke of Cumberland as he cautiously made his way north to Culloden and the final extinction of the Jacobite cause. It is ironic to think that Glamis may well have provided the same bed for both the Pretender and the man who finally put paid to his pretensions.

INFORMATION

ACCESS — Glamis Castle is signposted off the A928 just north of the village of Glamis
Public transport infrequent

RESPONSIBILITY FOR THE SITE
Private

TELEPHONE — 030-784-242

OPENING HOURS
Mid-April — mid-October:
12.00-17.00

ADMISSION PRICE
£3.00 (Senior citizens £2.40 & children £1.50)

FACILITIES — Disabled (limited)
Parking
Dogs (grounds only)
Toilets
Shop
Refreshments

BARONIAL STRONGHOLDS

The castle was a product of strictly hierarchical society. Wealth, power and influence were concentrated in the hands of comparatively few families, whose privileges were hereditary. Occasionally a new name forced its way into the list of aristocracy and from time to time ill luck or imprudence caused a great family to slip back into anonymity. But by and large the social order was fixed, and accepted as such. It was one of the ways of preserving a fragile stability during an age when war or the untimely death of a monarch could plunge the country into chaos.

A castle was a status symbol, an almost obligatory badge of a member of the ruling class. It delivered a clear message to the surrounding countryside: here dwells a great man, one whom it would be wise to respect and obey. Thus high walls and towers were not just defensive requirements. They enabled the castle to be seen for miles around, to dominate the landscape. Furthermore, a castle needed to be of a substantial size for other purposes. In medieval and early modern society there was a strong sense that obligation accompanied privilege. The laird's castle was the local law court, where one went for redress of grievance. It was also a place of safety, in which people could gather when danger threatened. The castle enabled its owner to fulfil his social obligations, too. In its broad halls dozens could sit down to eat at the same time and the many chambers could provide accommodation for guests and their retinue.

With this in mind, a category of castle is introduced which covers a broad sweep of location and type. The buildings described here all belonged to families who maintained a high profile in national affairs, and whose castles were physical manifestations of their self-esteem. They range from the great border stronghold of Hermitage, through Duke Murdoch's purpose-built fortress at Doune, to the celebrated five towers of Fyvie and the Duke of Maitland's expanded tower house at Thirlestane. Unfortunately many fine castles, such as Castle Campbell, Craigmillar, Bothwell, Brodie, Cawdor and others, have had to be omitted. But we are left with a distillation of distinction, linking us directly to fascinating episodes and characters from Scotland's past.

HERMITAGE CASTLE

North of Newcastleton, Borders Region

Hermitage must surely be the most forbidding castle in Scotland. The building is grim, its location bleak, and, not surprisingly, most of the stories

HERMITAGE CASTLE
A dour border fortress of evil reputation.

connected with it are gruesome. Those fortunate enough to find the monument on a sunny day, when the surrounding fells hold a certain Wordsworthian beauty, may come away with more felicitous memories; but generally the dark mass of the castle presses a sombre shadow on the imagination of all who behold it.

Liddesdale runs from the farmland above Carlisle, north-east towards Hawick. Hermitage Castle stands at the upper end of the dale, on a low bluff rising above the left bank of Hermitage Water. Although it is not apparent at first, the site guards a crossroads on the path from Newcastleton. A small metalled road leads west over Din Fell and Geordie's Hill. Eastwards there is a way between Arnton and Saughtree Fells to Riccarton Junction, Saughtree and the present border with England north of Keilder. For centuries Hermitage was a key stronghold in this troubled border region, and it was manned at different times by both Scottish and English garrisons. It is said that when Henry III heard that Hermitage was being fortified in 1343, he prepared for war. The story may not be true, but it is an interesting testimony to the castle's importance.

Hermitage relied for defence not on an elevated position but on the difficulty of dragging heavy siege machinery up the dale and on massive walls surrounded by marshy ground. With Hermitage Water running to the south and two flanking burns, named Castle Sike and Lady's Sike, to the east and west, it is difficult to approach the castle from any direction, other than along the raised path from the car park, without getting sodden feet. Even in the exceptionally dry summer of 1989 the area to the north of the castle, where no stream flows, remained treacherously boggy — as the author discovered, to the cost of a new pair of shoes.

The undulations around the castle are something of a mystery. Some are clearly associated with sixteenth-century artillery fortifications; others may well pre-date the present building. Since the oldest parts of the existing fortress were put up in the middle of the fourteenth century, and we have records of a castle at Hermitage in 1296, some of the ramparts possibly do relate to an earlier stronghold. However, there is a ruined chapel some 400 metres west of the castle and it too appears to have earthworks of its own. So it has been suggested that this is the true site of the original castle, the fourteenth-century one being built from scratch on a fresh site. Only careful excavation would reveal the answer.

It is not difficult to imagine foul deeds being perpetrated in the desolate hills around Hermitage. Sure enough, history and legend combine to bring us three sorry tales set in the vicinity of the castle. Not far away, in a stone circle known as Nine Staine Rig, the knight Barthram was done to death by the aggrieved brothers of a girl whom he had led astray. Closer to hand, Hermitage Water has a story of its own to tell.

Once, a gigantic Tyneside warrior named Cout of Keilder set out to destroy the master of Hermitage Castle, Lord Soulis. To increase his chances of

Stone machiolation at Craigmillar Castle near Edinburgh through which defenders could drop missiles and noxious liquids onto the heads of assailants. In the later Middle Ages such elaborate corbelling replaced temporary wooden galleries on the wall head. At Hermitage the joist sockets for the gallery are still visible, as are the rectangular openings through which the garrison had access to the platform.

The eastern flank of Hermitage Castle, showing the latrine, and the arch (rebuilt in the nineteenth century) which permitted the fighting platform to extend the full length of the wall.

In 1566 Mary Queen of Scots rode to Hermitage from Jedburgh in order to spend a few brief hours with her lover, the Earl of Bothwell. The couple could hardly have chosen a less felicitous spot in which to pursue their amorous adventures.

success the battling Geordie dressed in magic mail, through which no weapon could pass. The men of Hermitage strove in vain against him and eventually, leaving many of their number dead upon the grass outside, they turned and fled into the fastness of the castle. This was before the present fortress was built, so we must imagine a far less secure and imposing structure. With an apparently invincible giant pounding at his gate and roaring for his blood, Soulis grew anxious for his safety. Moreover, he was a cruel individual, who inspired little devotion in his retainers. Many probably had a sneaking sympathy for the ambition of their adamantine foe.

But Soulis was not a man to submit easily. He had one last ploy: giving up the pointless task of trying to wound his enemy, he ordered his men to seize him instead. After a tremendous struggle, like triumphant Lilliputians they succeeded in holding Cout down. They then carried him to Hermitage Water and held his head beneath the surface of the stream until the colossal body finally stopped its frantic convulsions. The 'Cout of Keilder Pool' can still be seen in the river beneath the castle.

Unchivalric though this behaviour might have been, it was one of the least dastardly of Soulis' acts. In the end his men would take no more. After consulting a wizard about how their lord might be slain, they bound him with ropes of sand, wrapped him in lead, and boiled him alive in a huge cauldron at Nine Staine Rig.

THE CASTLE

At first glance Hermitage gives the impression of being a simple design. It is in fact a rather complex building, which passed through five distinct stages of development to reach its present form. The earliest surviving work is that of the Dacres, an English family who controlled the Hermitage estates between about 1340 and 1365. They constructed a fortified manor house of the type very much in vogue at that time in northern England. It comprised two parallel blocks of accommodation, running north-south. The building became an oblong fortress when walls were placed across the openings and towers erected at the four corners. The modest Dacre castle was probably about the same size as the central part of the present castle. Since it was built in red sandstone remains of it can still be identified in the existing structure, particularly on the inside.

The next three phases of building were carried out by the Douglases, who came into possession of the castle in 1371 and held it for more than a century. Initially they turned the Dacre fortress into some sort of keep or tower house, perhaps resembling their castle at Threave. The main body of the new fortress was constructed on the ground plan of the manor, with an extension to the south-west in the form of a small wing (or jamb) which contained the entrance. The L-plan keep was later strengthened by the addition of three towers on its unprotected corners. Finally the Douglases built a new block over the jamb. It acted as a corner tower but was in fact considerably larger than the other three.

This left a roughly symmetrical building, resembling in form a thickened swastika.

The castle was extensively repaired by the Duke of Buccleuch in the early part of the last century. This work included the addition of the corbelled parapet at the wallhead, the crowstepped gables on the two eastern towers, and the rebuilding of most of the eastern side of the castle, including the flying arch between the towers. The arches on the eastern and western flanks are the castle's most unusual feature. They not only added structural strength to the building but also enabled the bretach, which jutted from the walls at the third floor level,to run straight across above them. It would otherwise have had to follow a more complicated crank-shaped path between the towers. The presence of this fighting platform can be deducted from the small square holes, which housed the floor joists, and the larger doors through which the garrison emerged from inside the walls.

The interior of the castle is almost completely ruinous. This makes it very difficult to understand the configuration of the rooms, particularly as at times the floor levels were altered to suit the requirements of the occupiers. It is still possible to make out the dungeon and pit prison, the kitchen, at least one hall, and an elaborate drainage system culminating in a cesspool below the south-west tower. It is always mildly surprising to a twentieth-century observer, raised on scornful notions of medieval sanitation, to find a castle's engineers paying such close attention to the efficient disposal of waste. They clearly realised that to neglect this aspect of a castle's design would render the building most unpleasant as a residence, and increase considerably the chances of the whole garrison being struck down by debilitating disease.

T Y R A N T S   A N D   L O V E R S

Hermitage changed hands several times during the Wars of Independence, finally ending up in the possession of Sir William Douglas, the Knight of Liddesdale. He had captured the castle from the Englishman, Ralph Neville, an ally of Edward Balliol. The Knight is remembered for his vigorous campaigning on behalf of the Bruces. Unfortunately, there was also a less noble side to his character. This became apparent when he captured Sir Alexander Ramsay of Dalhousie, a fellow patriotic warrior, and starved him to death in Hermitage's airless pit prison. The deed was made more reprehensible by the fact that Sir Alexander was seized while kneeling defenceless at his devotions in St Mary's, Hawick. The prisoner took an unconscionable long time to die: he was able to sustain himself for seventeen days on a dribble of grain leaking from a granary situated above his place of incarceration. About ten years later the Knight of Liddesdale was murdered in Ettrick Forest by his kinsman William, the 1st Earl Douglas. The squabble between relatives at least ensured that Hermitage remained in the family.

As has already been made clear, the Stewarts had little love for the

Douglases, and they were understandably anxious about leaving so major a fortress as Hermitage in the hands of potential rebels. In 1492 James IV ('James of the Iron Belt') ordered Archibald Douglas, 5th Earl of Angus, to exchange Hermitage for Bothwell Castle in Lanarkshire. The new master of Liddesdale was Patrick Hepburn, 1st Earl of Bothwell. The Hepburns were scarcely less unruly than the Douglases, and in 1540 Hermitage was taken over by the crown, although the former owners continued to live there.

We have so far avoided more than passing reference to Mary Queen of Scots, but the story of her visit to Hermitage is too well-known to be omitted. Besides, it provides a touch of warmth to what is otherwise a chapter of unrelieved barbarity.

By 1566 Mary's relations with her ineffectual husband Lord Darnley were at rock bottom. She could hardly stand the sight of the man. Much more to her liking was the robust James Hepburn, 4th Earl of Bothwell, with whom it seems she was already having a passionate affair. Her son James, the result of a short-lived reconciliation with Darnley in the autumn of the previous year, was born on 19 June. In October the queen went to Jedburgh to hold a justice in eyre. Darnley remained at Stirling and talked sulkily of going abroad.

At Jedburgh Mary received news that Bothwell had been quite badly wounded in a fight with a border reiver named 'Little Jock' Elliott, and was laid up in his castle at Hermitage. She did not, as some accounts would have us believe, immediately set out to visit him, fired by a combination of compassion and sexual desire. Instead, she waited almost a week before making the journey. But Hermitage was twenty-five miles away, and in order to spend a few happy hours with her lover she rode there and back in a single day. We do not know why she refused to spend the night at the castle. It may have been too small to accommodate her retinue, or she may have wished to avoid further scandal. Alternatively, it is possible that she and Bothwell had had some sort of quarrel. Whatever the reason, the long ride in inclement October weather, undertaken four months after the debilitating experience of childbirth, made her seriously ill.

For several days it was thought that the queen would die. Bothwell came to visit her, and a day or so later even Darnley appeared at her bedside, although this can have brought the patient little comfort. However, Mary eventually recovered to pursue her impetuous reign once more. Years later she was often heard to say that she wished she had died at Jedburgh.

ACCESS The castle can be seen to the right of the B6399 about 13 miles south of Hawick

RESPONSIBILITY FOR THE SITE
Scottish Development Department

OPENING HOURS
April-September: 9.30-19.00 (Sun 14.00-19.00) October-March: Sat 9.30-17.00, Sun 14.00-17.00

ADMISSION PRICE
60p (Senior citizens & children 30p)

FACILITIES Parking
Dogs
Guided tours by special request

DOUNE CASTLE

Doune, Central Region

King Robert II (1371-1390), grandson of Robert the Bruce and first Stewart monarch of Scotland, lived to the age of seventy-four, and his eldest son did not inherit the crown until he was in his mid-fifties. By this time Robert III (1390-1406) was both a mental and physical cripple. The man already in control of the government was one of the king's younger brothers Robert Stewart, Earl of Menteith and Fife and, after 1398, Duke of Albany. He served as Governor of the Realm during the last two years of his father's reign then took up the title again upon his brother's death in 1406, holding it for the remaining fourteen years of his life. The duke was an ambitious, competent politician and it is very likely that he wanted the crown for his own branch of the Stewart family. In 1402 his brother's eldest son David, Duke of Rothesay and heir to the throne, died in mysterious circumstances while under detention on Albany's orders. From this time onwards only the young King James (the boy who gazed upon Tantallon — stood between the Duke and the throne. But the lad was a captive in England, safe from his uncle's grasp.

Doune was built by Duke Robert at the heart of his Menteith earldom sometime towards the close of the fourteenth century. The narrow neck of land between the confluence of the River Teith and Ardoch Burn was well selected: there had possibly been an earlier castle on the site and the Romans, who knew as well as anyone how to choose a defensive position, had constructed a fort one hundred metres or so to the north-west of the location favoured by Albany. Since the living moats around Doune form less impenetrable barriers than, for example, those at Threave, the castle was further protected by earth ramparts to the north and south. There may also once have been an outer curtain wall around the whole building. The strategic positioning of Doune was also important. The Teith runs from the Firth of Forth deep into the Highlands, providing one of the chief highways between the nation's capital and the north-west. By constructing a fortress astride this route, Albany was guarding access to the territory controlled by his nephew Donald, Lord of the Isles. Doune was also well placed to oversee the lines of communication running north-east from Glasgow and Dumbarton, along the Highland line, to Perth and Aberdeen.

Doune is an unusual castle, built at a time of transition in fortification design and therefore incorporating features of several different styles. Furthermore, its imposing bulk is extremely well preserved, having undergone extensive restoration in late Victorian times. The Historic Buildings and Monuments Directorate presents the castle with its customary balance of information and imagination, including a slide and music presentation in one of the castle's vaults. This happy combination of factors guarantees that a visit to Doune is well worthwhile.

THE CASTLE

The first thing to remember about Doune is that it was never finished. The original plan may well have been for a quadrangle of buildings within a high encircling curtain wall; but the latter, if it was ever built, has been pulled down and within it only the northern range of buildings was completed. We are left with what looks like two tower houses, linked by a Great Hall surmounting vaulted cellars, and a freestanding wall to the rear enclosing a trapezium-shaped courtyard. The northern section of the castle was built first. It closed the neck between the river and its tributary, afforded immediate defensibility for the site, and provided accommodation for the duke and his retinue. The large windows in the southern curtain wall suggest that Albany planned eventually, perhaps when he had the full resources of the crown at his command, to erect an even more palatial residence. As it turned out, he died before he could realise his dreams, and those of his son Duke Murdoch were cut short by the return of James I from involuntary exile.

The larger of the two towers is that on the left as one faces the castle. It is a massive construction, almost thirty metres high, with walls three metres thick. The five storeys and garret contained the gatehouse, two halls and a number of smaller chambers. It is topped with attractive corbelled bartizans, or small turrets, which may well have been added in the sixteenth century to give the building a less bleak appearance. Notable features are the large yett, the rectangular protrusion on the eastern wall, which houses with curious economy both chimney flues and latrine chutes, a rounded tower beside the entrance and the restored Lord's Hall on the first floor. There is a school of thought which holds that Albany had so little confidence in the trustworthiness of his garrison, mercenary or otherwise, that he designed his part of the castle so that it could be held against attack from within as well as without. It is true that the tower's principal entrance is above a doubly defended stone stairway from the courtyard, but there are other ways in (notably from the wall head and through a door from the Great Hall). And the tower has no independent water supply. It is unlikely, therefore, that it could have held out for long if the rest of the fortress had been in hostile hands. Moreover, Albany's largely successful career, spanning several decades, suggests that he was quite capable of surrounding himself with loyal servants. Though the 'paranoid' interpretation of the castle's design has obvious appeal, it does not really accord with the facts.

The Great Hall now has a somewhat spartan appearance, although when filled with feasting guests and lit by innumerable candles and firelight it must have looked altogether more grand. The lord sat on a raised dais at the east end, flooded with light from an oriel window in the southern wall. A door behind him led to the smaller hall and his private accommodation. In the wall to his left was a latrine within easy reach of those sitting at the high table. The wall opposite him was hidden by wooden screens, behind which a door led to the servery and kitchens. These occupied the first floor of the second, or Retainers' hall. Above the servery there is large bedroom supposed to have been used by Mary Queen of Scots. The kitchen is distinguished by wide serving hatches, not unlike those at Elcho and resembling a modern factory canteen.

Doune is clearly more than a tower house. And though security was crucial in its design, we have also moved away from the enceinte castle of the high Middle Ages; internally at least there is a more homely feel about Doune than about earlier strongholds, which may be why, perhaps, three monarchs in succession made a gift of it to their queens.

HUNTING AND KNOTTED SHEETS

As we saw when looking at Caerlaverock, the career of Albany's son Murdoch did not long survive the return to Scotland of James I. In 1424 Doune was taken over by the crown and for several generations it served as a sort of Scottish Camp David, a place where the monarchs could go to get away from the hassle of court and enjoy the excellent local hunting. The resident castle captain was also keeper of the forest nearby. Mary of Gueldres, Margaret of Denmark and Margaret Tudor, the respective wives of James II, III and IV, all enjoyed the castle's secure comfort. In the sixteenth century it suffered a three-day siege when its Keeper, Sir James Stewart (a descendant of Duke Robert), refused to hand it over to the Earl of Lennox, who was acting as regent for the young James VI. The castle was soon repaired, however, and the Stewarts retained their charge. King James, for whom hunting was almost an obsession, enjoyed the facilities of Doune and the surrounding countryside much as his predecessors had done.

Doune remained with its hereditary keepers after the removal of the Scottish court to England in 1603. In 1580 the Stewarts had acquired the Earldom of Moray through marriage, and when in 1984 the Secretary of State for Scotland took over Doune on a 999-year lease, it was with the Earl of Moray that the agreement was made.

Only in the 1745-6 Jacobite rebellion did Doune once again come into national prominence. It was taken by the followers of Bonnie Prince Charlie, garrisoned by a nephew of Rob Roy and used as a prison. Among those held in the castle was the author John Home, whose tragedy *Douglas* is reputed to have drawn from its first-night audience the famous cry: 'Whaar's yer Willie Shakespeare noo?' History has given its answer. Although Home's reputation as a leading dramatist may not have endured, he is still remembered as a daring escapologist. One night he and some other prisoners escaped in classic schoolboy fashion from the Retainers' Tower by scaling down a rope of knotted bedding.

INFORMATION

ACCESS   The castle is signposted from the A820 in Doune
Public transport

RESPONSIBILITY FOR THE SITE
Scottish Development
Department

OPENING HOURS
April-September: 9.30-19.00 (Sun 14.00-19.00) October-March:

Mon, Tues, Wed, Thurs am, Sat 9.30-16.00, Sun 14.00-16.00

ADMISSION PRICE
£1.00 (Senior citizens & children 50p)

FACILITIES   Disabled (Limited)
Parking
Dogs
Toilets
Guided tours by special request

CRICHTON CASTLE

Crichton Village, Lothian Region

T he direct route from Newcastle to Edinburgh proceeds from Lauderdale through a broad pass between the Moorfoot and Lammermuir Hills, known as the Middleton Gap. Two castles once commanded this important gateway to the capital. One, Borthwick, has been turned into an hotel; the other, Crichton, is now just an imposing ruin.

The castle has to be approached on foot, along a track leading south-east from the small car park by Crichton church. The most impressive view of the fortress though is to be had from the other side of the valley cut by the river Tyne. Crichton rests in august isolation on the hillside. Bracken-strewn slopes rise gently behind it, and sheep safely graze on the rich grass extending to the castle's broken walls. The scene would serve as a poignant illustration to the first chapter of the Book of Ecclesiastes: 'What profit hath a man of all his labour which he taketh under the sun? One generation passeth away, and another generation cometh.'

THE CASTLE

Crichton began life as an ordinary tower house, built in the late fourteenth-century by John de Crichton. Although a simple structure, the early castle was imposing. Its thick walls, enclosing an area of about 150 square metres, rose some twenty-five metres above the ground. The lower storeys were vaulted and held the usual arrangement of store rooms, prison, kitchen and hall. A walled barmkin, part of which can be identified in the north wall of the

From one of the high windows in Doune's Retainers' Tower the playwright John Home claimed to have escaped from his Jacobite captors by scaling down a rope of knotted sheets.

Crichton Castle, once a formidable fortress guarding the approach to Edinburgh from the south through the Middleton Gap.

present ruins, surrounded the central keep. In the next century the tower was incorporated into a much larger structure, and later still its upper storeys were dismantled as they had become unsafe. The stump which remains can be seen to the right of the present entrance.

Little is known of the man responsible for the early tower. His son, on the other hand, rose to become one of the most powerful and respected men in the realm. William Lord Crichton, a loyal and efficient servant of both James I and James II, was appointed Chancellor of Scotland in 1439. His career was not without its difficult moments — he was outlawed for a while in 1444 — but by the time of his death ten years later his authority was probably second only to that of the king himself. Clearly a man in his position could not possibly continue to live in a tower. To begin with, the kitchens were far too small to manage the amount of entertaining expected of him, and there was simply not enough space to accommodate the stream of guests, friends and clients who came to his door. He had either to build an entirely new castle on a fresh site, or extend the present one considerably. He chose the latter option, probably because it was cheaper.

Chancellor Crichton refurbished the whole castle. His principal addition was a new three storey block on the south side, which served as both gatehouse and keep. Above the entrance passage, flanked by cellars, was a large hall served by a flight of stone steps from the courtyard. It was surmounted by a lesser hall or great chamber, reserved for the private use of the lord and his family. Ancillary rooms were housed in a new building incorporating the western wall of the barmkin. On the northern side of the courtyard the Chancellor adapted the original structure to suit the needs of a much grander residence. The external walls were splayed at their base and topped with daring machiolations, constructed as much for display as for defence. From the outside, therefore, the fine stronghold must now have given the desired impression of power and prosperity, while internally it offered all modern comforts.

The final alterations to Crichton were made towards the end of the sixteenth century. By this time the castle was no longer in the hands of the Crichton family. The 3rd Lord Crichton lost it for his involvement in treasonable activities during the reign of James III, and the Crichton estates passed to the Hepburn Earls of Bothwell. James the 4th Earl was the man who replaced Darnley in the affections of Mary Queen of Scots, and when her reign came to its unhappy close the estates were again forfeit. In 1576 James VI granted them together with the title Earl of Bothwell to Francis Stewart, a descendant of James V and nephew of the 4th Earl. Francis, the 5th Earl, was a cultured adventurer, who combined Renaissance learning with a streak of energetic irresponsibility. He had travelled widely in several European countries and determined to transform the medieval castle at Crichton according to his cosmopolitan tastes. The result was an unexpected but harmonious juxtaposition of Scottish and continental styles, reminiscent of the

Earl of Nithsdale's later work at Caerlaverock.

The area of the building to benefit most from Earl Francis' attentions was the northern side of the courtyard, which had been least altered by Chancellor Crichton. Here a splendid new residential block was constructed, the facade of which is one of the delights of castle architecture. At ground level the earl arranged an arcade or piazza of eight bays (seven facing south and one east), above which rose an Italianate curtain of diamond facets, interspersed with plain windows and topped with a moulded frieze. It fronted three storeys of ancillary rooms, public chambers and sleeping accommodation. Lying in its grey shell of medieval stone, the piazza gleams in the sunshine like a bright pearl revealed.

Earl Francis also overhauled the rest of the castle, though time and the despoliation of later generations unfortunately have left the work much marred. Still visible, however, are exciting corbelled bartizans and dramatically overhanging stonework at the wallhead on the northern side. Curiously, the enigmatic earl did not furnish his mansion with an entrance commensurate with the grandeur of the residence he had created. He blocked the southern doorway and replaced it with the smaller one still in service today. However elaborate the palace within, the narrow entrance reminds us that the building was still a fortress.

King James was a man of learning and culture. An invitation to dine amid the refined beauty of Crichton delighted him, for he valued the earl's company and appreciated his exquisite taste. But there was a less attractive side to Francis' nature. Since his arrival in Scotland in 1581 he had dabbled in witchcraft and raided royal residences on several occasions, terrorising the king. He also became heavily embroiled in the fighting between various religious factions.

In the end James' patience ran out, and in 1595 the master of Crichton was forced to flee abroad, never to return. He died in Naples seventeen years later. His gorgeous castle at Crichton began to decay from the time of his departure. Only when Sir Walter Scott took an interest in the place more than two centuries later was the neglect halted, and in 1926 it was put into the care of the state. From that time forward adequate funds and technical expertise have preserved for all time this arresting monument to man's vanity and endeavour.

THE AMBITIOUS EARL

Twice forfeited and once abandoned, Crichton was unfortunate in the men chosen to care for it. It was besieged in 1444 and 1559, on each occasion falling without undue exertion on the part of the attackers, and the damage sustained in the assault was soon repaired. The second incident involved James Hepburn, the 4th Earl, the headstrong magnate whom we have already met at Hermitage and who played such a major part in the reign of Queen Mary.

Earl James (b 1535) took the usual course for one who endorsed the cause of the Reformation of siding with the French faction during the minority of Queen Mary. He seems to have been motivated by a fervent desire to prevent the English from using Scotland's domestic troubles to further their own ends. When in 1559 Regent Mary of Guise (the queen mother) faced a Protestant uprising, Queen Elizabeth of England acted with uncustomary speed and decision. She sent the rebels military and financial assistance with which to free themselves from French influence.

To the Earl of Bothwell this looked distinctly like yet another attempt by the English to win control over his native land. There was little he could do to prevent Admiral Winter's fleet from sailing into the Firth of Forth, but when he learned that a large sum of English gold was making its way north, and that the convoy was likely to pass close by his seat at Crichton, he saw his opportunity to strike a blow for Scottish independence. He seized the money, 4000 crowns in all, and locked it in the vaults of his castle.

Before long he found himself besieged by his own countrymen, furious at being denied the wherewithal to continue their struggle against the French. The castle was taken and sacked, and the money handed over to the Protestant lords. It took some careful explaining on the part of the earl to restore his political career.

The remaining chapters in Bothwell's story are well-known. The only detail worth mentioning here is that Mary Queen of Scots and Lord Darnley may have spent some of their honeymoon at Crichton, under the very roof of the man who before long was to bring the marriage down and play a leading part in Darnley's murder. If stones could smile at the folly they have witnessed, then those of Crichton would surely be cracked from side to side.

INFORMATION

ACCESS   The castle lies just outside the village of Crichton, on the B6367 running between the A7 and the A68 a few miles south of Edinburgh

RESPONSIBILITY FOR THE SITE
Scottish Development Department

OPENING HOURS
April-September: 9.30-19.00 (Sun 14.00-19.00) October-March: Sat 9.30-17.00, Sun 14.00-17.00

ADMISSION PRICE
60p (Senior citizens & children 30p)

FACILITIES   Parking
Dogs
Guided tours by special request

HUNTING TOWER

Near Perth, Tayside Region

For hundreds of years Huntingtower was known as the House of Ruthven, after the family who lived there. The present name was bestowed upon it in 1600 by Act of Parliament. Today it is difficult to imagine the sport of kings being pursued in the area, for though it is set in well tended grounds, Huntingtower is wedged between the A85 and the A9, in a district increasingly favoured by light industry. A deer would now look almost as incongruous here as in the centre of Perth, three miles away.

The castle is all that remains of a complex of buildings which at one time occupied the site. Markings on the exterior walls of the principal block indicate the position of these secondary structures, the largest of which was a long and lofty hall abutting the northern side of the western tower. It terminated in a substantial two-storey building of unknown function. Although standing two hundred years ago, the foundations of this wing now lie buried beneath the lawns to the rear of the castle.

Clearly the site of Huntingtower was not chosen primarily for its defensive qualities. To the south and east the land is level, although it falls away quite steeply on the other two sides. There is no record of the existence of a moat or other earthwork which might have strengthened the position. Nowadays only the corbelled parapet at the wallhead reminds the visitor that the structure once had military pretensions. The staggered southern facade, relieved by large rectangular windows, gives the impression of a country house rather than a castle.

By the end of the eighteenth century Huntingtower was no longer inhabited by its owners, and in 1805 it was converted into accommodation for cloth workers. It was then allowed to fall into a sorry state of repair. Shortly before it was taken into the care of the state at the beginning of this century, a single woman, with only chickens for company, took up residence amid the crumbling stonework and rotting boards.

The situation was ripe for scandal and, sure enough, before long tongues began to wag. The God-fearing locals did not condemn their lonely neighbour for witchcraft, as they might have done in earlier centuries. Instead they accused her of something equally wicked in their puritanical eyes. They whispered that on a bed of straw in her shabby mansion she entertained men friends. Dozens of them. And, not surprisingly, once a year the cries of a new-born baby could be heard within the castle. Yet no one ever saw these infants. An explanation was soon concocted: the harlot cast them down a well so that she could resume her wicked profession in peace. To this day, old folk

Huntingtower, originally known as Ruthven Castle, was once two separate towers standing only some three metres apart.

A long hall once extended northwards from the rear of Huntingtower Castle. Its position is clearly visible from the line of the roof above the raised doorway.

dwelling in the nearby hamlet will not visit the castle. They believe it to be an evil place.

THE CASTLE

Huntingtower was created by the amalgamation of two medieval tower houses. This makes it an interesting and unusual castle, particularly as no one is quite sure why the towers were built so close to each other in the first place. The original one, containing the present rear entrance, is at the eastern end of the building. It was an oblong structure, put up in the fifteenth century but extensively altered in about 1500, and it served as both accommodation and gatehouse. It is surmounted by an open parapet with neat rounded half-turrets at the corners. The room which excites the most interest is the hall, situated on the first floor above a vault inserted at the time of the reconstruction. Shortly before the First World War men working on the building uncovered simple but charming decoration painted on the wooden ceiling and on part of the walls. The former was executed about 1540 and is one of the earliest examples of its kind in Scotland. The murals may be slightly earlier. Loose black knots on a white background cover most of the ceiling panels, with more colourful figurative representations on the joists and beams. Though the fragmentary wall painting is much faded, a delightful picture of a hare can be made out above a window in the west wall.

At about the same time as he was rebuilding the original castle, the 1st Lord Ruthven constructed a second tower house, only three metres to the west of the first building but aligned slightly differently. It seems clear that one of the buildings was for his son William. The only link between the two towers was a wooden bridge at parapet level, so the separation may have been for reasons of security: if one tower fell, the defenders could retire to the other. By pulling down the bridge after them, they made themselves almost as safe as they had been when in possession of both keeps. On the other hand, the reason for the split-site residence may have been more mundane, such as an inability of father and son (or their wives) to live together under the same roof. The new tower was an L-shape, in three storeys, with a turnpike stair housed in a semi-circular turret in the north-west corner. It too contains ancient murals.

In the later seventeenth century the 2nd Earl of Tullibardine finally united the two towers with a low three-storey block containing a grand staircase. The south wall continued the line of the western tower and the roof of the linking segment was less steeply pitched than the one adjacent to it. The earl made no attempt to continue a parapet round the wallhead, and he opened large windows facing south, changes which suggest that by his time defensive requirements could safely be ignored. The completion of this work successfully transformed Huntingtower from a castle into a small but comfortable stately home.

RAID, REVENGE AND FILIAL REBELLION

Huntingtower is best remembered for the part it played in the celebrated Raid of Ruthven. The minority of the orphaned James VI produced the inevitable struggle between rival noble factions for control of the young king and the organs of government. James was a sensitive and lonely youth, starved of love and inclined towards homosexuality. As a result, he was susceptible to the attentions of attractive men of culture. One of the first to benefit was James Stewart, a soldier of fortune who in 1578 returned to Scotland from the continent and rapidly rose to political prominence. In 1581 he was created Earl of Arran. The success of a second visitor from continental Europe was even more meteoric. Esme Stewart, a cousin of Lord Darnley, had spent most of his early life in France, where he acquired sophisticated court graces and made himself master of the art of flattery. He arrived in Scotland in 1579, and before long James was lavishing admiration and affection on him. In 1581 the new favourite was made Duke of Lennox.

The startling success of the Arran-Lennox axis swiftly aroused the suspicious jealousy of their rivals, foremost among whom was William Lord Ruthven, 1st Earl of Gowrie. Resented for his personal hold over the king and mistrusted for his Catholicism, Lennox was the target of their bitterest hatred. Eventually, what the frustrated Protestant lords could not achieve by charm and diplomacy, they determined to bring about by force.

On 22 August 1582 the fifteen-year-old King James was at Perth, returning home after a hunting trip to Atholl. The Earls of Gowrie and Mar, accompanied by a number of lesser nobility, visited him there and with a mixture of force and persuasion prevailed upon him to stay the night at the House of Ruthven. In the morning James was surprised to find the House full of retainers and his own movements politely but firmly curtailed. Then his captors appeared and presented him with a remonstrance condemning Lennox and Arran. Protests, pleas and tears failed to move the conspirators. John, Gowrie's second son, upset the king most by suggesting that it was better for a boy to shed tears at the loss of his freedom, than for grown men to do so as a result of bad government. James harboured the tactless remark in his heart.

As a result of the 'Raid of Ruthven' Lennox was banished. He died in France the next year, leaving his embalmed heart to the king who loved him. After a captivity of ten months, with Arran's help James escaped from the Raiders while out hunting. The Earl of Gowrie was executed in 1584. Arran was murdered in 1596. Four years later, John (now the 3rd Earl) and his brother were slaughtered at the Ruthven town house in Perth. James claimed that the killings were self-defence, as the Ruthven brothers had been trying to assassinate him. Whether this was true or not, the king had finally taken his revenge for the humiliation he suffered at the House of Ruthven eighteen years before.

The 1st Earl of Gowrie had a headstrong and vigorous daughter, Dorothea. To the irritation of her family she developed a strong affection for John Wemyss, a pleasant enough fellow but not her equal in either rank or fortune. Marriage between the two was out of the question. Nevertheless, unwilling to risk an open confrontation with her daughter, Lady Gowrie permitted John to visit them at Huntingtower and a bed was found for him in the tower opposite that in which Dorothea had her apartment. Since there was at this time no bridge linking the two sides of the house, the family believed the arrangement to be both decent and safe.

At the close of an enjoyable but formal evening, during which the young couple were closely chaperoned, Dorothea managed to give her mother the slip and hide in the tower where accommodation had been arranged for her admirer. When members of the household had retired to bed and all was still, she emerged from her place of concealment and quietly made her way to John's room. Once she was inside and the door securely locked, the couple threw themselves onto the bed, their passion heightened by the illicit nature of their meeting. However, scarcely had John begun to fumble his way beneath Dorothea's elaborate dress, when the unmistakable sound of Lady Gowrie's footsteps was heard approaching up the stone stairs outside the room. The lady had been alerted to what was going on by a suspicious member of the family. Now, having locked all possible ways of escape, she planned to surprise the couple at their illicit lovemaking, and so end the relationship once and for all.

But before her mother reached the room, Dorothea quietly slipped out and fled up the stairs. At the top of the tower she made her way to the parapet. She then gathered her skirts about her and leapt over the divide between the two towers, landing safely on the other side. A minute later she was back in her own room, tucked up beneath the bedclothes and feigning sleep.

Meanwhile, Lady Gowrie had stormed into John's room. Finding the young man alone, she muttered a few words of explanation and set off to find her daughter. When eventually she met up with her, seemingly fast asleep in bed in the neighbouring tower, she apologised for her lack of trust and, still muttering to herself, she stumped back to bed.

The very next night, however, the suspicions of the Ruthven family were confirmed in the most concrete manner possible. Dorothea eloped with her lover and secretly married him, thereby freeing herself to employ her remarkable athleticism in less hazardous pursuits.

INFORMATION

ACCESS   The castle is signposted from the A85 3 miles west of Perth

RESPONSIBILITY FOR THE SITE
                Scottish Development Department

TELEPHONE   0738-27231
OPENING HOURS
                April-September: 9.30-19.00 (Sun 14.00-19.00) October-March: Mon, Tues, Wed, Thurs am, Sat

9.30-17.00, Sun 14.00-17.00
ADMISSION PRICE
          60p (Senior citizens &
          children 30p)

F Y V I E   C A S T L E

Fyvie Village, Grampian Region

Although opened to the public only a few years ago, Fyvie has rapidly established itself as one of the most popular castles in Scotland. In the summer its ancient harled walls are lapped by a ceaseless tide of tourists, while the many fine rooms resound to the muffled tread of a thousand feet and the gasped admiration of expert and amateur alike. The democratic intrusion, however, produces no discernible reaction from the generations of lairds who gaze impassively down upon the multitudes from their grand portraits on the walls. Is it with scorn or total surprise that they view the rude interruption upon their secret and sinister residence? We cannot tell. Nor do we know whether popular ownership has finally ended the curse of the three weeping stones, or driven away the green lady whose appearance foretold doom for Fyvie's owners.

The reason for Fyvie's popularity is obvious. It has everything a visitor could possibly wish for. The majestic southern facade is one of the finest examples of baronial architecture in the country. The well-kept policies (probably laid out by Robert Robinson, the man who remodelled the grounds of Glamis) are a delight to behold. The building itself, which dates back to the rich era of peace and prosperity before the Wars of Independence, is a treasure house of paintings, furniture and objects d'art. And no other castle can match Fyvie's macabre anthology of curses and sinister stories.

Extensive drainage and landscaping have so altered the land around the castle that it is not easy to see that Fyvie ('Deer Hill' in Gaelic) stands upon a terrace which once afforded considerable defensive potential. The ground slopes steeply away to the north, and all flanks except that to the south were protected by the marshy ground which drains into the River Ythan. The site was once occupied by a medieval castle of enceinte, the north and east walls of which have completely disappeared. It was a large castle, with two-and-a-half-metre thick walls rising eight metres above the ground and enclosing an area of about 2,500 metres square. This early building was a royal stronghold, lying at the heart of the Thanage of Formartine, and did not pass into private hands until Robert III gave it to Sir James de Lindsay in 1380. Records show that long before this William the Lion, Alexander III and Robert I had all stayed here, the Bruce holding court beneath the spreading beeches which grew outside the walls. In 1296 the Hammer of the Scots halted at Fyvie during his progress through the conquered kingdom. It is said that he ordered the fortress to be strengthened with a new gatehouse, a command which, as we have seen, he repeated before several other newly-acquired strongholds.

THE CASTLE

Five families owned Fyvie since the fourteenth century. Each one is remembered in a tower bearing its name, although, contrary to what legend would have us believe, only two of the towers can be directly attributed to the work of a particular family. As it now stands the castle is in the shape of a figure 2, the base and the upright being on the lines of the south and west walls of the medieval courtyard fortress. The upper part of the figure, known as the Leith tower, was added in the last century by John Bryce, acting for Alexander Forbes-Leith. Before this the castle was in a more familiar L-shape.

The oldest part of the structure is probably the tower at the eastern end of the southern wing, known as the Preston Tower. The Prestons were assigned the castle in 1390, through the marriage of Sir Henry Preston with Lady Elizabeth Lindsay. Sir Henry is supposed to have raised the height of the walls when the castle finally came into his possession in 1402, although we cannot be certain that he ordered the construction of the tower which bears his name. It appears to have been a simple vaulted structure, with a stairway set in a projecting jamb to the west. Upon Sir Henry's death the castle passed through his daughter to Alexander Meldrum, whose family retained Fyvie until 1596, when financial difficulties forced them to sell to Sir Alexander Seton. The extent of the work undertaken by the Meldrums is not clear, but they too have a tower named after them, at the opposite end of the southern facade. The work of Sir Alexander Seton, later Lord Fyvie and 1st Earl of Dunfermline, is much more apparent. He transformed what must have been a largely medieval structure into a partly-defended country house of palatial proportions, the grandest example of what has become known as the Scottish Baronial style.

Seton rose to become one of the most powerful men in the kingdom. Having made a strategic switch from Catholicism to the reformed religion, his scholarship and cultured ways attracted the attention of James VI. An able lawyer and politician, Seton became a Privy Councillor in 1585, Lord Fyvie twelve years later and Chancellor of Scotland in 1601. He was also entrusted with the guardianship of the sickly Prince Charles, who spent some time at Fyvie before following his father to London in 1604. We thus owe a considerable debt of gratitude to the percipient king, whose patronage enabled the Earl of Dunfermline to accumulate the means with which to demonstrate his refined taste in durable form at Fyvie, to the delight of subsequent generations.

The celebrated southern facade of the building is largely the work of the 1st Earl of Dunfermline. It is a masterpiece of unification, produced by harling the whole front, thereby bringing together the eastern and western towers, the Edwardian gatehouse and the linking curtain wall. An exciting skyline was sculpted by decorating the towers with corbelled, cone-capped bartizans, and interpolating the pitched roof with neat dormer windows. The central towers, now known singly as the Seton Tower, were embellished with a flying arch and furnished with a new doorway in red ashlar. The pointed turrets and narrowly rectangular windows emphasise the vertical line of the towers and so bring lightness to what otherwise might appear to be a rather overbearing fifty metres of fortification. The elaborate remodelling results in a balanced and harmonious broken sweep of sand-coloured roughcast, vast in scale yet fine in detail. Though the building as a whole might lack the near-perfect unity of Craigievar, it presents a facade of unparalleled nobility.

The 4th Earl of Dunfermline became entangled with the Jacobites and fled following the collapse of his cause in 1690. For some forty years Fyvie remained in the possession of the crown, and no doubt fell into a poor state of repair. The man responsible for saving the building was William Gordon 2nd Earl of Aberdeen, who bought it for his third wife Lady Anne Gordon, sister of the celebrated Jacobite Lord Lewis Gordon. When the earl died in 1745, he left Fyvie to his nine-year-old son, the Hon. William Gordon. The Gordons were responsible for draining the marshy areas around the castle and landscaping the policies. They also dismantled what was left of the old north and west wings, and built a new tower at the northern end of the west block to improve the accommodation. Needless to say, in due course it became known as the Gordon Tower. Another Gordon innovation was the grand entrance on the eastern side of the west wing, opening onto what was once the castle courtyard. This lessened the importance of the Seton gateway and it was reduced in size.

The Gordons held Fyvie for more than a century before they too were forced to sell it, owing to the unbusinesslike behaviour of Sir Maurice Duff-Gordon, a notorious spendthrift. The castle and its 10,000 acre estate were purchased for £175,000 by Alexander Leith, a local man who had made his fortune in the American steel industry. He changed his name to Forbes-Leith and was raised to the peerage in 1905 by the time-honoured means of making judicious donations to appropriate causes. Lord Leith's descendants lived as lairds of Fyvie until Sir Andrew Forbes-Leith sold the castle to the National Trust for Scotland in 1984.

Lord Leith's principal contribution to Fyvie's heritage was a remarkable collection of paintings and other works of art. He was also responsible for the fifth tower, built at the north-west corner of the mansion. The appropriate-sounding 'five towers of Fyvie' were now complete. It was apt, therefore, that when the Forbes-Leiths found it necessary to part with the castle, they should hand it over to the nation rather than to a private individual. No one would welcome a sixth tower.

Since we are here concerned with buildings rather than with their contents, it is neither possible nor appropriate to do more than hint at the

Fyvie Castle. The building has recently been acquired by the National Trust for Scotland and is already one of the organisation's most popular attractions.

collection of treasures held within Fyvie's walls. However, mention needs to be made of some delightful plasterwork and panelling, and of the broad sweeping staircase put in by the 1st Earl of Dunfermline. The latter, modelled on an original at Chaumont, is daringly suspended on a series of arches set at right angles to each other. Its graceful ascent was employed to lend elegance to the interior of the Renaissance building, though some unruly Gordons are supposed to have found another benefit in the design: they rode their horses up it. Like so many castles, Fyvie rattles with a vast assemblage of armour and weaponry. More memorable are the numerous Raeburns, the Batoni portrait of the Hon. William Gordon (wrapped in a sort of tartan toga and standing before the ruins of ancient Rome) and Millais' *The Sound of Many Waters*. Broad tapestries and superbly-crafted English furniture from the eighteenth century complete a collection which makes the interior of the castle just as memorable, in its own way, as the dramatic exterior.

THE CURSE OF THE WEEPING STONES

Thomas the Rhymer was a thirteenth-century minstrel with the reputation of being something of a sage and prophet. Contemporaries explained his unusual gifts by the fact that he had spent seven years living with the Elves. Like many whose talents are widely praised, however, he developed an irascible and intolerant nature, as the owners of Fyvie found out to their great cost.

The celebrated seer apparently expressed a wish to visit Fyvie castle and, unwilling to offend a man capable of showing his annoyance in no uncertain terms, the owners ordered the castle gates to be left open until Thomas turned up. Unfortunately, on his rise to stardom the Rhymer had allowed punctuality to join tolerance among his discarded virtues, and the castle gates swung idly on their hinges for seven years before he appeared. Then, just as he was about to pass through the entrance, a mighty tempest arose, uprooting trees and, as luck — or some more sinister force — would have it, slapping shut the gates in his face. Furious at such a reception, and no doubt suffering acutely from rheumatic pains after a night in the open, Thomas the Rhymer gave vent to his spleen by laying a curse upon the castle of Fyvie and its masters.

Like modern horoscopes, Thomas' curses were worded with skilful ambiguity. Several versions of what he uttered have come down to us, all equally obscure. They concern three boundary stones of the Fyvie estate, which mysteriously weep of their own accord and thereby bring ill-luck upon the castle and its inhabitants. This misfortune is usually said to manifest itself in the inability of a father to pass the estate to his eldest son, a situation which has occurred time and again in the castle's long, unhappy history. The Forbes-Leith family, the last private owners of the castle, provided sufficient examples to give the prophesy at least a fleeting plausibility.

The family's founder, Lord Leith, left the estate to his daughter Ethel, as his only son had died of enteric fever during the Boer War. Ethel's first son was slain in the Great War, so the estate passed to her younger son Ian. Ian's elder son died in Malaya in 1949, so Fyvie was inherited by Sir Andrew Forbes-Leith, the second son. He sold it to the National Trust for Scotland before Thomas the Rhymer could wreak any more havoc on the family.

Fyvie also has a ghost, in the form of a Green Lady. She is a capricious spectre, who not only appears to herald a moment of doom for the owners of Fyvie, but also insists that the reigning laird breathe his last in the room where she herself had passed away. She is supposed to be the spirit of the second wife of Alexander Seton, 1st Earl of Dunfermline. For some reason the earl incarcerated her in a tiny chamber at the top of the wheel stair. When lengthy imprisonment had finally caused her to lose her reason, she was transferred to a room known later as the Gordon bedroom. Here she was starved to death.

A few weeks later the earl married Grizel Leslie, a famous local beauty. On their wedding night, spent in the Drummond Room, the couple's enjoyment was interrupted by dreadful sighs outside the window. Assuming the sounds to be those of the wind, they ignored them. In the morning, however, when the window was opened to air the room, the name of the earl's second wife was found carved on the sill from the outside:

D LILIES DRUMMOND

It remains there to this day.

There is room here to mention only a few of the numerous tales surrounding Fyvie and its owners. The remarkable story of Lord Leith, who at the age of six arrived at the castle and explained that he had come to view the property as one day it would be his, and how he came to fulfil his precocious prophesy, requires a chapter to itself. So let us conclude with a brief look at the charter room, on the first floor of the Meldrum Tower, which served as the laird's office and strong room. Beneath it lies a secret chamber which may on no account be entered. A laird who attempts to do so brings death upon himself and blindness to his wife. There is a story that the room's existence was once confirmed by hanging towels at all the castle windows. When the exercise was completed, two windows remained unadorned. General Gordon once broke into the cursed vault, said to house a considerable treasure. He died shortly afterwards and his wife lost her sight. Later Sir Maurice Duff-Gordon, who professed to care more for wealth than superstition, ordered workmen to force a way into the chamber. But when he suffered a broken leg from a fall in the drawing room and his wife developed a painful eye complaint, he revised his priorities and commanded that the investigations go no further.

INFORMATION

ACCESS   Fyvie is on the right of the
             A947, 8 miles north of its
             junction with the A920
             Public transport (infrequent)
RESPONSIBILITY FOR THE SITE
             National Trust for Scotland
TELEPHONE   06516-262
OPENING HOURS
             May-September: 11.00-18.00;
             October: Sat, Sun 14.00-16.00

ADMISSION PRICE
             £2.10 (Children £1.05)
FACILITIES   Disabled (limited)
             Parking
             Dogs (in grounds)
             Toilets
             Guided tours
             Shop
             Refreshments

THIRLESTANE CASTLE

Lauder, Borders Region

The Maitlands are one of the few British families who can genuinely trace their descent back to the Conqueror. Originally based in Northumberland, in the thirteenth century they acquired the estates in Berwickshire where their principal seat, Thirlestane Castle, now stands. The present castle was not built until the late sixteenth century. It was erected by John the 1st Lord Maitland to replace Old Thirlestane Castle, a medieval L-shaped tower house standing some four kilometres east of Lauder, beside Boondreigh Water.

When the Maitlands moved to their new residence they took the name of their original castle with them. The site of the present building was once occupied by a structure known as Fort Lauder, said to have been put up by Edward I to guard the vital route into Edinburgh through Lauderdale, now the path of the A68. Edward II rebuilt the fort in 1324, and over two centuries later it was again reinforced at English expense, this time by the command of Lord Protector Somerset. The street in Lauder known as the Row ('rue du roi') may follow the route once used by English kings to approach the stronghold. A little of Fort Lauder was incorporated into the lower works of the new Thirlestane Castle.

The patronage of two soldiers as skilled as Edward I and the Duke of Somerset is adequate testimony to the excellence of Thirlestane's fine defensive position on a rocky crag above Leader Water. This aspect of the castle is best appreciated by following the pleasant river-bank footpath beneath the fortress' northern walls. Nevertheless, Thirlestane is not really a castle any more. Extensive rebuilding and landscaping in the seventeenth and nineteenth centuries have transformed it into an impressive country house, graced with one of Scotland's most magnificent frontages. To view this at its best advantage the visitor has to risk the wrath of the authorities by climbing into the field in

Thirlstane Castle near Lauder, the seat of the Maitland Family for the last four hundred years.

The original gatehouse at Thirlstane. It was extensively remodelled by the first Duke of Lauderdale, the 'uncrowned King of Scotland' for much of the reign of Charles II.

front of the mansion and threading his way among the sheep towards the distant woods.

THE CASTLE

The broad sweep of Thirlstane's south-west facade contains little of the residence erected by the 1st Lord Maitland in about 1590. This was an unusual building, rectangular in shape, with massive rounded towers at the four corners. It can be seen clearly from the garden and raised picnic area situated south-east of the castle, although it must be remembered that the parapet and much of the upper work is of a later date. The three storeys and garret of the sixteenth-century castle were served by no less than six stairways, four in segment towers set between the walls and the corner towers, and two more in semi-circular towers positioned mid-way along the side walls. The two towers at the north-eastern end are corbelled after the second storey to accommodate square summit rooms with crow-stepped gables, in the manner of Claypotts.

Lord Maitland's grandson, the 2nd Earl of Lauderdale, was not a particularly likeable person. But he had a quick and able mind, a memory like a computer and of all his contemporaries perhaps only his master, Charles II, was a more skilful judge of character. Moreover, Earl John was exceedingly ambitious. He became a prominent Covenanter in the 1640s and was one of those responsible for handing over Charles I to Parliament in 1647. Yet he viewed with distaste and alarm the direction which affairs then took in England, and in 1650 he placed himself among the Scots supporting Charles II in his attempt to win back his throne by force of arms. As a result of this bold display of loyalty the earl was captured at the battle of Worcester (1651) and spent the next nine years in prison in England. At the Restoration he was rewarded for his pains by the office of Secretary of State for Scotland. Within three years he had made himself the most powerful man in the kingdom, a position he was to retain for a further seventeen years. When Charles appointed him Lord High Commissioner in 1669, Maitland's position became well-nigh unassailable; contemporaries christened him the 'uncrowned King of Scotland'. Charles II expressed his approval of the Commissioner's services by turning a deaf ear to the numerous complaints he received about his servant's corrupt and high-handed methods and, later, by creating him a Duke. John Maitland is remembered in the last letter of Charles' 'Cabal' government, a title formed from the initial letters of the names of the five ministers who comprised it. It is appropriate that Lauderdale's should be the final letter, for he outlasted his political partners by many years.

The Duke of Lauderdale's tastes were straightforward, almost crude. He once confessed to Samuel Pepys that he preferred to hear a cat mew than listen to concert music. Had he been left to his own devices, therefore, goodness knows what he might have made of Thirlestane. As it was, he employed the leading architect of the day, Sir William Bruce, to help him and his second wife,

and Duchess of Lauderdale. No children were born of the marriage, though it gave rise instead to a more enduring offspring: the rebuilt castle at Thirlestane.

INFORMATION

ACCESS   The castle is clearly signposted
                from Lauder
                Public transport to Lauder
RESPONSIBILITY FOR THE SITE
                Private
TELEPHONE   05782-430
OPENING HOURS
                Easter Sun & Mon, May, June &
                Sept: Wed, Thurs, Sun

14.00-17.00; July & August: daily
(except Sat) 14.00-17.00

ADMISSION PRICE
                £2.00 (Senior citizens & children
                £1.50)

FACILITIES   Parking
                Dogs (in grounds)
                Toilets
                Guided tours
                Shop
                Refreshments ?

THE HEART OF SCOTLAND

The elaborate complexes of fortification at Edinburgh and Stirling stand at the very heart of the kingdom, two rocks around which the tide of history has swept for many hundreds of years. Though they are strikingly different from all other Scottish castles, they strongly resemble each other, both in appearance and in their experiences over the centuries. The decision to include them in a separate chapter of their own requires no further justification.

The most obvious similarity between Edinburgh and Stirling castles is a physical one. Each stands on a towering volcanic outcrop, three sides of which were scoured to a precipitous steepness in the last Ice Age, while the fourth side, sheltered from the full force of the ice flow, trails more gradually towards the plain below. Although we have little direct evidence on the subject, it seems certain that these splendid natural fortresses have been in use since at least Iron Age times.

Unlike all the strongholds examined so far, well-established urban communities have grown up around the castles at Edinburgh and Stirling. There are small settlements near Dirleton, Crichton, Inverary and Hunting-tower. Thirlestane and Floors have towns in the vicinity, and Claypotts has recently been swamped by urban sprawl. But not one of these is an urban castle, in the same sense as Edinburgh or Stirling. The reasons for this are complex, though an important factor was that the two castles featured in this chapter were popular royal seats, which acted like magnets in drawing around them members of the aristocracy and business community who wished to be near the patronage and influence of the court.

So great was their natural strength and strategic importance that, long after most other castles had either been abandoned or converted to purely domestic purposes, both Edinburgh and Stirling were continually being modified in accordance with the latest military requirements. This has resulted in their now being veritable jig-saw puzzles of military and domestic architecture, within which it is often difficult to distinguish the work of different epochs. As a consequence, while they are obviously impressive structures, they are not easy castles for the tourist to master.

Finally, no other Scottish fortresses have featured so often and so importantly in the nation's past. Without too much difficulty one can construct a satisfactory political history of Scotland, from the thirteenth to the eighteenth century, solely around the stories of Edinburgh and Stirling castles. Few other countries have buildings of comparable significance.

EDINBURGH CASTLE
The towering citadel which has for centuries stood guard over the city sprawling beneath its mighty walls.

Stirling Castle from the north-west, showing the Royal Palace and the Old King's Building.

The unusual Renaissance decoration on the southern facade of the palace at Stirling. The castle was popular with the later Stewarts, who spent considerable sums turning it into a residence worthy of a king.

STIRLING CASTLE

Stirling, Central Region

Until the Forth Road Bridge was opened in 1964, almost all those journeying between the Highlands and south-east Scotland had to pass by the towering, castle-capped rock at Stirling. The position is of crucial strategic importance. For several miles to the south-east the river Forth meanders inland along a broad valley, cutting across the waist of the country like a silvery belt. The reaches below Stirling are tidal and the castle guarded the first practicable crossing point for those not wishing to use one of the ferries downstream. In the Middle Ages the river was spanned by a vulnerable wooden bridge, replaced in the fifteenth century by a graceful construction of five semicircular stone arches. Despite temporary damage at the time of the 1745 Jacobite rebellion, it survives intact to this day, though it has not been open to heavy traffic for well over a hundred and fifty years.

Stirling, which has been likened to a broch fastening the Highlands to the Lowlands, guards not only the north-south route but also that running east-west, from Perth to the Clyde. It is significant that the Dukes of Albany, who harboured ambitions of seizing the crown for their own branch of the Stewart family, chose Doune, only a few miles north-west of Stirling, as the site for their new stronghold: the position was as convenient as any from which to dominate the whole country. Successive generations of English invaders were also acutely aware of the importance of controlling the region, and it is no coincidence that the most famous battle in Scottish history was fought just outside Stirling. It was in order to prevent the castle from falling into Scottish hands that on Midsummer's Day 1314 Edward II met the army of Robert the Bruce beside the Bannock burn. As it turned out, the English lost the battle, their army — and the castle.

It is curious that nature should have provided such a magnificent defensive position at so vital a crossroads. There was almost certainly a fort of some description here in prehistoric times and Stirling can probably be identified as the seventh-century city of Ludeu. There is no record of a stone building on the site, however, until the late thirteenth century. Before that it is likely that earth ramparts and timber palisades were considered sufficient to render the summit impregnable. The oldest part of the existing castle is contained within the North Gate, dating back to 1381. Since then the buildings on the sloping plateau have been altered so many times that it is almost impossible to discover what the stronghold looked like during the different stages of its development.

Edinburgh was not thought of as Scotland's capital city until the early modern period. Before that the seat of government was peripatetic, moving around the country with the king's court. Since most monarchs from the house of Stewart spent more time at Stirling than elsewhere, during their reigns the town came to be seen as Scotland's principal administrative centre, and acquired a complex of appropriately splendid domestic buildings. It is this close amalgam of the military with the domestic which makes Stirling so unusual.

There are visitors who find the castle something of an anticlimax, expecting to find a more exciting fortress in so dramatic a setting. It is true that Stirling lacks the clarity and unity of a fortress such as Caerlaverock and that years of vandalism by the army have give the place a somewhat drab air. But quite miraculous restoration is in progress; and the tourist with a little imagination will discover that Stirling affords just as many delights and surprises as a more straightforward monument.

THE CASTLE

The ground plan of Stirling Castle is best considered as bullet-shaped, with the town situated on a tail sloping away south-east from the flat end of the cartridge. At the tip of the site there is a large open area known as the Nether Bailey, containing some unexceptional nineteenth-century magazines and a punishment block of similar date. The Stewart palace stood at the centre of the castle, comprising four impressive buildings constructed over a period of a century and a half. The principal defences were concentrated at the vulnerable southern end of the rock, nearest the town. These consist principally of James IV's forework, which was extensively modified to accommodate artillery in the mid-seventeenth and early eighteenth centuries.

The Old King's Building, now housing a museum of the Argyll and Sutherland Highlanders, is the earliest part of a quadrangle of structures facing the court in the middle of the castle, known as the Upper Square. Unfortunately the building was much altered by Robert Billings after a fire in the middle of the last century, so that it is now difficult to see what the former Stewart palace looked like. It may well have taken a form widely copied in several later castles, with a vaulted basement, a hall and private chamber on the storey above, and accommodation on the second floor. There was a spiral staircase at the southern end. There is a tradition, unsupported by much in the way of evidence, which holds that it was from a room in this building that the mutilated body of the 8th Earl of Douglas was cast after the fateful dinner with James II in 1452. The incident is commemorated in a stained-glass representation of the Douglas arms in the Douglas Room.

Opposite the Old King's Building stands the Great Hall, one of the finest late-medieval structures in the whole of the British Isles. At present the hall is being lovingly restored to its former magnificence at great expense; when finished it will surely be one of the showpieces of the Scottish heritage. The hammer-beam roof was equalled only by that of Westminster Hall in London. Warmth was proved by five huge fireplaces and the building was lit by pairs of lofty windows, beneath which the plain stone walls were adorned with rich tapestries. The elevated dais was at the south end of the hall, where gigantic bay windows rose from floor to ceiling. The chamber may have been planned in the reign of James III, though most of the work was carried out by his successor, James IV, in the early years of the sixteenth century, at the same time as the reconstruction of the curtain wall. The hall was the last major example of its type in Britain and must have verged on the anachronistic even before it was completed. It represents a tradition stretching back to the monarchs of the House of Alpin, when the king was the great chief and feasting in his hall was the focal point of court life. There was still a need for huge refectories, where the king could entertain courtiers and foreign embassies with a lavish display of pomp and generosity — and such flamboyance was very much in keeping with the personality of 'James of the Iron Belt' — but throughout Europe there was a move away from such obvious public ostentation, towards a more private and domestic style of court. This is born out by the building on the third side of the Upper Square, the Palace.

Although completed less than forty years after the Great Hall, the Palace suggests a totally different approach to court life. The quadrangular building, linked to the Great Hall by a nineteenth-century neo-Gothic bridge (replacing what was almost certainly an original feature), contained separate suites of rooms for the king and queen. James V was provided with two public chambers, for the reception of guests and official functions, and a large Bed Chamber with a number of smaller rooms leading off it. Here he could attend to day-to-day matters of state relatively undisturbed. The open courtyard in the centre of the Palace is known as the 'Lion's Den' and may have been where the king allowed a real lion, the central motif of the royal coat of arms, to roam free — to the horror of unwary servants and guests. The Palace is famous for two aspects of its decoration. The ceiling of the Royal Presence Chamber was once embellished with a large number of carved wooden heads. When in the eighteenth century one of these fell and injured a soldier standing below, they were removed and preserved through the good offices of the governor of Stirling prison, Ebenezer Brown. He had the good sense to realise that they were rather too precious to be used as firewood. They were recovered almost two centuries later, when most were returned to the castle. They are now displayed on the walls of the queen's apartments, where they can be clearly seen and no longer endanger passers by.

The carvings on the outside of the building are even more noteworthy than the 'Stirling Heads' within. The Palace was essentially a Gothic structure, but it was one of the first buildings in Britain to exhibit a facade decorated in the new Renaissance style. Though much of the work must have been executed by native craftsmen, the influence of French designers is clearly apparent in the twisted columns and blatantly secular statues arranged along the building's south face. Some show mythical beasts, others are more realistic representations of Planetary Gods and even of King James V himself.

The Chapel Royal completes the complex of buildings surrounding the Upper Square. It stands on the site of a previous chapel and was built in 1594 by James VI for the christening of his first born son, Prince Henry. The chamber's plain, rather cold appearance probably reflects the haste in which it was built and the king's unwillingness to offend puritan sensibilities. The interior was brightened in 1628 with paintings by Valentine Jenkin, fragments of which have survived the various sub-divisions made to the building in the eighteenth and nineteenth centuries.

James IV was responsible for the Forework, the last traditional reworking of the castle's defences, completed in about 1508. Like his Great Hall, these too were probably out of date as soon as they were finished: the massive towered curtain wall, thrown flat across the 'cartridge' end of the rock, would have been of little use against artillery bombardment. The wall was flanked by a square tower at either end, the Prince's Tower in the west and the Elphinstone Tower (now just a stump) in the east. The central gatehouse is still visible, though it has been considerably reduced in height and two of its four towers have been demolished. The crenellations are nineteenth-century work. James' outmoded defences were re-worked within forty years of their completion, when two artillery batteries were constructed in front of his wall. The one on the right as one enters the castle, known as the French Spur, is still intact, but the larger, central projection was incorporated in an even more complete programme of reconstruction (the Outer Defences) begun in 1707 by Theodore Drury, in anticipation of trouble following the Union with England. He provided the front of the castle with substantial gun emplacements and a series of dry moats, the outer of which was flanked by caponiers — galleries from which the defenders could shoot down assailants in the ditch.

Despite the clutter of functional nineteenth-century buildings left over from the time when Stirling was employed as an operational military garrison, the castle defences still present a resolute appearance. It is not hard for the visitor to see why it was regarded as one of the kingdom's most doughty strongholds. Nor is it difficult to understand the affection in which the place was held by many Stewart monarchs. Not only did they feel safe here, but the pleasant combination of fine buildings, quiet gardens and unsurpassed views made it a delightful place in which to live.

A S Y M B O L O F S C O T L A N D ' S I N D E P E N D E N C E

Such was the importance of Stirling that its fortunes tended to mirror those of the nation of which it was the principal fortress. This was never more apparent than during the Wars of Independence. The origins of this conflict go back to 1290, when the seven-year-old Queen Margaret died as she was travelling back from Norway to take up the Scottish crown. Since the succession was not clear, all interested parties agreed to accept Edward I of England as their feudal overlord and arbitrator between the claims of the rival Competitors.

A view from Stirling's lofty battlements towards the ancient bridge over the River Forth. The occurrence of a natural defensive position at the river's lowest fordable point gave Stirling tremendous strategic importance.

Edward was an ambitious and shrewd politician. He had already subjugated the Welsh and was not one to let slip such an opportunity of extending his sway further north. After John Balliol had been chosen king of Scotland in 1292, Edward made such unreasonable demands of him that within four years John felt compelled to renounce his fealty to the English king and declare war. This was, of course, precisely what Edward had been angling for. The Scottish forces were crushed and King John compelled to abdicate in 1296.

For the next ten years Scotland was a kingdom without a king. There was continual conflict between the Hammer of the Scots and hard-pressed patriots who fought to preserve Scottish independence, foremost among whom was

William Wallace. Following Wallace's capture and execution in 1305, his place was taken by Robert Bruce, who had himself proclaimed King of Scotland in 1306. Although Bruce had not shown any particular enthusiasm for his country's cause before this, he was fortunate in the moment he chose to discover his latent patriotism — Edward I died the following year and was succeeded by a son who had no stomach for the expansionist policies of his father. Bruce beat off a major English invasion in 1314, and by the time of his death in 1329 he was undisputed master of his kingdom.

Unfortunately the dispute did not end here. King John's son Edward returned to Scotland with English backing, and in 1334 Robert I's young son David II was sent to France for safe-keeping. Upon his return in 1441 David became involved in yet another war with England, which led to his defeat and capture at Neville's Cross in 1346. He remained a prisoner in England for eleven years, during which time Robert Stewart, the future Robert II, came to prominence.

During this conflict Stirling castle changed hands no less than eleven times, although not every change of ownership involved a fight. For example in 1291 Edward I, in his capacity as guardian of the realm, demanded and received the keys of all Scottish castles, including Stirling. On two other occasions when he moved to seize the castle he found it abandoned before his arrival. At other times, however, Stirling did not fall into his hands so easily. The most famous resistance occurred in the summer of 1304.

Edward was at the peak of his power. He had just quelled a nationalist uprising and almost all the major Scottish families had either come to terms, or were in exile. Only Stirling held out against him. The castle was manned by Sir William Oliphant and a tiny garrison of some thirty men. They fought for no king — Scotland was without one at the time — but swore allegiance to the lion rampant, which they flew proudly over Stirling's ramparts. Though they knew that their cause was hopeless, they were fired by an inner spirit which urged them to uphold the pride of the Scottish nation.

Edward, on the other hand, was determined to enjoy himself and make the siege a demonstration of modern military techniques. He did not play into Scottish hands by ordering his men to attack the castle directly, but camped on the plain below where he set up his mighty engines of war. There were twelve or thirteen of these machines, each known by name, including a terrible device for hurling fire at the castle above them. To load the counterweights of these huge catapults lead was stripped from the roofs of all large buildings in the vicinity, including two cathedrals and an abbey. Furthermore, Edward's engineers were working on a still more frightful weapon, a gigantic catapult known as 'Warwolf' ('loup de guerre'), and he was determined that the siege should not end before the Wolf had demonstrated its destructive capabilities. To make the most of the spectacle the king ordered a special stand to be built from which the ladies accompanying his army could view the proceedings in comfort and safety. He was making the Anglo-Scottish clash a social event, rather like a Calcutta Cup match.

While the English were enjoying themselves on the plain below, the conditions inside Stirling grew steadily worse. There was plenty of fresh water, but food supplies soon ran out and the garrison was reduced to eating dogs, cats and anything else remotely edible which they could lay their hands on. And all the while they were subjected to a ceaseless bombardment from the English catapults, steadily knocking down their defences and inflicting ghastly wounds on the enfeebled garrison. Edward was, in fact, playing with Sir William and his tiny band. Given his immense numerical superiority, the English king could have taken Stirling whenever he wished. Instead, he was taking the opportunity to demonstrate to the Scots that even their mightiest fortress was but a castle of sand before his great engines of war. Even when the Scots finally capitulated, exhausted and starved to the point where they could resist no more, he refused to accept their surrender until the Wolf had spent a day hurling huge boulders at the ruined castle in an orgy of wanton destruction, to the applause of awe-struck spectators. When the wretched garrison finally appeared before the king, he made them grovel and beg for mercy. The next year Wallace was executed as a traitor in London and his quarters exhibited on gibbets in northern England and Scotland. The humiliation of the Scots was complete.

Edward's tactics did not break Scottish resistance but stiffened it. After the siege of 1304 the English held Stirling for ten years, but in 1314 the castle walls witnessed a military humiliation even greater than that which had been meted out to Sir William Oliphant and his garrison. And this time it was the English who suffered. After Bannockburn Stirling passed back into Scottish hands and Bruce slighted it so that never again could it be held against them by a foreign power. But the site was too important to be left undefended for long, and soon the castle was rebuilt stronger than ever. Since then it has been fought over many times, including a half-hearted and unsuccessful assault by Bonnie Prince Charlie in 1746. The Prince knew as well as anyone that he could not to secure himself in Scotland without first seizing the key to the kingdom, the great castle at Stirling.

INFORMATION

ACCESS   The castle is clearly visible in the centre of Stirling Public transport

RESPONSIBILITY FOR THE SITE
    Scottish Development Department

TELEPHONE   0786-62517

OPENING HOURS
    April-September: 9.30-17.15 (Sun 10.00-16.45) October-March: 9.30-16.20 (Sun 12.30-3.35)

ADMISSION PRICE
    £1.75 (Senior citizens & children 85p)

FACILITIES   Disabled (limited)
    Parking
    Toilets
    Guided tours by special request
    Shop
    Refreshments

The rock upon which Edinburgh Castle stands has been continually inhabited for almost thirty centuries, although the present buildings have been in existence for only a fraction of that time.

The precipitous south-eastern face of the castle rock, surmounted by the Royal Palace rising above the massive Half Moon battery.

EDINBURGH CASTLE

Edinburgh, Lothian Region

Not many capital cities are dominated by a fortress. It says something about the suspicious nature of the Scots and the ceaseless turmoil of their history that the great black rock in the centre of Edinburgh is not surmounted by a church or cathedral, but by a castle, whose forbidding form looms over the city like a gigantic war memorial. It serves as a reminder to both citizen and visitor alike that here dwell a proud people who set great store by their independence.

Castle Rock is the plug of an extinct volcano, rasped to its present shape by the action of ice, wind and rain over millions of years. Archaeological evidence has recently confirmed what has always been believed: that the site has been occupied since prehistoric times. It now appears that Man recognised the summit's potential as soon as he was able to organise himself for defence. There are not many natural positions which are so readily defensible. The uneven plateau on top of the rock, which stands some ninety metres above the ground below, is roughly oval in shape. The vertical south face of the crag is best appreciated from Johnson Terrace, a broad road which passes directly beneath James IV's Great Hall, perched precariously on the adjacent cliff. The most common view of the castle is from Prince's Street Gardens to the north. On this side too the rock rises with a daunting verticality. Though the terraced north-western approach is less precipitous, by far the easiest route to the castle follows the line of the High Street westwards up Castlehill to the Esplanade and the Victorian Gatehouse. The highest point of the rock, known as Crown Square, rises to one's left, beyond the vast sweep of the Half Moon Battery. The path to the Square spirals anti-clockwise from the outer ditch like a snail shell.

There is evidence of the rock's occupation comes from the sixth century and there was certainly a castle of some sort here in the eleventh century. The oldest structure still standing is St Margaret's Chapel, probably erected during the reign of David I (1124-1153). Very little medieval fortification remains and most of the present castle buildings are comparatively recent, although the basic plan is still that established by David II at the end of the Wars of Independence. In a sense the site has been the victim of its own importance. The great majority of castles we have examined so far were either neglected when they ceased to be of military use, or the earlier work was incorporated into domestic additions and thereby saved for posterity. Unfortunately, Edinburgh Castle remained in active service long after most other medieval strongholds had been abandoned, and those responsible for the site were understandably more concerned with maintaining its defensibility and providing accommodation for the soldiers than with preserving ancient stones. Even when the Victorians took it upon themselves to give the fort what they considered to be a more authentic look, their confident work was not always appropriate. As a consequence, although the castle makes a splendidly picturesque backdrop for the city, many of the buildings which appear so impressive from the streets and parks below turn out upon closer inspection to be to be rather unexceptional.

THE CASTLE

Edinburgh Castle is best considered in three parts: the main defences in the south-east, the quadrangle around Crown Square, and the remaining structures on the north-west side of the plateau.

Although the castle featured many times in the Wars of Independence, the fortress was demolished in 1313 and not rebuilt on a grand scale until David II, the son of King Robert Bruce, returned from captivity in England in 1357. David constructed a large tower house on the site of the Half Moon Battery and a gatehouse, known as the Constable's Tower, on the northern side of the vulnerable eastern flank. The two were linked by a curtain wall which ran approximately along the line of the present Forewall Battery. All David's work has vanished beneath later modification designed either to strengthen the castle or simply to lend it a more dignified air.

The outer ditch was begun by soldiers of the New Model Army but not finished until almost a century later. The Gatehouse, featuring the last drawbridge to be installed in Scotland and statues of Bruce and Wallace, is barely more than a century old. The Constable's Tower was replaced in the 1570s by a structure known as the Portcullis Gate, or Argyll Tower (after the 9th Earl of Argyll, who was supposed to have been executed in one of the rooms). The lower part of the gate is embellished with Renaissance decoration, while the upper part is an incongruous nineteenth-century reconstruction. The dominant feature of the whole castle is the Half Moon Battery. It was aligned with the Forewall Battery so that they could pour fire upon anyone attempting to reach the castle entrance, placed at a right angle to them. The Half Moon battery was raised on vaults, incorporating David II's tower, well above the natural level of the rock. Some idea of the scale of the project can be gathered from the fact that the present platform is at the height of the second floor of the original tower house. Regent Morton constructed these defences after a lengthy siege to dislodge Sir William Kirkcaldy, who objected to the dispossession of Mary Queen of Scots and held the castle on her behalf between 1571 and 1573. The three batteries to the right of the Portcullis Gate, which until the eighteenth century commanded a view over open countryside, are a combination of several periods of work. The Argyle Battery is noteworthy as it was built by General Wade, better known for his road building in the Highlands.

Crown Square does not compare favourably with Stirling's Upper Square, though the two have undoubted similarities. This part of Edinburgh castle was originally approached up the Lang Stairs, from the head of which one looked across at St Mary's Church. The site was cleared to make way for a barrack block in 1755, then again altered in 1924-7 to create the Scottish National War Memorial. The outside of the building is not remarkable. The interior was designed by Sir Robert Lorimer, the man who transformed Dunrobin after the fire of 1915. What one feels about his work here is very much a matter of personal taste, although most would agree that it compares favourably with the majority of such memorials raised in the 1920s. To the building's right is an officers' block put up in 1708, now housing part of the Scottish United Services Museum.

The south side of the square is occupied by James IV's Great Hall, famous for its wonderful hammer beam roof. The delights of the building were lost on Cromwell's soldiers, however, and they sub-divided it to provide accommodation for the garrison. Subsequent generations continued their work. All vertical and horizontal partitions were eventually cleared out during an enthusiastic though somewhat fanciful restoration undertaken between 1887 and 1891 at the expense of the publisher William Nelson. Fortunately, the roof has survived both military vandalism and Victorian improvement. In order to provide a level platform for the hall, the area beneath it was built up with a series of massive vaults, which are well worth a visit. They contain not only the graffiti of prisoners of war held there in the eighteenth and nineteenth centuries, but also the great gun, Mons Meg, sheltering here to prevent further deterioration of its ironwork. This mighty Burgundian cannon was presented to James II and remained operational until 1680, when it burst. It weighs six and a half tons and was hauled around the country at an average rate of four miles per day. The effort required to drag it up to the top of Castle Rock must have been worth seeing.

The Royal Palace lies along the fourth side of Crown Square. The building was originally an extension of David II's tower, and dates back to the reign of James I. It was modified by James IV (who else?), and again for Queen Mary and Lord Henry Darnley. The couple's initials and the date 1566 can be seen above the door to the right of the tower. Further alterations were made for James VI. In the last century the tower was heightened and battlements added to give the building a more martial look. Two rooms are of especial interest. One is the chamber in which Mary Queen of Scots bore James VI, protesting from the moment of birth that her husband, and not the Earl of Bothwell, was the boy's father. The second room contains the Scottish Regalia, those highly-prized symbols of independent nationhood which we have already met at Dunnottar. They were walled up in this room following the Union with England in 1707, but rediscovered and put on display again in 1818. Though not as glorious as the regalia flaunted by some other monarchies, they have the restrained beauty of great age and simplicity. The crown was made for James V and incorporates gold from that worn by Robert I. The sword was presented to James IV by Pope Julius II in 1507.

With the exception of St Margaret's Chapel, erected by the queen's youngest son in memory of his mother, the rest of the castle is unremarkable. The twelfth century chapel was extended and used as a magazine at one stage and the building we now see is the product of a nineteenth-century recreation, incorporating what was left of the medieval structure. The exterior is dull but the plain whitewashed interior, with a fine Romanesque arch between the apse and rebuilt nave, captures the mystery of a place of worship which echoed to the Latin chants of the Mass over 800 years ago.

The largest and ugliest building on the rock is the barrack block put up in the 1790s. Opposite these New Barracks is a second entrance to the upper part of the castle, probably dating from the seventeenth century, and mysteriously entitled Foog's Gate. The garrison looked after a Military Prison, in use until 1923 and still able to teach us something about the amount of space required for a prisoner to live decently. A pleasant eighteenth-century Governor's House stands at the foot of Hawk Hill, near the cart sheds which have been converted into a souvenir shop. The Western Defences have some attractive corbelled sentry boxes and a battery named after Theodore Drury, the man who redesigned the artillery fortifications at Stirling. This completes the somewhat motley collection of buildings which crowns the Castle Rock. Though not matching the splendour of the position, they form a tangible panorama of the history of a mighty fortress over eight eventful centuries.

SAINT MARGARET

Margaret was the second wife of Malcolm III (1058-1093), known to his subjects as 'Canmore'. The epithet means Big Head and may refer either to the king's looks or, more kindly, to the fact that he was a great leader. Shakespeare favoured the latter interpretation, as this was the Malcolm, son of Duncan, whom the bard made the hero of *Macbeth*.

Malcolm first married Ingibjorg, daughter of the powerful Earl Thorfinn of Orkney. In 1068, however, the king received four uninvited guests at his court. They were the Saxon pretender to the English throne, Edgar Atheling, his mother and two sisters, Christine and Margaret. Malcolm was clearly smitten by Margaret's fair good looks and charming personality, and when the next year Ingibjorg died he lost no time in making the English princess his second wife. Though the union did little to endear Malcolm to his powerful southern neighbour, William the Conqueror, if we are to believe Margaret's biographer the marriage turned out to be unusually felicitous. Malcolm respected his wife's learning and saintly ways, and treated her with a courtesy most unusual for the time. Margaret, for her part, was equally devoted to her man of action and bore him seven children.

The small party of Saxon royalty had arrived in Scotland by accident, having been shipwrecked on their way to the continent. Hitherto Margaret had spent most of her life in exile, as first the Danes then the Normans had barred her from her native land. She may well have been born in Hungary, and only during the reign of Edward the Confessor had she been able to live in England for any length of time. As a consequence she brought to the Scottish court a welcome breath of continental air. In manners and thinking she became the model upon which other ladies fashioned themselves. She is also reported to have devoted much of her time to improving the church, weeding out some old-fashioned practices and introducing Benedictine monks to the abbey at Dunfermline.

Sadly, the queen's life ended in tragedy. Relations between Malcolm Canmore and his powerful Norman neighbours were rarely cordial. Five times during his reign the Great Chief swept over the border into England on raids of rape and pillage, usually drawing equally bloody responses from the Conqueror and his sons. Malcolm moved south for the last time in 1093, pricked into action by the refusal of William Rufus to accept the King of Scotland at his court. The Scots laid siege to Alnwick Castle. One dank day in late autumn a band of English knights ambushed Malcolm and his eldest son Edward on a low wooded hill overlooking the river Aln. The king and his bodyguard were heavily outnumbered and the fight was brief. Before it was over Malcolm lay dead upon the grass, with Edward mortally wounded beside him.

News of the disaster was brought to Margaret by the gentle Edgar, the son who most resembled his mother. He had hardly recovered from his journey, however, before he was obliged to leave again on an equally doleful mission. This time he bore the body of his mother from the castle at Edinburgh through the November mists to its final resting place at Dunfermline. On hearing the terrible news from Alnwick the queen had given up all wish to live, and died within a few days.

Edgar became king himself four years later but he never married, and when he died in 1107 the crown passed in turn to his brothers Alexander and David. Although it was David who eventually built the chapel dedicated to their saintly mother, it is tempting to believe that he was only carrying out Edgar's wishes.

INFORMATION

ACCESS — The castle is in the centre of Edinburgh. Public transport

RESPONSIBILITY FOR THE SITE — Scottish Development Department

TELEPHONE — 031-225-9846

OPENING HOURS — Mon-Sat 9.30-4.20, Sun 12.30-15.35

ADMISSION PRICE — £2.20 (senior citizens & children £1.00)

FACILITIES — Disabled (limited) Parking Toilets Guided tours by special request Shop Refreshments

INVERARY
The Campbell's fairy-tale headquarters set deep in the heart of Argyll.

Floors' riotous mock-Tudor skyline, produced by W H Playfair for the 6th Duke of Roxburghe in the early nineteenth century.

Inverary Castle, the distinctive home of the Dukes of Argyll since the late eighteenth century.

ROMANTIC RETREATS

By the eighteenth century the castle was obsolete as a place of refuge. Where military fortifications were needed, they took the form of forts, such as those built by the Hanoverians at Fort William, Fort Augustus and Fort George. Perversely, however, long into the nineteenth century well-to-do Scots continued to build castles, or at least romantic pseudo-military buildings which they called castles. The appellation was pure sentimentality. By this time the castle, along with whisky, tartan and bagpipes, had become part of the nation's heritage. The English gentleman might live in his manor, his hall or even his abbey, but the Scotsman of substance had a castle. In what was to prove the final phase of castle construction in Scotland, scores of older structures were rebuilt and entirely new ones commissioned in a mock-baronial style. When Prince Albert and Queen Victoria were looking for a little place north of the border where they could establish themselves as the laird and his wife, it was a castle, Balmoral, which caught their fancy. Indeed, if the royal residence (rebuilt 1853-5) were open to the public, it would make an excellent addition to this chapter.

Though several of the castles already examined, such as Glamis, Thirlestane and Dunvegan, were altered or extended in the nineteenth century, the essential character of the buildings was not radically changed. On the other hand, the four castles included here are all of predominantly late eighteenth or nineteenth century construction. Dunrobin and Culzean incorporate the remains of medieval castles, but these have been almost entirely subsumed in later work so that they are now virtually invisible from the outside.

Selecting castles for this chapter, unlike some that have preceded it, has not been difficult. A few may resent the exclusion of the proud white walls of Blair, and a case can be made for including the stately Drumlanrig. But neither represents as well as the four chosen here the final flourish of a proud Scottish aristocracy before the onset of democracy, in architecture as well as politics.

These stately homes were retreats in the sense that they were the country mansions of families who owned several houses. Sometimes the proprietors stayed away from their castles for months on end, leaving the day to day maintenance to factors and an army of local servants. When the family returned it was to relax, away from the social, political and business interests which filled most of their lives. With a few notable exceptions, the struggling owner-manager is a relatively modern phenomenon.

The country seat is a tangible reminder of an era already slipping away at the dawn of this century, when the luxurious living of a handful of grand families contrasted pointedly with the relative poverty of the majority of citizens. As a consequence, these manifestations of aristocratic privilege are still capable of arousing feelings of outrage. But to regard Floors, Inverary,

Dunrobin and Culzean as vulgar symbols of exploitation is merely to rehearse a condemnation relevant to almost all castles. The contrast between the hut of the peasant and the glory of a building such as Kildrummy raises little indignation, for time is a powerful amnesiac. Moreover, the buildings studied in this chapter are now all open to the public, the ultimate humiliation for any castle and a powerful statement that their exclusivity is at an end.

Like the tower house and the baronial stronghold, the Romantic Retreat was built to display power and insulate its owner from the rough realities beyond its walls. It is not, therefore, a mere postscript to the history of the Scottish castle, but an appropriately splendid conclusion to an epic tale.

FLOORS CASTLE

Kelso, Borders Region

Floors castle occupies one of the loveliest sites in all Scotland. It stands on sloping hills above the ancient market town of Kelso, with a grand arch of woodland enfolding it on three sides, and open park and farmland falling gently away towards the Tweed and the distant abandoned ramparts of Roxburgh Castle in the south. Even the obligatory car park is tucked away out of sight beneath the trees, like a shady Continental campsite.

Beautiful though the position may be, it has no defensive potential whatsoever, which explains why there has not been a substantial building on the site for very long. Floors castle grew out of an early eighteenth-century Georgian mansion, and the estate's only military association is provided by its proximity to the site of Roxburgh castle.

James II, known as 'Fiery Face', was disfigured by a large red birthmark. This, together with a traumatic upbringing, made him shy of human company, and he rather pathetically transferred his affection to a siege train of massive cannon, upon which he lavished both money and attention. In 1460 he was given the opportunity of putting his beloved weapons to the test. The occasion was a siege of Roxburgh castle, then in the hands of the English. At first the bombardment went well and James watched delightedly as his cannon steadily reduced the mighty castle's defences. Then, to mark a visit to the front by his queen, Mary of Gueldres, the king arranged for his artillery to fire a special salute. He took personal charge of the operation, ensuring that each gun was fully loaded to provide as impressive a noise as possible. At the moment of firing he positioned himself beside his favourite weapon, a gun known as the 'Lion'. Unfortunately, in his enthusiasm he had allowed the cannon to be packed with more gunpowder than the breach could safely contain, so when a lighted match was applied to the charge the gun exploded, killing the king and several soldiers. It is claimed, with somewhat dubious authenticity, that a holly tree in the grounds of Floors marks the spot where James II met his death.

Floors is owned by the Innes Ker family, who rose to national prominence during the reign of James VI. Sir Robert Ker of Cessford was a close friend of the king and became a Privy Councillor in 1599. He accompanied James to London in 1603 and in 1616 was created Earl of Roxburghe. The former lands of Kelso Abbey, upon which the present castle stands, came into the possession of the family at this time.

THE CASTLE

The architecture of Floors Castle is not to everyone's taste. It is said that the original house, the neat design of which was influenced by William Adam (father of the more famous Robert), was no match for the grandeur of the position. Visitors can decide for themselves upon the veracity of this observation by studying William Wilson's 1809 painting of the castle, which today hangs in the Sitting Room. Whatever one thinks, the architect W.H.Playfair (1790-1857) certainly took to heart the command of the 6th Duke of Roxburghe to transform Floors into a building more appropriate for the site. Indeed, some would claim that Playfair took his instructions too literally and produced a sprawling mass of a mansion, whose cluttered decoration speaks more of ostentation than good taste.

The Georgian building was a plain rectangle, with a tower at each corner, a forecourt and two pavilions. Beginning in 1841, Playfair added spreading wings to the east and west. These extended some fifty metres to the north, so forming a huge, partially enclosed court on that side of the house. On the southern side of this space, against the main block, he built a large covered porch, known as a porte-cochere. The basic design is elegant and balanced. In the decoration to the building, however, Playfair cast aside all restraint. Walter Scott once described the setting of Floors as 'a kingdom for Oberon and Titania'. Taking up this Shakespearian theme, the architect covered the castle with a riot of mock-Tudor adornment. The windows were surmounted with hood-moulds, and the skyline transformed with a stubble of paired chimneys, corbelling, elaborate water spouts, castellation and innumerable pepper-pot turrets. The effect is more impressive than beautiful, and all the more surprising since it comes from the drawing board of the man responsible for the clean classical lines of the National Gallery in Edinburgh. Nevertheless, the visitor is left in no doubt that this was the residence of a man of considerable consequence and wealth, which is just what the 6th Duke would have wished.

Sir Henry Innes-Ker, the 8th Duke of Roxburghe, adopted the manner fashionable at the turn of the century for re-endowing his estate. He married the daughter of an American millionaire. The influence of Mary Goelet upon Floors was extensive. She added many pieces, notably tapestries, to the castle's collection of artistic treasures and supervised an extensive remodelling of the interior. Any feelings of misgiving engendered by the castle's exterior are instantly evaporated as one steps inside and encounters her work.

The striking feature of the Floors collection is its variety and breadth. The priceless display contains, among other items, Brussels and Gobelins tapestries, Chinese vases, pieces of sculpture, Meissen and Coalport porcelain, British, Dutch and French furniture, clocks by Faberge and Cartier, and even a collection of stuffed birds. The paintings include works by Gainsborough, Raeburn, Turner, Matisse and Bonnard. There can not be many finer exhibitions of masterpieces from three and a half centuries of European high culture.

THE DISPUTED INHERITANCE

Although Floors is not a castle of ghosts and bloodshed, conflict once played an important part in its history. The story begins with John the 3rd Duke and William the 4th Duke, who both died childless within a year of each other. The succession to the Duchy and the Floors estate was now hotly contested by a number of claimants before the House of Lords' Committee of Privileges. Like the foggy Jarndice v Jarndice case in *Bleak House*, the issue dragged on for many years, the only beneficiaries being the lawyers accumulating fat fees from their clients. Finally, after seven years of wrangling and procrastination, the Committee decided in favour of the seventy-six year old Sir James Innes.

The aged duke now faced two pressing problems. Firstly, he could not pay his lawyers. Secondly, and more worrying in the long run for it suggested that shortly the whole issue would be before the House again, he had no children. He solved the first difficulty by selling off the immensely valuable collection of books and manuscripts he had inherited from the 3rd Duke. The second challenge was less easily met. However, having waited so long to come into their inheritance, the septuagenarian and his young wife were determined not to allow their family be dispossessed without a struggle. Their efforts were rewarded four years later with the birth of a son. So in 1823, thanks to his father's perseverance and unusual vigour, the young James Innes Ker duly became the 6th Duke of Roxburghe. His descendants remain at Floors to this day.

ACCESS The clearly-signposted castle is a mile north-west of Kelso Public transport to Kelso

RESPONSIBILITY FOR THE SITE Private

TELEPHONE 0573-23333

OPENING HOURS May, June, September: Sun-Thurs 10.30-16.45 July & August: every day 10.30-16.45

ADMISSION PRICE £2.50 (Senior citizens £2.00, children £1.50)

FACILITIES Disabled Parking Dogs (on lead & in grounds only) Toilets Guided tours by special request Shop

INVERARY CASTLE

Inverary, Strathclyde Region

Inverary Castle has always been something of an oddity. It does not possess the authenticity of a medieval fortress or the grandeur of a stately home. Set amid the glorious scenery of Argyllshire, it looks more like a overblown model fort than a castle, the figment of a toy-designer's imagination rather than a serious piece of architecture. It is an enigmatic building, too. When the southern front is bathed in sunshine it can look almost beautiful. Yet the grey-green slabs of which it is constructed turn black in the rain and since the entrance is on the gloomy and undistinguished northern side, the visitor's first impression is often of a dark, sinister place. This is not completely alleviated when one enters the pleasing interior because of the incongruous emphasis upon weaponry in some of the rooms.

Inverary is the home of the Dukes of Argyll and headquarters of the Campbell clan. The castle and the small town beside Loch Fyne were both the brainchild of Archibald Campbell, the third Duke. Until the seventeenth century, when they became absentee landlords, the family had lived in a fifteenth-century L-shaped tower house beside the Aray. If the 'Gothick' castle in a highland wilderness strikes us as a little out of place today, how much more incongruous it must have appeared when first built, in the middle of the eighteenth century. In 1743, when the sixty-two year old Archibald inherited from his brother the Argyll title and the estates he had not visited for nigh on thirty years, there was no carriage road within forty miles of Inverary. The old castle was a ruin and the town a squalid little collection of insanitary huts beside the loch. But the age of conscience and philanthropy was dawning. No self-respecting Duke could inhabit a brand new castle and leave his tenants in mean and sordid dwellings. So while the mottled green castle rose on the hill, beneath it the town of Inverary was rebuilt with comfortable houses and public buildings in the classical style (more attractive than the laird's own place, some would say), and the townspeople were enabled to prosper from the Duke's patronage, tourism and a newly-established spinning industry.

THE CASTLE

The design of Inverary arose out of an original concept by Vanbrugh, but the exterior of the castle as it stands today is principally the work of Roger Morris, assisted by William Adam and his sons John and Robert. A serious fire in 1877 led to some very unfortunate reconstruction of the upper parts by Anthony Salin, which destroyed the wholeness of the eighteenth-century plan. The classical interior was arranged by Robert Mylne.

The castle is rectangular in shape, with tall, battlemented drum towers lightly attached at each corner. The windows in the towers and on the first two floors are round-headed, with pointed gothic mouldings above. The door in the south front, originally intended as the principal entrance, is well proportioned and hooded with a fine ogee arch. A broad dry moat follows the contours of the walls. The third floor is entirely Salin's work and replaces the original castellated wall head. The architect probably had Chateau Rambouillet in mind when he undertook the rebuilding, but he patently failed to capture the grace of his model. The garret obscures much of the tower behind it, and its rectangular dormers, each set back from the sharp shape of a surmounting equilateral triangle, upset the balance of Morris' original design. The lofty cones on the towers, which help give the castle its Never-Never Land look, are another of Salin's ideas. Unfortunately, they too detract from the height of the central tower. In fact, the rectangular tower in the centre of the building is not altogether a successful concept anyway, partly because it was completed later than the original castle and the builders employed granite of a different hue, and partly because of the insubstantial narrow tracery on its large gothic windows. Before we dismiss Salin as nothing but an architectural vandal, however, it is worth pointing out that he did draw up plans for a complete reconstruction and extension of the castle in the baronial style, including a gigantic new tower in one corner. The relatively minor alterations he eventually made were only the remnants of this grander design, within which they would undoubtably have appeared far more appropriate.

Unkind though it may seem, mention must be made of the iron appurtenances which have been added to the outside of the castle. These include the inappropriate drainpipes, which, together with horizontal moulding between the storeys, serve to divide the facades into square blocks, and the extraordinary wedge-shaped entrance porch in the north. The best that can be said for the latter is that it enables visitors to enter the castle from their vehicles without getting wet, though whether it was necessary to produce a piece of railway station to enable them to do this is a debatable point. Better the occasional wet feet or ruined hair-do than that the castle should have been so marred.

Fortunately, allowing for the reservation already made, the castle interior is a delightful contrast to the bizarre external elevations. Particularly attractive are the State Dining Room, with its exquisitely painted wall panels and ceiling design by Robert Adam, the elaborate Tapestry Drawing Room, and the form (but not the bloodthirsty display — even the bills have 'Argyll' engraved on them) of the Armoury Hall. The castle's wonderful collection of Oriental and European porcelain is arranged in cabinets within a China Turret, whose light Wedgewood-style papier mache ceiling is the very antithesis of the buildings jumbled exterior. There are many treasures, including eighteenth-century Beauvais tapestries, superb furniture (there are ten sets of gilded chairs, some even upholstered with Beauvais tapestry), and paintings by Kneller and

Gainsborough. Particularly eye-catching are four nefs: German silver-gilt table decorations in the form of wheeled ships.

LITERARY ASSOCIATIONS

Inverary was completed just when it was becoming fashionable for visitors from the south to venture into the Highlands, and it was not long before the castle and the new town had become a popular stopping point on the tourist route. Fortunately, Duke Archibald had allowed for this, and even encouraged it, by constructing the Great Inn at Inverary — reputed then to be the finest hostelry in the whole of Scotland. From this comfortable base, now mundanely renamed the Argyll Arms Hotel, visitors could view the town and castle (and, if they were fortunate, be invited inside), before moving north to Oban, the Great Glen and the Western Isles.

Two early visitors were Dr Johnson and his travelling companion, James Boswell, who spoke well of the 'excellent inn' they found on the shore of Loch Fyne. During their stay Johnson produced his celebrated description of whisky. 'We supped well', reported Boswell, 'and after supper, Dr. Johnson, whom I have not seen taste any fermented liquor during all our travels, called for a gill of whisky. "Come," (said he) "let me know what it is that makes a Scotchman happy."' Since the opinionated literatus drank all but a drop of what he was proffered, we may safely assume that the beverage made him happy too.

Johnson also praised the castle, although not so much for its architectural merits as for its display of opulence. 'What I admire here,' he observed to Boswell, 'is the total defiance of expense.' He subsequently enjoyed a grand dinner with the fifth duke and his beautiful wife, who made a fuss over Johnson but rudely snubbed his Scottish side-kick.

Fourteen years later Robbie Burns stayed at the Great Inn. His reception was a great deal less lavish than that afforded to Johnson, for he arrived unrecognised and, as all the principal rooms were taken, he had to spend the night in a chilly attic. 'Who'er he be that sojourns here', he scratched on the window, 'I pity much his case'. Keats also tried his hand at composition after a night at the inn, although, to judge by the result, the great romantic had probably enjoyed too much of 'what it is that makes a Scotchman happy' to allow the muse to soar much above floor level on this occasion. The poem was inspired by hearing a bagpipe playing during a performance of a drama entitled *The Stranger*, and concerns the poet's inability to decide which of the two is the more beautiful. 'O Bag-pipe thou didst steal my heart away' is not one of Keats' most memorable lines.

Our final literary story concerns that fine travel writer, H.V. Morton. Standing at the door of Inverary post office one day, he glanced up the street to see a cyclist careering down the hill at considerable speed:

He wore a kilt. It was the first time I had ever seen a kilted cyclist.

'Who is that?' I asked the girl in the post office.
'Oh,' she said, 'that's his Grace. '

The Campbells are one of the great Scottish families, and the Dukes of Argyll still among the most influential men in the country. It is pleasing, therefore, to find them as charmingly eccentric as their extraordinary castle.

INFORMATION

ACCESS — The castle is clearly signposted from the loch- side at Inverary Occasional public transport

RESPONSIBILITY FOR THE SITE — Private

TELEPHONE   0499-2203

OPENING HOURS — April-October: Mon-Sat 10.00-18.00; Sun 13.00-18.00. But NB April-June & September-October closed on Fri; April, May, September & October closed 13.00-14.00

ADMISSION PRICE — £2.50 (Senior citizens £2.00 & children £1.50)

FACILITIES — Disabled (limited) Parking Dogs (in grounds only) Toilets Guided tours by special arrangement Shop Refreshments

DUNROBIN CASTLE

One mile north-east of Golspie, Highland Region

Dunrobin Castle, the most northerly of Britain's great houses, stands looking out over Dornoch Firth towards the grey expanse of the North Sea. It is a bleak spot and certainly an unusual one in which to find a French chateau. But that is what Dunrobin is, or rather it comprises an old fortress encased in a chateau-like shell. It is a huge building, too, with 189 rooms. The castle's size and alien architecture are very much in keeping with its history, for over the centuries it has been the seat of the Earls and Dukes of Sutherland, outsiders who came to control and, on occasion, exploit the Norse-Gaelic inhabitants of this wild region.

The 1st Earl of Sutherland was William Lord Duffus, from the family which built the early motte and bailey castle of that name near Elgin. His symbol was the great cat, from which the name Caithness derives. Dunrobin is supposed to have been named after Robin, the 6th Earl ('dun' meaning a fortified place). There may have been a castle of sorts on the site as early as the eleventh century, and there was certainly a keep here in about 1275. The oldest part of the present building, most of which is hidden by nineteenth-century rebuilding, dates from the beginning of the fifteenth century.

The fairy tale southern facade of Dunrobin produced by Sir Charles Barry the architect of the Houses of Parliament.

Dunrobin Castle. The most northerly great house in Britain and the residence of the House of Sutherland since the Middle Ages.

Though originally from south of the border, by the late Middle Ages the Sutherlands had made themselves into Celtic chieftains. In the sixteenth century they were supplanted by another family of ambitious southerners, the Gordons, whose Machiavellian take-over, involving murder, intrigue and brieves of idiocy, was effected over a number of years. It was finally concluded in 1550, when the severed head of Alexander Sutherland, a relative of the neighbouring Rosses of Balnagown, was pierced with a spear and displayed on the battlements of Dunrobin.

For a while things did not run smoothly for the Gordons. The 11th Earl and his wife were poisoned, and while still a minor the 12th Earl was forced to marry a woman twice his age. Nevertheless, when he reached maturity he divorced his fading Katisha and re-married, this time making his own choice of bride. She was Jane Gordon, the ex-wife of the Earl of Bothwell. After the briefest of marriages she had been discarded by her first husband to make way for Mary Queen of Scots. Her union with the Earl of Sutherland produced a formidable partnership between two branches of the Gordon family which, with one hiccup, survived at Dunrobin into the present century. In the eighteenth century the family name was changed to Sutherland. Countess Elizabeth, the heiress of the 18th Earl, restocked the family coffers by marrying the Marquess of Stafford, quipped at his funeral to be the 'richest man who ever died'. The couple, who were not short of places to live, spent little time at Dunrobin but did enough in the eyes of the government to earn themselves the titles of Duke and Duchess of Sutherland. In Scotland they were far less favourably regarded, for they were the couple who presided over the Sutherland estates during the infamous 'Highland Clearances'.

THE CASTLE

In the middle of the seventeenth century an L-shaped block was built opposite the medieval tower at Dunrobin to form a courtyard castle. Though a new wing was added in 1785, the present building is largely the creation of the 2nd Duke, who succeeded his mother as Earl of Sutherland in 1839. The design was by Sir Charles Barry, who built two other houses for the Duke and earned himself undying fame as the architect of the Houses of Parliament. Having been converted for use as a military hospital on the outbreak of the First World War, Dunrobin was badly damaged by a fire in 1915. The restoration was undertaken by Sir Robert Lorimer, who redesigned much of the interior and altered some of the roofs.

What are we make of this hotch-potch of a castle? Barry's long Neo-French front, with its tall, tapering cones, balconies and multitude of rectangular windows is a delightful concept. But the crow-stepped gables, no doubt added to give the castle an authentic Scottish flavour, do not sit easily in such a setting. And the other sides of the building also contrast strangely with the symmetrical facade. They are dominated by two towers, the larger of which is a massive display of reconstructed military features, including false machiolation, battlements and bartizan turrets with neat acorn-shaped caps. An upper section, which springs from within the parapet after the fourth storey, appears to draw its inspiration more from Flemish architecture than from anything found in Scotland. The second tower is smaller, sporting a large clock beneath an ogee roof and a broadly corbelled walkway two-thirds of the way up its square height. Although the overall effect is impressive, it is disconcerting in its lack of harmony.

Lorimer's interiors are spacious yet comfortable, and succeed in producing a homely atmosphere in what might otherwise be overpowering rooms. The panelled library and dining room, notable for the exquisite craftsmanship of their decoration and fittings, are two of the best examples of the architect's work. He formed a new drawing room by joining two smaller chambers, thus creating a space large and light enough for the castle's tapestries and broad Canalettos to be seen to best effect. Several pieces of priceless furniture are on display, as well as paintings by Romney, Reynolds, Ramsay and Michael Wright. The house and nearby museum also contain fascinating miscellanea, ranging from a nineteenth-century fire-engine to a unique collection of Pictish stones.

DUNROBIN'S GHOST

On occasion bitter weeping can be heard issuing from a small, empty room high in the attics of Dunrobin. The sobs are those of Margaret Gordon, daughter of the 14th Earl, who one night tragically fell to her death while trying to escape from the castle.

Margaret was young and beautiful, as all heroines of such tales must be. She was also headstrong, and in love. The object of her devotion was Jamie Gunn, the handsome but low-born son of one of the earl's tacksmen, who reciprocated Margaret's sentiments with equal passion. From time to time the two contrived to steal away and spend a few hours alone in each others' company. But secrets do not remain hidden for long in the close-knit community of a castle, and in due course the earl came to hear of his daughter's unsuitable attachment. His furious reaction was to dismiss Jamie and banish him from Dunrobin for ever. By so doing, he believed he was concluding the whole embarrassing episode.

Margaret had other ideas. She scornfully rejected the suitors suggested by her father, and planned to run away to join her beloved Jamie. But there was within the castle one whose sense of loyalty to the earl, mixed with jealousy at the amorous success of a mere servant, gave him an excuse to spy on Margaret. She was betrayed to her father before she could make good her escape.

This time the earl was taking no chances. He locked Margaret in a dark room at the top of the castle and commanded that a guard stand at her door night and day. She would not be permitted to come out, he swore, until she renounced her love for Jamie and promised to marry a man of her father's choosing. So a prolonged battle of wills began. Each day the father stood outside his daughter's place of confinement and asked her whether she was ready to submit to his wishes. He offered rich rewards and threatened dire punishment, but all to no effect. The girl would not give way. She grew weak from lack of exercise and, although she put on a brave and defiant face when confronting her captors, at night she gave vent to her despair in hours of wretched crying. She passed her days in reading and gazing wistfully from her small window at the distant hills, where in the past she and Jamie had spent such happy moments together.

Meanwhile, her lover had not been idle. With a resourcefulness which matched his good-looks, the young man had used his charm to befriend Morag, the maid who daily attended on Margaret in her lonely room. After much cajoling, he finally persuaded the girl to hide a length of rope about her person and deliver it to his love when next she waited on her. He also sent careful instructions that, on hearing a prearranged signal, Margaret was to secure one end of the rope to a piece of furniture, cast the other end out of the window and climb down it to the courtyard below. Here Jamie would be waiting with two fast horses. They would be miles from Dunrobin before anyone discovered that she was missing, by which time there would be little point in giving chase.

The plan was sound, though somewhat unoriginal. But alas it fared no better than the previous proposed elopement. Morag's suspicious behaviour was carefully noted. So a few nights later, as Jamie crept quietly into the castle yard and whistled gently beneath Margaret's casement, he was observed by a sinister figure standing in the shadows of the battlements. While Jamie waited for his lover to arrange her means of escape, the spy limped away and betrayed the couple to his master.

The earl burst into his daughter's room just in time to see her squeezing through the narrow window, and he lunged forward to grab her. Weakened by her long captivity and terrified by the sudden intrusion, the girl slipped from the rope and, with a faint cry, fell to her death on the hard cobbles many feet below.

Horrified, the earl staggered to the window and peered down to where his daughter had fallen. In the moonlight he saw her crumpled and broken body lying at the foot the tower. Jamie was kneeling over it. When he glanced up and saw the earl, the young man's face contorted with anguish and hatred. Their eyes met for a brief, bitter second. But the lad had not a moment to lose, for already the earl's men were running towards the scene of the accident. He sprinted to one of the horses tethered nearby and sprang into the saddle. Slowing as he passed through the castle gate, he turned and looked up towards the head of the earl, still framed in the high dark window. With a terrible scream he cursed the man and his castle, 'May she haunt you for ever more!' Then, setting spurs to his horse, he disappeared into the night.

Jamie was never seen or heard of again at Dunrobin. But Margaret's presence can still be felt in the tiny chamber where she had been held, and it is her sad crying that can be heard echoing down the gloomy passages and stairways of the castle.

INFORMATION

ACCESS Dunrobin stands one mile north-east of Golspie on the A9 Limited public transport
RESPONSIBILITY FOR THE SITE Private
TELEPHONE 04083-3177
OPENING HOURS
May: Mon-Thurs 10.30-12.30;
June-September: 10.30-17.00
(Sun 13.00-17.00)

ADMISSION PRICE
£2.40 (Senior citizens £1.50, children £1.20)
FACILITIES Parking
Dogs in grounds only
Toilets
Guided tours
Shop
Refreshments

CULZEAN CASTLE

North of Maidens, Strathclyde Region

Culzean commands a fine cliff-top position overlooking the entrance to the Firth of Clyde a few miles south of Ayr. Its name derives from 'Cuilean', meaning place of caves, for the shore hereabouts is honeycombed with natural caverns carved by the action of the sea. Robert Adam, who rebuilt the castle for the 10th Earl of Cassillis in the later eighteenth century, had to arrange for those directly beneath his new building to be filled in, lest they collapse under the weight of the structure above. Further down the coast, near Ballantrae, are the caves supposed to have been inhabited by the notorious Bean family, who robbed unwary travellers and ate their bodies. By this means they not only provided themselves with nourishment, but also removed trace of their crimes.

Like Dunrobin, Culzean consists of an older castle incorporated within more recent additions. The first building on the site was a medieval tower, formed into an L-shape by placing the stairway in a tower of its own at right angles to the main block. A barmkin extended along the rocky plateau to the north. This castle was replaced in the seventeenth century by a fortified complex of buildings of no particular architectural merit, but which served well enough to house in reasonable comfort and security the family and household of successive generations of Kennedys. A wing built by the 9th Earl to extend his castle westwards towards the sea was knocked down when Adam began his improvements a few years later.

THE CASTLE

Robert Adam began his work at Culzean in 1777. For the outside of the building he employed a 'Gothick' style, fashionable at the time but not a mode with which he was entirely happy. He reserved his best skills for the interior, where he was able to indulge his more restrained classical tastes. The older parts of the castle which Adam was asked to work on were roughly in the shape of a flattened U, with the base facing inland. The 1760s extension passed along to top of the uprights, facing the ocean. First Adam reworked and extended the wings of the castle. Then he cleared away the 9th Earl's building to leave room for a massive drum tower overlooking the sea. This became the central feature of the cliff-top facade. Finally, in the 1780s he designed a magnificent oval staircase to fill the rectangular space between the old and new building. In the nineteenth century the Edinburgh firm of Wardrop and Reid carried out a number of tasteful alterations, including the construction of an entrance hall on the east end and a new west wing.

Culzean has been heralded as a masterpiece of Scottish Gothic Revival architecture. It is indeed a most attractive example of that genre and is undoubtably more successful than the other examples of revivalist building featured in this chapter. There is sufficient symmetry about the castle to avoid the impression, given by Dunrobin, of a kit-built house put together by someone who had lost the instructions. It also displays none of the simple, almost naive uniformity of Inverary. Military features — machiolation, bartizans, battlements and the like — are presented with restraint and not permitted to dominate the form of the building. There is no attempt to clutter the skyline with a romantic excess of turret and cone. If the house had to be rebuilt in a form resembling a genuine castle, then the design probably could not have been better executed.

Within this romantic shell, the interior of Culzean is a Georgian delight. The only feature that jars is the obsession with weapons, something already noted at Inverary. An armoury may be permissible, but it it really necessary to place cannon at the foot of Adam's glorious staircase, the very epitome of harmony and cultured development?

As was his custom, Robert Adam concerned himself with every detail of the building for which he was responsible, designing the furniture, the decoration, and even, in one or two cases, the carpets. The craftsmanship is of the highest possible quality. Two rooms of contrasting style may be singled out. One is the Old Eating Room, a comfortable sitting room set in the base of the original tower house which exudes an atmosphere of relaxed security. It contains a number of pieces of Adam furniture and probably incorporates some medieval masonry. The circular Saloon on the first floor of the drum tower is an altogether different proposition. It is one of the most delightful rooms of any house in the country. Part of its effect is achieved by the juxtaposition of the wild coastal scenery outside the windows with the clean elegance within. The delicate ceiling has recently been restored according to Adam's design and on the floor the National Trust for Scotland, whose superb work at Culzean is a credit to both themselves and the nation, have laid a locally-made carpet, a close copy of Adam's original. The crimson-carpeted oval staircase, supported on Corinthian and Ionic columns (the usual order is cleverly reversed to emphasise the height of the structure) and lit by daylight streaming in from above, is another unforgettable piece of Culzean artistry.

THE KENNEDYS

The Kennedy family came to national prominence in the fifteenth century, when James Kennedy married a daughter of Robert III. David, James' great-grandson, was fortunate enough to have a sister who became mistress to James IV, a proximity to royal favour which undoubtably helped him to acquire the title of Earl of Cassillis. The earl and his immediate successors led violent lives: Earl David himself died at Flodden, the 2nd Earl was murdered, the 3rd was poisoned and the 4th started a bitter family feud by roasting alive the Abbot of Crossraguel to force him to sign away the church properties at his disposal.

The 7th Earl agreed to an arranged marriage with the spirited Jean Hamilton, daughter of the Earl of Haddington. Such pragmatic liaisons were not uncommon at the time, but they frequently brought unhappiness to the parties concerned. If we are to believe an ancient ballad, this marriage was just such a one. Jean was in love with another man, Johnny Faa the gypsy king, and was prepared to cast aside all her wealth and position in society to be with him.

One day Johnny and a band of his men arrived at the Kennedy seat of Cassillis Castle and took their leader's high-born lover away with them into the wilderness. Enraged at such an insult from a mere gypsy, the earl set off in pursuit. Ere long he caught up with his wife and her new companions on the banks of the Doon. There all the gypsies except Johnny Faa were killed. The vagabond king was dragged back in chains to Cassillis and hanged on a tree growing beneath the castle walls. The heart-broken Countess was cruelly forced to witness the execution, then imprisoned for the remainder of her brief, wasted life.

Following the death of the 8th Earl there was a lengthy court dispute to decide his successor, who was eventually declared to be Sir Thomas Kennedy, the man who first chose to live at Culzean rather than Cassillis. When Thomas's brother died without leaving an heir the title moved again, this time to a Kennedy living in New York. The 12th Earl was created Marquess of Ailsa, a title he held concurrently with that of Earl of Cassillis. In 1945 the 5th Marquess gave the Culzean estate to the National Trust for Scotland, who have cared for it with exemplary devotion ever since.

Unfortunately the castle's exposed position has led to serious decay of the stonework over the years, and an appeal has recently been launched to help pay for the cost of restoration.

In the hands of the Trust the extensive Culzean estate has been developed into a delightful Country Park, centred on Adam's Home Farm which lies to the

Robert Adams remarkable castle at Culzean stands on the cliffs overlooking the ocean south of Ayr. The gothic style was not the architect's first love and within the building's laudably restrained shell he designed a classical interior of singular beauty.

north of the castle. In the top floor of the castle a National Guest flat has been created, in which hospitality can be offered to distinguished overseas visitors. The first guest was General Eisenhower, who was given the use of the flat for the duration of his lifetime as a gesture of thanks for the part he played in commanding the Allied forces during the Second World War.

INFORMATION

ACCESS   Culzean is four miles west of
                Maybole, just off the A719
                Public transport
RESPONSIBILITY FOR THE SITE
                National Trust for Scotland
TELEPHONE   065-56-274
OPENING HOURS
                April-October: 10.30-17.30

ADMISSION PRICE
                £2.40 (Senior citizens & children
                £1.20)
FACILITIES   Disabled
                Parking
                Dogs (in grounds only)
                Toilets
                Guided tours
                Shop
                Refreshments

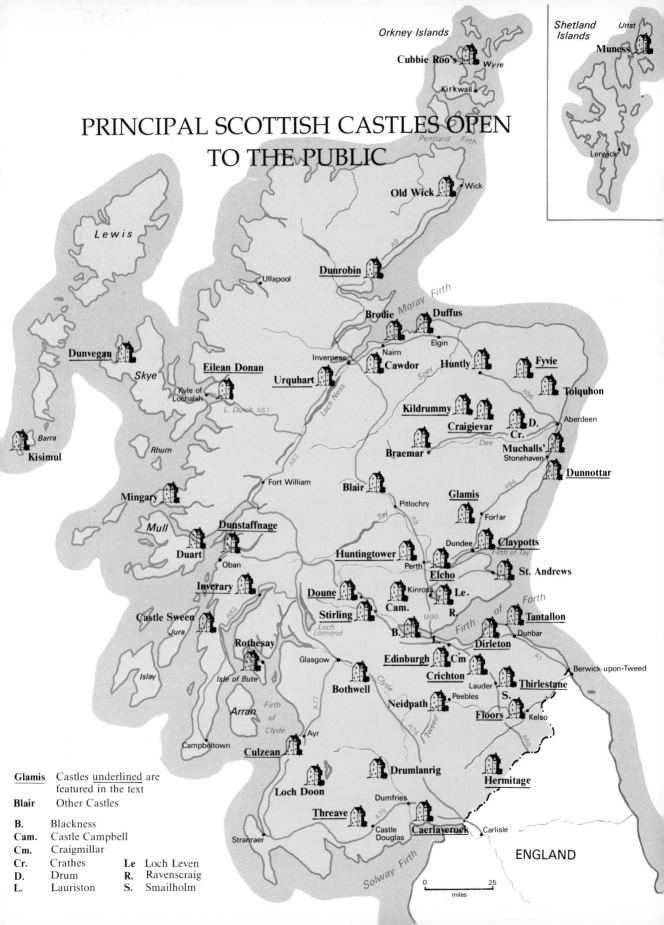

FURTHER READING

CASTLES

The standard work of reference is still MacGibbon, D. and Ross, T., *The Castellated and Domestic Architecture of Scotland* (5 vols., Douglas, Edinburgh, 1887-92). A more recent scholarly introduction is Cruden, S., *The Scottish Castle* (Spur Books, London, 1981). Tourists will also enjoy the beautifully presented *Exploring Scotland's Heritage* series (8 vols., HMSO, Edinburgh, 1985-7) and Christopher Tabraham's *Scottish Castles and Fortifications* (HMSO, Edinburgh, 1986). A broader perspective is taken in Ian Grimble's *Castles of Scotland* (BBC, London, 1987), which is full of fascinating comment and anecdote. Guide books are, of course, on sale at each site. Those for monuments in the care of the Historic Buildings and Monuments section of the Scottish Development Department are particularly good.

HISTORY

The best history of Scotland is Donaldson, G. (ed.), *The Edinburgh History of Scotland* (4 vols., Mercat Press, Edinburgh, 1987). Useful single-volume works are Mackie, J.D., *A History of Scotland*, the lively *Scotland's Story* (Fontana, London, 1985) by Tom Steel, and Caroline Bingham's accessible *Land of the Scots* (Fontana, London, 1983). In *Monarchs of Scotland* (Lochar Publishing, Moffat, 1990) Stewart Ross gives Scotland's rulers a treatment similar to that afforded castles in this book.

GLOSSARY

ASHLAR	Prepared (or 'dressed') stone with smooth surfaces and square edges
ATTIC	The small top storey of a house or castle
BAILEY 1.	An enclosed courtyard; or 2. an early term for a castle's surrounding wall
BAILIE (Scots)	A bailiff
BARBICAN	The outer defences of a gateway
BARMKIN (Scots)	A sturdy enclosure around a castle or tower, originally for penning cattle
BARTIZAN	A corbelled turret
BATTER	The outward splay of the foot of a wall
BATTLEMENT	A crenellated parapet at the wall head
BRETACH (Scots)	An overhanging wooden gallery at the wall head
CORBELLING	Stepped projection from a wall
CRENEL	A notch in a parapet
CROW-STEPPED GABLE	The end wall of a building, rising above the pitched roof in a series of steps
CURTAIN (WALL)	The tall outer wall of a castle, usually running between towers
DONJON	A keep
ENCEINTE	1. A line of fortification around a castle; or 2. the area within such an enclosure
FACTOR (Scots)	One who manages an estate on behalf of another
HARL (Scots)	Roughcast which is hurled onto a wall to protect it from the elements
HOARDING	The same as Bretach, see above
JAMB (Scots)	A projecting wing or buttress
KEEP	A castle's central tower
MACHIOLATION	Holes in the floor of an overhanging parapet through which those below can be bombarded
MOTTE	A tall mound, usually of earth
MOULDING	A surface decorated with raised or recessed work-manship
OGEE	A pointed arch made of two S-shapes laid on their sides
PARAPET	A low wall shielding the defenders at the wall head
POLICIES (Scots)	Grounds or estate
PORTCULLIS	A wooden or metal grille which can be lowered from above to close an entrance passage
RAMPART	A defensive line built outside a castle wall, usually of earth

RUBBLE	Stone blocks that have not been dressed (see Ashlar)
SHELL KEEP	A keep comprising only a curtain wall
SLIGHT	To demolish a castle deliberately, in order to prevent its use by anyone else
SOLAR	A private living room for the lord and his family
TURRET	A small tower attached to the upper part of a building
TYMPANUM	The space above an arch
WALL HEAD	The top of a wall
YETT (Scots)	A hinged iron grille, used like a door to close an entrance or passage

INDEX

Juin 20

Cher Logan

Bienvenue dans la famille
Peters
Je t'ai attendu très, très longtemps.
Mais tu es là, Je t'ai aimé
avant ton arrivée et je t'aime
encore plus depuis que tu es là.
N'oublie jamais que je t'aime
Huguette, Benny, Yogi
Grand-maman, mémère,
mamie.

Logan
We are so happy to have
you with us. We love you
and hope to be able to be
with you often.
Grand dada Bob

Ce livre
appartient à :

_____

Contes et comptines

Le Grand Livre des tout-petits

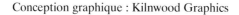

Réalisation : The Templar Company Plc

Conception graphique : Kilnwood Graphics

© 2005 Copyright pour l'édition française : Parragon
Réalisation : InTexte Édition, Toulouse
Traduction et adaptation : Sylvie Astorg

Imprimé en Chine
Printed in China
ISBN 1-40545-213-7

Contes
et comptines

Le Grand Livre des tout-petits

Histoires de Caroline Repchuk, Claire Keen et Andrew Charman

Sommaire

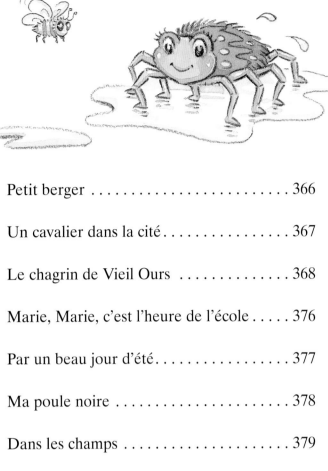

Danse, danse, petit bonhomme

Danse, danse, petit bonhomme,

Pomme, pomme, c'est l'automne,

Danse, danse, petit bonhomme,

Ou fredonne deux ou trois notes.

Chante, chante, blondinette,
Brosse tes jolies bouclettes,
Chante, chante, blondinette,
Ou fredonne deux ou trois notes.

Tape, tape dans tes mains,
Siffle, siffle pour tes copains,
Tape, tape dans tes mains,
Ou fredonne deux ou trois notes.

Tombe, tombe sur l'oreiller,
Oreiller doux, oreiller douillet,
Tombe, tombe sur l'oreiller,
ou fredonne deux ou trois notes.

Mandarines et citrons

Mandarines et citrons,

Sonnent les cloches du Panthéon.

Danse avec ton ami Léon,

Sonnent les cloches de Meudon.

Écoute le chant du petit grillon,

Sonnent les cloches de Tarascon.

Il chante dans tes oreilles,

Sonnent les cloches de Marseille.

Dis, joli caneton !

Dis, joli caneton, les trois hommes dans leur bain,

Sais-tu qui ils sont ?

Le boucher, le boulanger et le bougonnier.

Mais un bougonnier, ça n'existe pas, joli caneton !

Cet homme avec sa casquette, c'est le bourrelier.

Les abeilles
tournent en rond

Les abeilles tournent en rond
Autour d'un petit ourson.
Elles appellent les papillons
Et se moquent des grillons.
Miam-miam ! Un, deux, trois,
Butinons, butinons !

Une souris guette
La porte de la maisonnette.
Depuis belle lurette,
Elle n'a pas mangé de noisettes.
Miam-miam ! Un, deux, trois,
C'est l'heure de la dînette.

Dessiner un cercle
dans la main

Faire monter
ses doigts sur le bras

Miam-miam !

TOURNE EN ROND

UN, DEUX, TROIS

CHATOUILLE !

19

Bêê ! Bêê !
Joli mouton noir

Bêê, bêê, joli mouton noir,

Me donneras-tu ta laine ?

Oui, tu n'as qu'à t'asseoir,

Je te donnerai trois grandes poches pleines :

Une pour tricoter un gilet,

Une pour remplir un oreiller,

Et une pour tisser un manteau,

À moins que tu ne préfères un poncho.

Beignets chauds !

Beignets chauds !

Beignets chauds !

Tout chauds, mes beignets à un euro.

Beignets chauds !

Je ne les sors pas de mon chapeau,

Ils sortent de mon four tout chaud.

Tout chauds, mes beignets à un euro.

Beignets chauds !

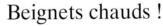

As-tu déjà vu ?

As-tu déjà vu

Une cuillère et une assiette qui volent dans la brume ?

Un petit chien qui rit et mange des bonbons ?

Une vache qui saute sur la lune ?

Ou un chat qui joue du violon ?

Mam'zelle Pompon

Mam'zelle Pompon a perdu ses moutons.

Elle ne les voit pas, cachés derrière les buissons.

Mam'zelle Pompon est en colère et rentre à la maison.

Eh bien, ils rentreront tout seuls, tans pis pour les moutons !

Le sourire du crocodile

« Dis CHEESE ! » dit le photographe.

« CHEESE ! » grimaça Croquemalin, le crocodile. Les flashes et les appareils photo crépitèrent tandis que le crocodile souriait de toutes ses dents.

« Tu es formidable ! » cria le chef de l'expédition venu avec toute une équipe de reporters. Croquemalin sourit en apercevant son image dans l'eau de la rivière.

« Hé ! Hé ! Je suis vraiment très séduisant ! » dit-il en paradant et en grinçant des dents avec jubilation.

Croquemalin était extrêmement fier de ses deux belles rangées de dents blanches et acérées. Il se pavanait sur le bord de la rivière pour être sûr qu'on le voie bien.

« Je suis une star ! s'écria-t-il. On va me connaître dans le monde entier ! »

« Merci pour cette photo », dit le chef.

« Pas de problème, dit Croquemalin. C'était un plaisir ! »

« En récompense, voici la cargaison de chocolat que tu avais demandée », dit le chef.

« Oh ! Quelle chance ! dit Croquemalin. C'est tellement gentil de votre part. Merci beaucoup. »

Quand tout le monde fut parti, Croquemalin resta sur le bord de la rivière, se prélassant au soleil, rêvant de gloire et de fortune, tout en avalant les carrés de chocolat les uns après les autres. Un chocolat, puis un autre, puis un autre…

C'est à ce moment-là qu'arriva le serpent.

« Mais, qu'essst-ce que csssss'est ? siffla-t-il. Un crocodile qui mange du chocolat, ça n'exissste pas. Bizzzarre ! »

« Pas du tout ! rétorqua Croquemalin. Tous les crocodiles aiment le chocolat. Seulement, les autres ne sont pas assez futés pour s'en procurer. »

« Eh bien, si tu es sssi intelligent, tu dois sssavoir aussssi que, quand on mange trop de chocolat, on perd toutes sssses dents ! » siffla le serpent.

« Balivernes ! ricana Croquemalin. Pour ta gouverne, sache que, moi, j'ai des dents absolument parfaites. »

« On verra, on verra ! » ricana le serpent en se faufilant dans les buissons.

Croquemalin continua à croquer goulûment chocolat après chocolat, piochant sans arrêt dans la montagne de friandises. Chocolat au petit déjeuner, chocolat au déjeuner et… chocolat au dîner.

« Hum, miam-miam ! » soupira-t-il de bonheur avec un grand sourire tout chocolaté. « C'est vraiment le paradis. »

« Ne t'étonne pas que ton ventre devienne si énorme que tu ne pourras plus flotter sur l'eau ? » lança le perroquet, qui le regardait depuis un moment, perché sur un arbre.

« N'importe quoi ! s'esclaffa Croquemalin. Ne vois-tu pas que je suis absolument magnifique ? »

« Si tu le dis », dit le perroquet en disparaissant dans la jungle.

Les jours passaient, puis les semaines, et Croquemalin continuait à manger et à manger chocolat après chocolat, jusqu'au jour où il n'en resta plus un seul.

Croquemalin commença à se lamenter. « Oh, la, la ! Je vais devoir retourner dans la rivière pour chercher mon prochain repas. J'aurais préféré manger encore du chocolat. »

Mais quand Croquemalin se glissa dans la rivière, au lieu de flotter doucement à la surface de l'eau, il coula à pic et son énorme ventre s'enfonça dans la vase.

« Quoi ? Quoi ? Mais que se passe-t-il ici ? se demanda Croquemalin. C'est bien difficile de nager aujourd'hui. »

« Même pour une personne aussi magnifique que toi ? » ricana le perroquet, qui l'observait. Croquemalin ne daigna pas répondre et s'enfonça un peu plus profondément dans l'eau. On ne voyait plus que ses deux petits yeux ronds qui jetaient un regard furibond au perroquet.

Le lendemain matin, quand il se réveilla, il ressentit une violente douleur dans la bouche. Il avait l'impression que quelqu'un lui arrachait les dents avec des tenailles. « Aïe, aïe, aïe, mes pauvres dents ! » gémissait-il.

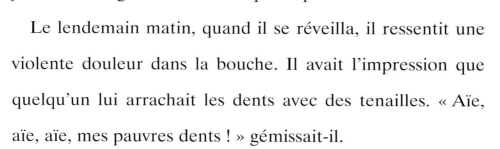

« Ah ! Sssça alors ! » gloussa le serpent en descendant d'un arbre. « Je croyais que toi, le magnifique Croquemalin, tu avais des dents sssi parfaites ! » Puis, il ondula sur le sol, moqueur, et s'enfuit.

Croquemalin savait ce qu'il devait faire. Il sortit de la rivière et se dirigea vers la demeure de M. Dembelles, le dentiste.

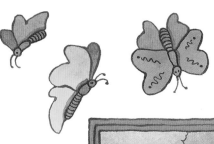

Le chemin lui paraissait si long, si long. Croquemalin soufflait, haletait, et soufflait encore.

« Ouvre bien grand ! » dit M. Dembelles, le fourmilier, qui examina la bouche de Croquemalin en fourrant son long museau à l'intérieur. « Hé, bien ! Tout ça ne se présente pas très bien. Qu'as-tu donc mangé, Croquemalin ? Bon, montre-moi où tu as mal. »

Piteux et honteux, Croquemalin dit : « Ici, en montrant une pauvre dent malade, et ici, et ici, et encore ici… »

« Bien, bien… Hum, je crains qu'il n'y ait pas grand-chose à faire, malheureusement, dit M. Dembelles. Il va falloir arracher les dents malades. » Et c'est ce qu'il fit.

Peu de temps après, une nouvelle expédition de reporters arriva dans la jungle.

« Dis CHEESE ! » dit le chef de l'expédition.

« CHEESE ! » dit Croquemalin, quittant timidement l'arbre qui le dissimulait. Mais, au lieu de flashes et d'appareils photo, d'énormes éclats de rire l'accueillirent. Les photographes en pleuraient tellement ils riaient.

« Tu nous avais dit que Croquemalin était un magnifique crocodile avec des dents superbes ! crièrent-ils en s'adressant au chef. Ce n'est pas Croquemalin qu'il faut l'appeler ton crocodile, mais Croquevilain ! »

Le pauvre Croquemalin se faufila dans les buissons et se mit à pleurer. Tout était de sa faute. Il avait été trop glouton.

« Là, là, dit M. Dembelles, en lui tapotant la patte. Ne t'inquiète pas, je te mettrai bientôt de belles dents toutes neuves. »

Croquemalin jura alors que, jamais plus, il ne mangerait de chocolat !

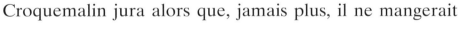

Si tu es joyeux...

Si tu es joyeux le soir et le matin,

Tape dans tes mains.

Si tu chantes souvent avec entrain,

Tape dans tes mains.

Si tu es heureux d'avoir des copains,

Tape dans tes mains.

Si maman console tous tes chagrins,

Tape dans tes mains.

Si tu aimes la bicyclette,

De droite à gauche, remue la tête.

Si tu as déjà vu un scarabée,

Le plus haut possible, lève le pied.

Si tu aimes le son de l'harmonica,

En chantant, dis : « Ha, ha ! »

Et si tu aimes la comptine que voilà,

Fais les quatre à la fois !

Pourquoi pleures-tu ?

Pourquoi pleures-tu, petite ?

Un corbeau a volé mes chapeaux.

Un corbeau avec un chapeau, c'est rigolo !

Oui, mais avec deux chapeaux, c'est insolite !

Trois souris myopes

Une, deux, trois souris myopes

Courent, courent dans la cuisine

Pour échapper au couteau de la voisine.

Regarde comme elles galopent.

Si ça continue, les trois souris myopes

Vont courir, courir jusqu'en Chine !

Les cinq canetons

Un, deux, trois, quatre, cinq,

Une cane cancane guidant ses canetons,

Six, sept, huit, neuf, dix,

Ils ont tourné en rond et rentrent à la maison !

Pourquoi la cane guide-t-elle ses canetons ?

Pour ne pas les perdre au milieu des joncs !

Ils vont à la queue leu leu sous l'œil des papillons.

Te souviens-tu où ils vont ?

Chats chanteurs

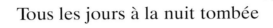

Tous les jours à la nuit tombée

Nous commençons notre soirée,

Et si vous avez beaucoup de chance,

Vous pourrez entendre notre romance :

Miaou ! Miaou ! chat gris, chat roux,

Chats des rues et chats poètes, nous chantons pour vous !

Coco est la soprano,

Titor, le ténor,

Pompon, le baryton,

Annibal, le chef de chorale.

Nous connaissons les chansons

D'hier et d'aujourd'hui.

Tous les quatre blottis,

Nous chantons en toute saison.

Gaspard, l'ourson vantard

Gaspard était un ourson extrêmement vantard.

« Regardez comme ma fourrure est belle et douce, disait-il aux autres jouets. Regardez comme elle brille ! »

Gaspard aimait plus que tout parler de lui. « Je suis le jouet le plus distingué de cette salle de jeux ! disait-il. C'est une évidence et tout le monde le sait. »

Ce qu'il ne savait pas, c'est que tous les autres se moquaient de lui dès qu'il avait le dos tourné.

« Cet ours se croit le plus intelligent et le plus beau, grommelait Choupi le Chien. Mais il n'est pas assez futé pour comprendre que plus personne ne le supporte ! »

« Un de ces jours, il va prendre une bonne leçon », dit Simbo le Singe, et c'est exactement ce qui arriva.

Ce jour-là, il faisait beau et très chaud. Les jouets paressaient dans la salle de jeux. « Et si nous allions faire une petite balade », dit Paméla la Poupée.

« On pourrait faire un pique-nique dans les bois ! » dit Papy Ours.

« Encore mieux ! et si nous partions dans la voiture à pédales ! » dit Lapinot.

« Mais aucun d'entre nous n'est assez fort pour la conduire », dit Paméla la Poupée, d'une voix un peu triste.

« Moi, si ! » lança une voix depuis le fond de la pièce. C'était Gaspard, qui avait tout entendu.

« Je sais conduire la voiture et, en plus, je connais le coin idéal pour pique-niquer dans les bois », dit-il.

Soupçonneux, Lapinot dit : « On ne t'a jamais vu conduire une voiture ! »

« C'est parce que je conduis la nuit, quand vous dormez tous, dit Gaspard. Je suis même un excellent conducteur. »

« Bon, alors on y va ! » cria Paméla la Poupée. Et, en moins de temps qu'il ne faut pour le dire, ils avaient préparé le pique-nique et s'étaient assis dans la voiture, prêts à partir.

« Euh ! Je ne me sens pas très en forme pour conduire aujourd'hui, marmonna Gaspard. Il fait vraiment trop chaud. » Mais les autres ne voulaient pas le savoir et, bien à contrecœur, Gaspard dut se résoudre à s'installer au volant et à démarrer.

Évidemment, Gaspard n'avait jamais conduit de sa vie et il était vraiment mort de peur. Mais, voulant faire l'intéressant, il n'en laissa rien paraître et fit semblant de maîtriser parfaitement la situation.

La voiture commença à descendre le chemin du jardin. « Tut, tut ! » Gaspard donna deux petits coups de klaxon en s'engageant sur la route. Bientôt, la voiture roula tranquillement dans la campagne tandis que la petite troupe chantait à tue-tête.

Tout allait bien, quand Paméla la Poupée s'exclama : « Hé, Gaspard, tu es sûr que tu n'as pas oublié de tourner pour prendre le chemin du bois ? »

« Je sais où je vais, rétorqua Gaspard. Laissez-moi donc faire. » Et il accéléra.

« Doucement, Gaspard ! Tu vas trop vite, cria Papy Ours, depuis le siège arrière de la voiture. Ma fourrure est tout ébouriffée. » Il commençait à avoir un peu peur.

« Je n'ai aucun besoin d'un coéquipier sur le siège arrière. Je te remercie », grogna Gaspard, et il accéléra encore.

Désormais, les autres commençaient à être vraiment terrifiés, mais Gaspard, lui, s'amusait beaucoup.

« Ne suis-je pas un merveilleux conducteur ? gloussa-t-il. Regardez : sans les mains ! » Et il lâcha le volant, juste au moment où ils atteignaient un virage à angle droit.

La voiture roula sur le bas-côté, zigzagua, puis finit sa course contre un arbre, éjectant tous les jouets dans le fossé !

Ils étaient un peu étourdis, mais heureusement aucun n'était blessé. Ils étaient très en colère contre Gaspard.

« Ourson stupide ! jura Lapinot. Tu aurais pu tous nous tuer ! »

« Nous allons être obligés de rentrer à la maison à pied, gémit Paméla la Poupée, en secouant la tête. Et puis, où sommes-nous ? »

Tout le monde regardait Gaspard.

« Ne me le demandez pas ! » dit-il à voix basse.

« Mais tu disais que tu connaissais le chemin ! » dit Papy Ours, indigné.

« J'ai menti, dit Gaspard avec la voix tremblante. Je ne sais pas conduire et je ne sais pas où nous sommes ! » Et il fondit en larmes.

Les jouets étaient vraiment furieux contre Gaspard.

« Tu n'es qu'un ourson vantard et prétentieux ! dirent-ils en colère. Regarde maintenant dans quelle galère tu nous as entraînés ! »

Les pauvres jouets, perdus dans la forêt obscure, durent marcher toute la nuit, effrayés par les ombres qui surgissaient devant eux et se réconfortant mutuellement.

Jamais ils n'étaient sortis la nuit. Enfin, juste avant que le soleil ne se lève, ils aperçurent leur maison.

Épuisés, ils se précipitèrent dans la salle de jeux. Être enfin chez soi ! Quel bonheur !

Heureusement, la petite fille à qui ils appartenaient n'avait pas remarqué leur absence. Elle ne sut jamais ce qui était arrivé à ses jouets et quelle aventure ils avaient vécue. Elle se demanda juste où avait bien pu passer sa voiture à pédales.

Quant à Gaspard, il était vraiment désolé des ennuis qu'il avait causés à ses amis. Ceux-ci, pourtant, lui pardonnèrent. Depuis cette histoire, Gaspard ne s'est plus jamais vanté.

49

Doudi est un chat heureux

Doudi est le chat que j'aime tant.

Regard doux et pelage soyeux,

Doudi est un chat heureux.

Pelotes de laine et rubans

Chipés dans la corbeille de maman,

Doudi est un chat malicieux.

Quand dans mes bras il ronronne,

C'est de l'amour qu'il me donne.

Un arbre magique

Un arbre magique, tout près de la mer, s'élevait.

Noix d'argent et poire d'or, voilà ce qu'il donnait.

La fille du roi d'Espagne, à l'été, me rendit visite,

Fort attristée pour son fils atteint d'une otite.

Noix d'argent et poire d'or franchirent l'océan

Et, sur-le-champ, guérirent l'enfant.

Épouvantail clopinant

Les vaches sont au bercail
Et le soleil au lit,
Fugue l'épouvantail,
Et voici ce qu'il dit.

Épouvantail clopinant,
Chapeau de paille bringuebalant,
Je remue les bras de haut en bas,
Je lève les jambes comme ça !

LEVER LES BRAS

REMUER LA TÊTE

Les enfants sont dans les champs
Et le fermier travaille,
Fugue l'épouvantail,
Et voici ce qu'il dit doucement.
Refrain

SECOUER LES BRAS

LEVER LES JAMBES

Les oiseaux sont perchés
Et la lune bien cachée,
Fugue l'épouvantail
Et voici ce que dit cette canaille.
Refrain

Mon meilleur ami

Il me câline dans mon lit,
Et me protège la nuit,
Quand un vilain cauchemar
Me réveille dans le noir.

Toujours prêt à jouer,
Il partage mon goûter,
Et me laisse gagner la partie,
Avec une mine réjouie.

Je lui dis tous mes secrets,
Il n'a jamais l'air étonné,
Et comme il connaît mes soucis,
Je peux vraiment compter sur lui.

Si j'ai un gros chagrin,
Il me tient toujours la main.
C'est mon nounours, mais aussi
Oui, oui, oui, mon meilleur ami !

Les nounours

J'en connais des minis, des petits
Des grands et des géants,
Il y en a des dodus, des joufflus,
D'autres sont vraiment très élégants.

Certains sont doux comme des agneaux,
D'autres ont le poil comme du crin,
Parfois leur fourrure est de satin,
Comme la plume d'un oiseau.

Ils ont l'air tout content,
Ou gardent un air distant,
Des yeux pétillants
Ou un regard inquiétant.

Mais tous les nounours sont aimants,
Tous les nounours ont un cœur d'or,
Tous les nounours sont charmants,
Tous les nounours sont des trésors.

Cinq petits pois

Serrer ses mains l'une contre l'autre

Cinq petits pois blottis
dans leur cosse,

Lever les deux index et les deux pouces

L'un grossit, puis un autre,
puis tous les autres.

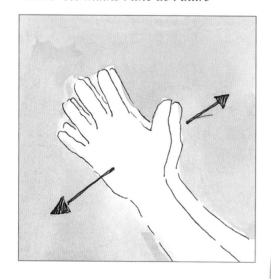

Écarter ses mains l'une de l'autre

Ils grossissaient, encore et
encore, et ne s'arrêtaient pas,

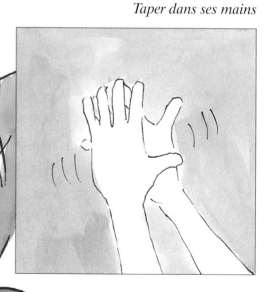

Taper dans ses mains

Jusqu'à ce que... POP !
la cosse éclatât.

Lève le pouce et l'index

Lève le pouce, l'index, et claque des doigts.
Lève le majeur, l'annulaire, et assieds-toi,
Lève le tout petit auriculaire et lève-toi,
Claque des doigts, assieds-toi et lève-toi.

Un doigt, deux doigts,
un bras, danse, danse.
Un doigt, deux doigts,
un bras, danse, danse.
Claque des doigts,
assieds-toi et lève-toi.

Un doigt, deux doigts, un bras,
un pied, danse, danse
et recommence.
Un doigt, deux doigts, un bras,
un pied, la tête, danse, danse
et recommence.

Pauvre petit chien perdu !

« Brrr », dit Pilou en frissonnant. Qu'est-ce qu'il fait froid. »

« Oui, blottis-toi tout contre moi », dit sa maman.

« Ce n'est pas drôle, maugréa Pilou. Pourquoi sommes-nous obligés de dormir dehors, dans le froid, alors que les chats, eux, dorment dans de jolis paniers bien au chaud ? »

« Nous sommes des chiens de ferme, mon chéri, dit Maman. Nous devons être solides et travailler dur pour gagner notre nourriture. »

« J'aurais préféré être un chat, bougonna Pilou. Tout ce qu'ils font, c'est manger, dormir et se frotter le bout du nez. »

« Nous ne vivons pas si mal, dit Maman. Alors arrête de te plaindre et dors maintenant. Demain, nous avons du travail. »

Le lendemain, Pilou se réveilla tôt et partit se promener sur le bord du chemin. Il trottinait dans l'herbe, faisant fuir les lapins et reniflant les fleurs.

Comme d'habitude, lorsqu'il arriva au bout du chemin, il s'arrêta dans l'intention de faire demi-tour. C'est alors qu'il aperçut un gros camion rouge, garé devant une maison. La porte arrière du camion était ouverte et Pilou fut pris d'une subite envie d'y monter et de jeter un coup d'œil à l'intérieur.

Le camion était rempli de meubles et, dans le fond, il y avait un gros fauteuil confortable avec des coussins moelleux. Pilou sauta sur le fauteuil. « Ah, je vais enfin pouvoir dormir toute la journée, comme un chat ! » se dit-il. Il ferma les yeux et s'endormit aussitôt.

Pilou se réveilla en sursaut quelque temps plus tard.

« Oh, non, je me suis endormi ! bougonna-t-il. Je ferais bien de me dépêcher. Aujourd'hui, j'ai du pain sur la planche ! »

Mais la porte du camion était fermée ! Pilou entendait des voix à l'extérieur.

« Oh, la, la, qu'est-ce que je vais prendre si on me trouve ici », pensa-t-il, et il se réfugia derrière le fauteuil.

La porte du camion s'ouvrit et Pilou jeta un coup d'œil. Deux hommes commençaient à décharger le camion.

Quand Pilou fut sûr que personne ne le voyait, il sauta du camion. Il se rendit bien vite compte qu'il était très loin de chez lui ! Il se trouvait dans une énorme ville bruyante, hérissée de buildings et grouillante de voitures.

Le pauvre Pilou n'avait aucune idée de l'endroit où il se trouvait !

« C'est le camion qui m'a amené jusqu'ici », pensa-t-il, effrayé.

Toute la journée, errant dans les rues, frigorifié, fatigué et affamé, Pilou chercha son chemin. À la fin, il se coucha sur le sol et se mit à gémir.

« Hé, que se passe-t-il, petit chien ? dit un homme gentiment. Tu es perdu ? Viens, je t'emmène chez moi. » Pilou, reconnaissant, lui lécha la main, sauta sur ses pattes et le suivit.

Quand ils arrivèrent chez son sauveur, Pilou s'assit sur le pas de la porte, espérant que celui-ci penserait à lui apporter quelque chose à manger. Mais l'homme lui dit : « Entre, tu ne peux pas rester dehors. »

Le lendemain, l'homme enfila une laisse autour du cou de Pilou et l'emmena en ville. Le petit chien détestait être ainsi traîné sans pouvoir renifler le moindre brin d'herbe.

Puis, sur la place du marché, Pilou entendit un aboiement familier et aperçut le museau de sa maman derrière la vitre de la camionnette du fermier, son maître ! Il se mit à gémir, entraîna l'homme jusqu'à l'endroit où était garée la camionnette, puis bondit en jappant bruyamment sous la fenêtre du véhicule. Le reconnaissant, le fermier n'en crut pas ses yeux – jamais Pilou n'avait été aussi propre. L'homme expliqua comment il avait trouvé Pilou, et le fermier le remercia chaleureusement.

Sur le chemin du retour, Pilou raconta ses mésaventures à sa maman.

« J'ai cru que tu t'étais enfui parce que tu ne voulais plus être un chien de ferme », dit-elle gentiment.

« Oh, non, Maman, s'empressa de répondre Pilou. J'aime ma vie à la ferme et il me tarde de rentrer pour déguster un bel os et retrouver notre lit sous les étoiles ! »

Dix petits doigts

J'ai dix petits doigts.

Ils sont tous à moi

Et il n'écoutent que moi.

Regarde ce qu'ils font.

Ils se ferment comme un cocon,

Et, pour s'ouvrir, ils sont champions.

Lever les mains

DIX PETITS DOIGTS

Agiter les doigts

ILS SONT TOUS À MOI

Serrer les poings

FERMÉS COMME UN COCON

Ouvrir grand les mains

ILS SONT CHAMPIONS

Je peux croiser les doigts,

Les cacher derrière moi

Ou les lever au-dessus de moi.

Je peux les diriger vers le bas.

Et, si je n'ai plus envie de jeu,

Ne plus m'occuper d'eux.

Croiser les doigts

CROISER LES DOIGTS

Mains derrière le dos

LES CACHER DERRIÈRE MOI

Lever et baisser les bras

AU-DESSUS OU VERS LE BAS

Mains sur les genoux

NE PLUS M'OCCUPER D'EUX

Je sais...

Je sais lacer mes souliers,

Je sais me coiffer,

Je sais me laver les mains et le visage

Et m'essuyer comme un enfant sage.

Je sais me brosser les dents,

Et boutonner mon pantalon.

Je sais dire, « Comment allez-vous ? »

En enfilant mes chaussettes jusqu'au bout.

Mimer les gestes et, à la fin, poser ses mains sur ses genoux

Chaussures

Chaussures de bébé,

Chaussures de maman,

Chaussures de papa,

Chaussures de policier,

Chaussures de géant !

Écarter les mains de plus en plus pour chaque paire de chaussures, et prendre une voix de plus en plus grosse

CHAUSSURES DE BÉBÉ

CHAUSSURES DE MAMAN

CHAUSSURES DE PAPA

CHAUSSURES DE GÉANT

Petit comme une souris

Petit comme une souris,

Large comme un pont,

Grand comme une maison,

Droit comme un clou.

Doucement, tout doucement

Doucement, tout doucement,
Rampe l'escargot des champs.

Dans le jardin, il progresse,
À toute petite vitesse.

Vite, vite, très vite,

Tout autour de la maison,
Elle file comme un avion.

Faire marcher ses doigts doucement sur le ventre de bébé

Chatouiller le bébé pendant le second couplet

Bouba, l'ourson fugueur

Pendant que Lucie dormait à l'ombre d'un arbre, Bouba partit se promener dans les bois et ne tarda pas à être perdu. Il ne savait pas du tout comment rentrer. Il s'assit et se mit à réfléchir.

Quand Lucie se réveilla, elle regarda autour d'elle et constata avec surprise que son ours Bouba avait disparu. Elle pensa que quelqu'un l'avait emporté. Elle ne pouvait pas imaginer que, lorsque les enfants dorment, leurs ours en peluche aient envie d'aventure et veuillent s'échapper.

« Bouba ! appela-t-elle. Bouba, où es-tu ? »

Il n'était pas bien loin. Lucie ne tarda pas à le trouver, reniflant un buisson de mousse.

« Ah, tu es là ! dit-elle avec soulagement. Je croyais que tu t'étais perdu. Où as-tu mis ton gilet ? »

En fait, Lucie avait vraiment perdu Bouba, car l'ours qu'elle ramenait à la maison n'était pas du tout son ours en peluche mais un véritable ourson ! Tandis qu'elle courait, dans ses bras, l'ourson ne bronchait pas. Il regardait droit devant lui, sans sourciller, et tâchait de ne pas éternuer. Bientôt, ils arrivèrent dans la chambre de Lucie. La petite fille jeta négligemment l'ourson sur son lit, puis alla prendre un bain.

« C'est le moment de filer ! » pensa l'ourson. Il se glissa au bas du lit en tirant les couvertures derrière lui. Il courut à la fenêtre et tenta de grimper aux rideaux, qui se déchirèrent aussitôt et s'écroulèrent sur le sol. Juste au moment où la maman de Lucie entrait dans la chambre. L'ourson se figea subitement. Puis Lucie apparut.

« Regarde-moi cette pagaille, dit la maman de Lucie. Tu as encore joué avec cet ours. Range-moi tout ça. »

Lucie ne comprenait pas comment il pouvait y avoir un tel fouillis. Elle emporta l'ourson dans la salle de bain et le posa sur le bord de la baignoire.

« Fais attention de ne pas tomber », dit-elle avant de sortir pour chercher une savonnette. L'ourson sauta dans l'eau du bain avec un grand plouf et se mit à battre des pattes, éclaboussant toute la salle de bain d'eau mousseuse. Quand il entendit des pas, il se mit sur le dos et fit la planche comme si tout était normal. C'était Lucie, suivie de sa mère. « Oh, Lucie ! Quelle pagaille ! »

Une grenouille se lamentait

Une grenouille se lamentait sur son sort,

Elle rêvait d'aventure et de chasse au trésor.

Bref, elle voulait changer de décor.

Je suis une grenouille

Et je vais en vadrouille !

Elle mit sur sa tête un tricorne qu'elle avait trouvé

Et enfila des chaussures à boucles dorées.

Sur son chemin, elle rencontra un rat musqué.

Je suis une grenouille

Et je vais en vadrouille !

Juste après minuit

Juste après minuit,

Quand tout le monde est endormi,

Les ours en peluche bâillent et s'étirent,

Sortent de leur lit et s'apprêtent à partir.

Ils quittent la maison par une porte discrète,

Et, dans la nuit, ils s'embarquent,

Déambulant dans les rues désertes,

À la recherche d'un parc.

Et, au clair de lune, commence la rigolade.

Ils grimpent sur les balançoires et enjambent le portique.

Ce sont alors cabrioles, voltiges et escalades,

Et c'est aux éclats que rient tous ces loustics.

Quand le soleil pointe à l'horizon,

Ils se dépêchent de retrouver leur maison.

Quand les enfants s'éveillent au matin,

Les ours, blottis contre eux, réclament un câlin !

Brille, brille, petite étoile

Brille, brille, petite étoile du soir.

Je voudrais tant savoir qui tu es,

Toi qui viens illuminer la nuit noire,

Tel un diamant dans l'obscurité.

La princesse Lisette

Bagues aux doigts et bottines à clochettes,

Sur son cheval blanc, c'est la princesse Lisette

Qui, par le bois, se rend à Barcelonnette.

Où qu'elle passe, lièvres et hérissons sont à la fête.

Dans sa maison...

Mimer le toit avec les mains

MAISON

Regarder à travers ses doigts

REGARDAIT PAR LA FENÊTRE

Lever deux doigts

LAPIN

Frapper en l'air avec le poing

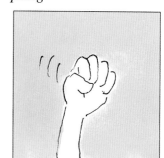

FRAPPER AINSI

Dans sa maison, un vieil homme

Regardait par la fenêtre,

Un lapin venir à lui et frapper ainsi :

« Grand-père, grand-père, ouvre-moi !

Ou le chasseur me tuera. »

« Lapin, lapin, entre et viens

me serrer la main. »

Agiter les bras de haut en bas

OUVRE-MOI !

Pointer un doigt

LE CHASSEUR ME TUERA

Incliner le doigt vers l'intérieur

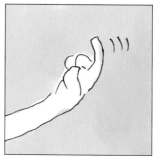

ENTRE ET VIENS

Serrer la main (du lapin)

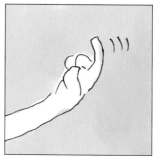

ME SERRER LA MAIN

Le secret d'Amédée

Amédée le porcelet avait un secret. Il se blottissait dans la paille chaude contre ses frères et sœurs, admirait le ciel sombre constellé d'étoiles et souriait secrètement dans l'obscurité. Peut-être, après tout, n'était-il pas si difficile d'être le plus petit des cochons…

Il n'y a pas si longtemps, Amédée en avait vraiment assez. Il était le plus jeune et, de loin, le plus petit cochon de la famille. Il avait cinq frères et cinq sœurs, et tous étaient plus gros et plus forts que lui. À cause de sa petitesse, la femme du fermier le surnommait Minus.

« Je ne crois pas que le petit Minus grandira beaucoup », disait-elle à son amie Daisy, en venant apporter de la paille fraîche aux petits cochons.

Ses frères et sœurs se moquaient de lui sans arrêt.
« Pauvre petit Minus minuscule, lui disaient-il en ricanant.
Tu dois être, c'est sûr, le cochon le plus petit du monde ! »

« Laissez-moi tout seul ! » disait Amédée, et il courait se
réfugier dans un coin de la porcherie, se roulait en boule et
se mettait à sangloter. « Si vous n'étiez pas aussi gloutons et
si vous me laissiez un peu à manger, peut-être serais-je plus
gros ! » disait-il tristement.

Tous les jours, au moment du repas, c'était la même chose. Les autres poussaient, tiraient et bousculaient Amédée jusqu'à ce qu'il ne lui reste que des miettes. À ce régime-là, jamais il ne grandirait.

Un jour, Amédée fit une découverte très importante. Il était pelotonné dans un coin de la porcherie, comme d'habitude, quand il aperçut un petit trou dans la clôture dissimulé derrière le baquet de nourriture.

« Je crois que je vais pouvoir passer par ce petit trou ! » pensa Amédée, tout excité.

Il attendit toute la journée. Quand la nuit fut tombée, il vérifia que ses frères et sœurs étaient profondément endormis, puis se faufila à travers le trou de la clôture. En un instant, il fut à l'extérieur, libre comme l'air et bien décidé à faire ce qui lui plairait. Et, en effet, quelle aventure !

D'abord, il courut jusqu'au poulailler et engloutit tout le grain destiné aux poules. Puis il fila dans la prairie, rampa sous la clôture et grignota toutes les carottes du petit âne.

Il se rendit ensuite dans le potager où il dévora toute une rangée de choux. Quel festin ! Enfin, quand son petit ventre fut plein à craquer, il prit le chemin du retour. Alors qu'il trottinait, il fut arrêté par un buisson. Quelle était donc cette délicieuse odeur ? Il tourna autour du buisson jusqu'à ce qu'il comprenne d'où provenait ce parfum – c'était un massif de fraisiers.

Amédée goûta une fraise, deux fraises, puis trois, et fut émerveillé. Jamais il n'avait mangé pareille chose. « Demain soir, je reviendrai ici », se promit-il tout en trottant vers la porcherie.

Il repassa discrètement à travers la clôture et s'endormit aussitôt, blotti contre sa maman et souriant de contentement et de béatitude.

Nuit après nuit, alors que tout le monde dormait, Amédée se faufilait dans le trou et poursuivait ses aventures gourmandes. Désormais, il ne s'inquiétait plus de ce que ses frères et sœurs lui faisaient endurer à l'heure des repas. Lui savait qu'à l'extérieur un festin succulent l'attendait. Il arrivait parfois qu'il tombe sur la gamelle du chien remplie des restes du dîner du fermier ou sur des seaux d'avoine destinés aux chevaux. « Miam-miam ! Tout ce que j'aime ! » disait-il en avalant goulûment.

Mais, les jours et les semaines passant, Amédée devenait de plus en plus gros et dodu. Il devenait difficile de se faufiler chaque nuit dans le trou de la clôture.

Amédée savait bien que, dans quelque temps, ses rondeurs l'empêcheraient de passer par le trou, mais à ce moment-là il serait assez fort pour affronter ses frères et sœurs. Et ce secret le réjouissait beaucoup !

Les roues de l'autobus

Les roues de l'autobus tournent, tournent,
Tournent, tournent,
Les roues de l'autobus
tournent, tournent.
Bon voyage !

Les essuie-glaces,
glissent, glissent,
Glissent, glissent,
etc.

Le klaxon de l'autobus
corne, corne.
Corne, corne, etc.

Faire tourner ses poignets

Frotter ses deux index l'un contre l'autre

Faire semblant de klaxonner

Presser ses pouces sur les autres doigts tendus

TOURNENT, TOURNENT

GLISSENT, GLISSENT

CORNE, CORNE

CAUSENT, CAUSENT

Les passagers de l'autobus causent, causent, etc.

Les enfants dans l'autobus sautent, sautent, etc.

Les bébés dans l'autobus pleurent, pleurent, etc.

Les grands-mères dans l'autobus tricotent, tricotent, etc.

Les roues de l'autobus tournent, tournent. Bon voyage !

Sautiller assis sur une chaise

Mettre ses mains autour de sa bouche et pleurer

Imiter les aiguilles à tricoter avec tes index

Reprendre au début

SAUTENT, SAUTENT

PLEURENT, PLEURENT

TRICOTENT, TRICOTENT

TOURNENT, TOURNENT

Un paysan vint dans son champ

Un paysan vint dans son champ, dans son champ,

Un paysan, avec son chien Chiffon,

Vint dans son champ.

Deux paysans vinrent dans leur champ, dans leur champ,

Deux paysans, un paysan avec son chien Chiffon,

Vinrent dans leur champ.

Trois paysans vinrent dans leur champ, dans leur champ,

Trois paysans, deux paysans, un paysan avec son chien Chiffon,

Vinrent dans leur champ.

Quatre paysans vinrent dans leur champ, dans leur champ,

Quatre paysans, trois paysans, deux paysans, un paysan avec son chien Chiffon,

Vinrent dans leur champ.

Cinq paysans vinrent dans leur champ, dans leur champ,

Cinq paysans, quatre paysans, trois paysans, deux paysans,

un paysan avec son chien Chiffon,

Vinrent dans leur champ.

 # Devine qui je suis !

PETITE

RONDE

ANSE

BEC

Devine qui je suis !

Je suis petite et ronde,

J'ai une anse et un bec,

Quelques feuilles

de thé et un peu

d'eau bouillante

qui chante !

Soulève-moi

et verse le thé.

Je suis une petite théière.

EAU BOUILLANTE

CHANTE

SOULÈVE

VERSE

110

Où vas-tu, Céleste ?

Où vas-tu, Céleste ?

Je vais à l'ouest.

Où vas-tu, Céleste ?

Je vais à l'est.

Que fais-tu, Céleste ?

Je lève un bras,

Que fais-tu, Céleste ?

Je tourne et j'étire mes bras.

*Commencer par le bras gauche, puis le bras droit,
puis faire la même chose avec les jambes*

JE VAIS À L'OUEST

JE VAIS À L'EST

JE LÈVE UN BRAS

JE TOURNE

… ET J'ÉTIRE MES BRAS

111

Les malheurs de Titours

M. et Mme Papeton possédaient une boutique de jouets fabriqués à l'ancienne. Tous étaient réalisés par eux à la main, dans l'arrière-boutique. Mais tous deux étaient âgés et leur vue devenait de plus en plus mauvaise.

« Il faut maintenant que nous prenions un apprenti pour lui apprendre la fabrication des jouets », dit M. Papeton à sa femme. Ils trouvèrent bientôt un jeune homme prénommé Tom. Il travaillait bien et beaucoup. La première semaine, il confectionna un nounours et, quand il eut fini, il le montra à M. et Mme Papeton.

« Il a l'air très affectueux, ton ours », lui dit Mme Papeton.

Tom était ravi que ses patrons aiment son premier ours et rentra chez lui en sifflotant.

« Il est joli son ours, dit M. Papeton, mais sa tête est un peu de travers. »

« J'ai vu, dit sa femme, mais c'est la première fois que Tom fabrique un jouet. Pose-le là-haut sur les étagères, avec les autres. »

Cette nuit-là, Titours, assis sur l'étagère, se mit à pleurer. Il avait entendu tout ce que M. et Mme Papeton avaient dit de lui.

« Qu'est-ce qui ne va pas », demanda Boulou, qui était assis près de lui.

« Ma tête est toute de travers », sanglota Titours.

« Est-ce que tu as mal ? » s'inquiéta Boulou.

« Non », répondit Titours.

« Alors, pourquoi pleures-tu ? » demanda Boulou.

« Parce que personne ne voudra d'un ours à la tête tordue. Je ne quitterai jamais la boutique et personne ne m'emmènera dans sa maison ni ne m'aimera », dit-il en larmes.

« Ne t'inquiète pas, dit Boulou. Nous avons tous des défauts et, moi, je te trouve plutôt mignon. Essaie simplement d'être le plus gentil et le plus câlin possible, et quelqu'un se prendra d'affection pour toi. » Ces mots rassurèrent Titours, qui s'endormit bientôt.

Le lendemain, la boutique était pleine de clients, mais aucun d'entre eux ne s'intéressait à Titours. Pourtant, un jeune garçon, passant devant l'étagère, s'écria : « Oh, qu'il est joli cet ours. Papa, je le voudrais, s'il te plaît ! »

Titours avait le cœur battant lorsque l'homme leva le bras pour l'attraper sur l'étagère. Mais c'est Boulou qu'il prit pour le tendre à l'enfant. Titours se sentit désespéré. Personne ne voulait de lui. Tous ses nouveaux amis seraient vendus, et lui restera là, sur son étagère, à prendre la poussière. Pauvre Titours !

  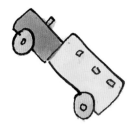

M. et Mme Papeton avaient une petite-fille prénommée Jessie qui aimait bien venir jouer à la boutique. Tous les jouets l'aimaient beaucoup parce qu'elle était douce et gentille.

C'est ainsi qu'elle vint à la boutique le jour de son anniversaire, et ses grands-parents lui permirent de choisir parmi les jouets le cadeau qui lui faisait plaisir.

« Je sais bien qu'elle ne me choisira pas, pensa Titours tristement, alors qu'il y a tant de jouets bien plus beaux que moi. »

117

Mais, à la grande surprise de Titours, Jessie leva les yeux et pointa l'étagère du doigt en disant : « Je voudrais ce petit ours à la tête toute de travers. Je trouve que c'est le plus mignon. »

M. Papeton sourit et tendit l'ours à la petite fille. Elle le serra dans ses bras et l'embrassa. Titours était si heureux qu'il en avait les larmes aux yeux. Une fois à la maison, Jessie lui mit un beau nœud papillon rouge autour du cou pour sa fête d'anniversaire. Titours n'avait jamais été aussi fier.

Bientôt les invités arrivèrent. Tous les enfants avaient apporté leur ours.

Titours n'en crut pas ses yeux quand il vit arriver le petit garçon qui avait acheté son ami Boulou !

« J'ai préparé un pique-nique spécial pour les ours », lui expliqua Jessie en l'embrassant. Les enfants ainsi que leurs ours passèrent une merveilleuse journée, particulièrement Titours. Il avait trouvé une maison douillette, rencontré son vieil ami et fait la connaissance de beaucoup d'autres.

« Tu vois, je te l'avais bien dit, il ne fallait pas t'inquiéter », dit Boulou.

« Je sais, répondit Titours. Je ne m'inquiéterai plus jamais. »

La ruche pointue

Voici la ruche pointue.

Mais où sont les abeilles ?

Cachées ? Personne ne les a vues.

Si tu attends qu'elles s'éveillent,

Tu les verras butiner les iris,

Un, deux, trois, quatre, cinq, six !

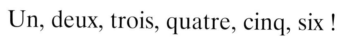

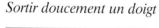

Joindre les mains pour mimer la ruche

Sortir doucement un doigt

... puis un autre, et un autre, et un autre encore

Tout d'un coup, chatouiller l'enfant

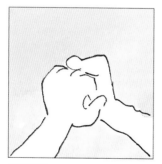
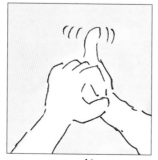

RUCHE

LES ABEILLES S'ÉVEILLENT

TROIS, QUATRE

CINQ, SIX !

La danse des rubans

C'est la danse des rubans,

Danse toute la journée,

Danse autour du mât,

En ce joli mois de mai,

C'est la danse des rubans,

Quelle joyeuse assemblée,

Danse autour du mât,

Jusqu'à l'heure du déjeuner.

C'est la danse des rubans,

Chante avec gaieté,

Danse autour du mât,

Jusqu'à l'heure du thé.

C'est la danse des rubans,

Même si tu es fatigué,

Danse autour du mât,

Jusqu'à l'heure du coucher.

Vogue, vogue, petit bateau

Vogue, vogue, petit bateau,

Et file gaiement au gré du courant.

Rame, rame, mon enfant,

La vie est un long cours d'eau.

Mimer l'action de ramer

Dans le jardin

Dans le jardin
Était assis un lapin.
Soudain, un chat vint
Et chassa le lapin,
Tout là-haut, là-haut !

Dessiner des cercles dans la main

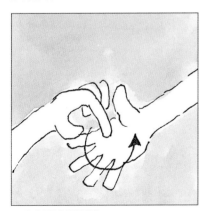

DANS LE JARDIN

Faire marcher ses doigts sur le bras

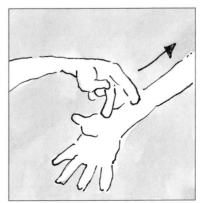

UN CHAT VINT ET LE CHASSA

Chatouiller !

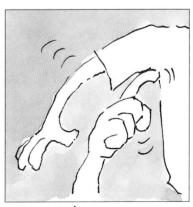

GUILI, GUILI !

Cinq grosses saucisses

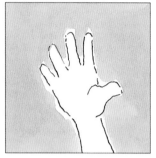

Lever les cinq doigts

CINQ GROSSES SAUCISSES

Taper dans ses mains !

L'UNE ÉCLATA – BANG !

Lever quatre doigts

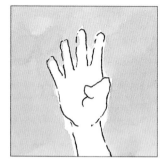

QUATRE GROSSES SAUCISSES

Taper dans ses mains !

L'UNE ÉCLATA – BANG !

Cinq grosses saucisses rissolaient,

Soudain, l'une éclata – « BANG ! »

Quatre grosses saucisses, etc.

Trois grosses saucisses, etc.

Deux grosses saucisses, etc.

Une grosse saucisse rissolait,

Soudain, elle éclata. « BANG ! »

et il n'y eut plus AUCUNE saucisse !

Continuer jusqu'à ce qu'il ne reste plus de doigts

UNE GROSSE SAUCISSE

Taper dans ses mains !

ELLE ÉCLATA – BANG !

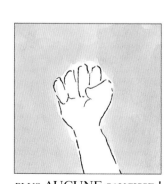

PLUS AUCUNE SAUCISSE !

128

Deux gros messieurs

Deux gros messieurs
se rencontrent dans la rue,
Se saluent poliment,
puis se saluent encore.
Comment allez-vous ?
Comment allez-vous ?
Comment allez-vous ?

Deux dames menues se rencontrent, etc.

Deux grands policiers se rencontrent, etc.

Deux jeunes écoliers se rencontrent, etc.

Deux petits bébés se rencontrent, etc.

*Changer de doigt à chaque phrase : l'index pour les dames, le majeur
pour les policiers, et ainsi de suite.*

Lever le pouce des deux mains

Incliner les pouces chacun leur tour

Tourner les pouces chacun leur tour

Tourner les deux pouces ensemble

DEUX GROS MESSIEURS

SE SALUENT POLIMENT

COMMENT ALLEZ-VOUS ?

COMMENT ALLEZ-VOUS ?

Une bouteille à la mer

Blizzi, l'ours polaire, plongea sa grosse patte velue dans l'eau à travers un trou creusé dans la glace. Il était sûr d'avoir vu quelque chose briller sous la surface. C'est à ce moment-là que Franklin, le pingouin, surgit de l'eau et sortit par le trou, serrant un objet sous son aile. C'était une bouteille de verre.

« Il me semblait bien que j'avais vu quelque chose de bizarre, dit Blizzi. Qu'est-ce que c'est ? »

« Je ne sais pas, répondit Franklin. Je l'ai trouvé dans la mer de l'autre côté des icebergs. Ça flottait sur les vagues. »

Les deux amis s'assirent et contemplèrent la bouteille.

« Il y a quelque chose à l'intérieur, dit Franklin. Sors-le. » Ils ôtèrent le bouchon et, avec son bec, Franklin atteignit le petit bout de papier et le sortit de la bouteille.

« Qu'est-il écrit ? » demanda Blizzi.

Franklin lut la note attentivement.

« C'est écrit : "Au secours ! Je suis échoué sur une île déserte. Mon bateau est cassé. Il fait très chaud. Amitiés, Attos, l'ours brun", lut Franklin. Il y a une carte au verso. Crois-tu que nous pourrions l'aider ? »

« Bien sûr, répondit Blizzi. Il semblerait qu'un de mes cousins soit en difficulté. De toute façon, ce sera une aventure ! J'ai toujours voulu savoir à quoi ressemblait la chaleur. »

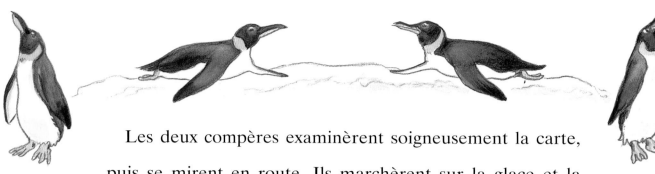

Les deux compères examinèrent soigneusement la carte, puis se mirent en route. Ils marchèrent sur la glace et la neige jusqu'à ce qu'ils atteignent la mer. Ils se retournèrent pour dire au revoir à la banquise, leur domaine, plongèrent dans l'eau glacée et commencèrent à nager vers le sud en direction de l'île déserte. Au bout de quelque temps, Blizzi commença à être fatigué. Jamais auparavant, il n'avait nagé aussi loin de chez lui.

« Reposons-nous un moment », dit Franklin. Tous deux se mirent sur le dos, faisant la planche à la surface de l'eau.

« Penses-tu que c'est encore très loin ? » demanda Blizzi.

« Oh, oui, très loin, dit Franklin. La mer n'est pas encore assez chaude. Quand nous y serons, l'eau sera aussi chaude que celle d'un bain. »

« Je n'ai encore jamais connu ça ! dit Blizzi, tout excité. Crois-tu que je vais aimer ça ? »

« Je n'en suis pas sûr », répondit Franklin.

Les deux amis continuèrent à nager en direction du soleil. Petit à petit, l'eau devenait tiède, puis chaude, puis de plus en plus chaude. Blizzi se mit à rire.

« Ma fourrure devient toute belle et ça me chatouille partout », gloussa-t-il.

Et les deux compères continuèrent à nager. Le chaud soleil tapait fort sur leur tête. Blizzi commençait à être essoufflé et chaque mouvement le faisait souffrir.

« Je crois que j'ai trop chaud, dit-il. Je ne vais pas pouvoir nager encore longtemps ! »

« Tu n'auras pas à le faire ! dit Franklin. Voici l'île déserte ! »

Sur le rivage, Attos sautait de joie et agitait ses pattes avec excitation.

« Vous m'avez retrouvé ! cria-t-il. Vous vous rendez compte que ma petite bouteille a vogué jusqu'au pôle Nord ! »

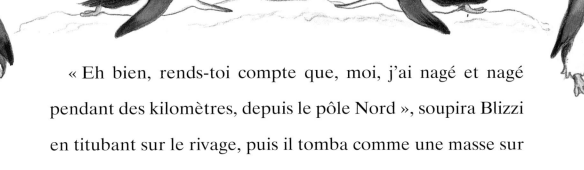

« Eh bien, rends-toi compte que, moi, j'ai nagé et nagé pendant des kilomètres, depuis le pôle Nord », soupira Blizzi en titubant sur le rivage, puis il tomba comme une masse sur le sable chaud. « Je suis littéralement épuisé ! »

Attos conduisit ses deux sauveteurs à l'abri, dans une grotte qu'il avait découverte non loin de là. Ils s'y allongèrent et dormirent tout leur soûl. À la nuit tombée, Attos alluma un feu sur la plage. Ils s'y réchauffèrent en se racontant des histoires. Attos leur expliqua sa découverte de la bouteille et la manière dont il l'avait jetée à la mer, ainsi que le naufrage de son bateau.

« J'avais vraiment peur de passer le reste de ma vie sur cette île ! dit Attos. Et je voulais rentrer à la maison ! »

« Ne t'inquiète pas, dit Blizzi. Nous allons rentrer chez nous. Mais, avant ça, nous allons passer une bonne nuit. »

Le lendemain matin, les trois amis jouèrent avec entrain sur la plage.

« Je ne suis pas sûr d'aimer beaucoup la chaleur, dit Blizzi. Ça me fatigue. Et puis ce sable qui s'infiltre partout ! » Les autres rirent en chœur.

« Bon, prenons la mer maintenant », dit Franklin.

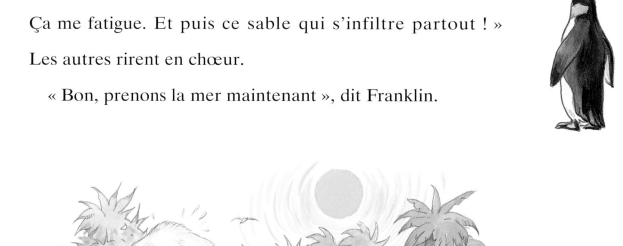

Attos n'étant pas aussi bon nageur qu'eux, ils firent le trajet du retour en remorquant leur ami sur un radeau qu'ils avaient fabriqué. Ce fut encore un long et difficile voyage, mais quand, enfin, ils atteignirent le domaine d'Attos, celui-ci était fou de bonheur. Ils comprirent alors que leurs efforts en valaient vraiment la peine.

« Promettez-moi de revenir me voir ! » cria Attos, alors que ses deux amis lui faisaient leurs adieux et prenaient le chemin du retour. Ils allaient retrouver leur chère banquise.

« Oui, c'est promis ! répondit Blizzi. Mais à condition que tu ne sois pas dans un endroit trop chaud. Quand je suis loin de chez moi, les glissades sur la glace me manquent trop ! »

L'autruche

Voici une autruche
douce et grande,

Elle est très élevée
avec sa tête perchée.

Voici un hérisson
aux poils qui piquent,

Il est tout petit,
et roulé en boule,
il est mimi.

Lever un bras

Remuer son poing

Entrelacer ses doigts

Fermer ses mains

UNE AUTRUCHE

TÊTE PERCHÉE

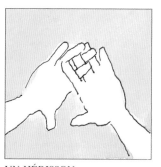

UN HÉRISSON

ROULÉ EN BOULE

138

Voici une araignée,

Elle a tant de pattes mais on ne voit

pas de nez.

Voici des oiseaux,

Aimant toujours voler là-haut.

Voici des enfants qui dorment,

Et, dans la nuit hulule un hibou

« Ououh ! Ououh ! Ououh ! »

Arrondir sa main
et ses doigts

Joindre ses pouces et
agiter les autres doigts

Faire semblant de dormir

Faire des cercles autour
de ses yeux

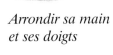

UNE ARAIGNÉE

DES OISEAUX

DES ENFANTS QUI DORMENT

UN HIBOU

Simon le simplet

Sur sa route, Simon le simplet rencontra un pâtissier

Qui allait à la foire,

Simon le simplet dit au pâtissier :

« Laisse-moi goûter tes tartes aux poires. »

Le pâtissier dit à Simon le simplet :

« Montre-moi d'abord ton porte-monnaie. »

Simon le simplet dit au pâtissier :

« Je n'en ai pas, je l'ai oublié. »

Remplis-moi un seau d'eau, lui proposa le pâtissier,

Et tu pourras goûter mon gâteau.

Mais Simon le simplet

Le puits ne sut trouver !

Saut en hauteur

Une souris dit au kangourou Kanga :
« Je peux sauter aussi haut que toi ! »
Kanga ricana : « Comment feras-tu ça ?
Toi, si petite, je t'en prie, dis-moi ! »

La souris répondit : « Je vais sauter
Si haut que tu seras étonné !
Mais, d'abord, tu dois accepter
De me montrer comment tu fais ! »

Kanga sauta donc tout en haut d'un bouleau,
Et ne vit pas, pauvre malchanceux,
Que la souris avait bondi sur son dos.
Ce n'était vraiment pas du jeu !

Kanga, en un bond, atterrit sur le sol.
« Où es-tu », dit-il, cherchant la bestiole.
« Ici ! » cria la souris perchée.
« D'accord, dit Kanga, tu as gagné ! »

Momo et son marteau

Momo bricole avec un marteau,

Un marteau, un marteau,

Momo bricole avec un marteau,

Gentil marmot.

Momo bricole avec deux marteaux,

Deux marteaux, deux marteaux,

Momo bricole avec deux marteaux,

Gentil marmot.

Momo bricole avec trois marteaux, etc.

Momo bricole avec quatre marteaux, etc.

Momo bricole avec cinq marteaux, etc.

Taper en rythme avec son poing sur ses genoux

Taper avec ses deux poings sur ses genoux

Taper avec ses deux poings et son pied

Taper avec ses deux poings et ses deux pieds

UN MARTEAU   DEUX MARTEAUX   TROIS MARTEAUX   QUATRE MARTEAUX

Momo est fatigué et a mal au dos,
Mal au dos, mal au dos,
Momo est fatigué et a mal au dos,
Gentil marmot.

Momo va se coucher aussitôt,
Coucher aussitôt, coucher aussitôt,
Momo va se coucher aussitôt,
Gentil marmot.

Momo se réveille frais et dispos,
Frais et dispos, frais et dispos,
Momo se réveille frais et dispos,
Gentil marmot.

Taper avec ses poings, ses pieds et remuer la tête

Se frotter les yeux et bâiller

Faire semblant de dormir

Faire semblant de se réveiller et de s'étirer

CINQ MARTEAUX

FATIGUÉ ET MAL AU DOS

VA SE COUCHER

SE RÉVEILLE

Miss Giroflée

Miss Giroflée,

Assise sur un tabouret,

Mangeait de la crème et buvait du petit-lait.

Arriva une énorme araignée,

Qui s'installa sous son nez

Et fit s'enfuir Miss Giroflée.

Le Père Bonsommeil

Le Père Bonsommeil arpente les rues de la cité,

Et, dans les ruelles, il monte et il descend,

Grattant aux fenêtres et criant derrière les volets :

« Il est plus de huit heures, les enfants,

Êtes-vous tous couchés ? »

Léo le paresseux

Rien ne faisait plus plaisir à Léo l'Ourson que rester douillettement dans le lit de Théo, bien au chaud.

Chaque matin, le réveil sonnait et Théo bondissait de son lit et tirait brutalement les rideaux. « J'aime le matin », disait-il en s'étirant, tandis que le soleil inondait la chambre de lumière.

« Tu es fou ! » marmonnait Léo l'Ourson, en s'enfonçant un peu plus dans le lit, sous l'édredon où il passerait le reste de la matinée à sommeiller avec délectation.

« Sors de là et va jouer, ourson paresseux », disait Théo. Mais Léo l'Ourson ne bougeait pas d'un pouce. Il ronflait, au contraire, encore plus fort.

Théo avait envie que Léo l'Ourson soit plus vif et plus actif, comme l'étaient les ours de ses amis. Il aimait les aventures et aurait bien voulu que Léo l'Ourson partage ses escapades avec lui.

Un soir avant d'aller se coucher, Théo décida d'avoir une conversation avec Léo l'Ourson. Il lui raconta la partie de pêche qu'il avait faite l'après-midi même avec ses amis, qui étaient accompagnés de leurs ours.

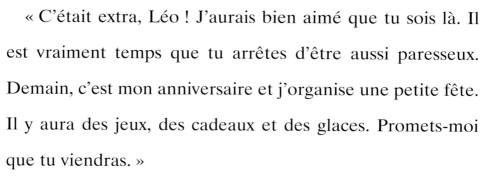

« C'était extra, Léo ! J'aurais bien aimé que tu sois là. Il est vraiment temps que tu arrêtes d'être aussi paresseux. Demain, c'est mon anniversaire et j'organise une petite fête. Il y aura des jeux, des cadeaux et des glaces. Promets-moi que tu viendras. »

« Ça ne me tente pas beaucoup, répondit Léo l'Ourson. Bon, d'accord. Je viendrai pour cette fois-ci. »

Le lendemain matin, Théo se leva tôt et en pleine forme. « Youpi, c'est mon anniversaire ! » hurlait-il en dansant tout autour de la chambre. Il arracha les couvertures du lit. « Viens, Léo, c'est l'heure de se lever ! »

« Encore cinq petites minutes ! » maugréa Léo l'Ourson
en tournant le dos. Il se rendormit instantanément.

Quand Théo revint dans la chambre, après le petit
déjeuner, Léo l'Ourson n'était toujours pas levé. Bien, Théo
allait employer la manière forte avec Léo. Il passa sa main
dans le lit et commença à chatouiller le ventre de Léo
l'Ourson. Celui-ci ouvrit un œil et grogna. « Debout, Léo !
Tu me l'avais promis. Tu te souviens ? » dit Théo.

Léo l'Ourson bâilla. « Bon, bon, s'il le faut ! » dit-il, et tout en grognant, ronchonnant et grommelant, il descendit du lit. Il se lava le visage et les pattes, se brossa les dents et enfila son plus beau gilet.

« Voilà, je suis prêt », dit-il.

« Bien, dit Théo. Ce n'est pas trop tôt. »

Juste à ce moment-là, la sonnette de la porte d'entrée retentit et Théo courut ouvrir. « Je reviens te chercher dans une minute », dit-il à Léo l'Ourson. Mais quand il revint, il n'y avait aucune trace de l'ourson, juste un léger ronflement s'échappant de sous l'édredon.

Théo était alors si fâché et même excédé à cause de Léo l'Ourson, qu'il décida de l'abandonner où il était.

« Il va rater la fête, tant pis pour lui ! » se dit-il. Il était profondément blessé que Léo l'Ourson n'ait pas tenu sa promesse de la veille.

Théo s'amusa beaucoup, mais il aurait préféré que Léo l'Ourson soit là. Cette nuit-là, quand il alla se coucher, il sanglota silencieusement sur son oreiller.

Léo l'Ourson, allongé près de lui dans l'obscurité, écoutait. Il savait que Théo pleurait parce qu'il l'avait laissé tomber. Il se sentit alors très honteux.

« Je suis désolé ! » murmura Léo l'Ourson. Il se blottit tout contre Théo et, de sa patte, lui caressa la tête jusqu'à ce qu'il s'endorme.

Le lendemain matin, quand le réveil sonna, Théo sauta de son lit, comme d'habitude. Mais, que se passait-il ? Léo l'Ourson était lui aussi levé et faisait sa gymnastique. Théo le regarda, stupéfait.

« Qu'est-ce qu'on fait aujourd'hui ? » demanda Léo.

« Heu, heu ! On… on va faire un pique-nique, bredouilla Théo, sidéré. Tu veux venir ? »

« Bien sûr ! » dit Léo l'Ourson. Depuis ce jour-là, Léo l'Ourson se leva tous les jours de bonne heure, jovial et prêt à vivre toutes les aventures avec Théo, et plus jamais il ne le laissa tomber.

Voici un ballon pour bébé

Voici un ballon pour bébé,

Beau, gros et rond.

Voici un marteau pour bébé,

Rouge, bleu et mignon.

Voici les soldats de bébé,

Alignés sur une rangée.

Voici la musique de bébé,

Il tape des mains et des pieds.

*Mimer une balle avec
les mains*

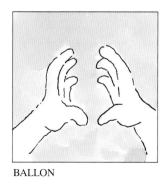

BALLON

*Taper du poing sur son
genou*

MARTEAU

Montrer ses dix doigts

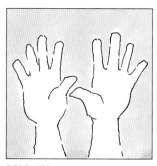

SOLDATS

Taper dans ses mains

CLAP ! CLAP !

Voici la trompette de bébé,
Tut ! tut !

Voici comment bébé
Joue à faire COUCOU !

Voici un grand parapluie,
Pour abriter bébé de la pluie.

Voici le berceau de bébé,
Berce-le toute la nuit.

Souffler à travers son poing

Boucher ses yeux avec ses mains

Faire semblant de porter un parapluie

Mettre ses bras en forme de berceau

TROMPETTE

COUCOU !

PARAPLUIE

BERCEAU

On dit de moi

On dit de moi

Que je suis une méchante oie.

Je ne sais pas pourquoi.

Ce matin, j'ai monté l'escalier

Et j'ai rencontré un vieil homme tout ridé.

Je l'ai attrapé par le pied

Et je l'ai fait tomber.

Suis-je une méchante oie ?

Hue, Dada !

Hue, Dada !

Ne t'arrête pas !

Bouba l'ourson

File sur son cheval.

À dada, à dada !

Crient ses compagnons.

Tous sortis du coffre à jouets,

Pour le voir filer.

Trois ours dans un baquet

Écoutez cette incroyable comptine :

Trois ours dans un baquet

De l'océan tentent la traversée !

Mais leur estomac crie famine,

Et une bonne odeur de beignets

Les ramène à la maison pour le thé !

Pâtissier

Pâtissier,

Prépare-nous un gâteau.

De la farine, des œufs

et un peu d'eau,

Puis du sucre et du lait.

Pétris la pâte et dessine un B,

C'est l'anniversaire de bébé.

Mets le gâteau au four.

C'est aujourd'hui un grand jour.

*Taper des mains
en rythme*

*Pétrir la paume
de sa main*

Tracer la lettre B

Enfourner le gâteau

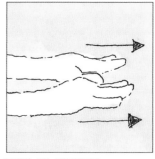

PRÉPARE UN GÂTEAU   PÉTRIS LA PÂTE   ÉCRIS LA LETTRE B   METS-LE AU FOUR

La tête, les épaules et les genoux

La tête, les épaules, les genoux

et les orteils, les genoux et les orteils,

La tête, les épaules, les genoux

et les orteils, les genoux et les orteils,

Et les yeux et les oreilles

et la bouche et le nez.

La tête, les épaules, les genoux

et les orteils, les genoux et les orteils.

Toucher toutes les parties de son corps, lentement puis de plus en plus vite.

Le pommier

Un arbre aux jolies feuilles vertes.

De belles pommes qui me sont offertes

Et tombent quand souffle le vent.

Pour les ramasser, le panier de maman.

Mimer l'arbre avec les mains

Fermer les poings

Mimer avec les poings les pommes qui tombent

Rassembler ses mains pour mimer un panier

UN ARBRE

DES POMMES

... QUI TOMBENT

LE PANIER DE MAMAN

164

Le cerisier

Un noyau de cerise, j'ai trouvé.

Dans la terre, je l'ai planté.

Quand je suis venu l'examiner,

Le petit noyau avait germé.

Un peu plus chaque jour, il a poussé,

Devenant bientôt un cerisier.

Toutes les cerises, j'ai récoltées,

Et, avec mon thé, je les ai mangées.

Mimer un trou avec la main et planter

Enfiler doucement les doigts dans le trou

Sortir sa main par le trou et attraper son poignet

Attraper des cerises au bout de ses doigts et les manger.

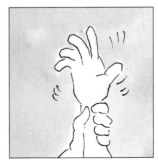

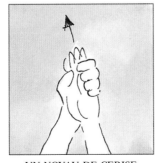

J'AI TROUVÉ…

… UN NOYAU DE CERISE

… DEVENANT UN CERISIER

… JE LES AI MANGÉES

165

Le chant de la baleine

« Joli matin ensoleillé ! » fredonnait Flippie, la baleine, en s'ébattant dans l'eau bleue de l'océan inondé de soleil. Sous une douce chaleur, elle nageait avec grâce et légèreté, tournoyant en cabrioles et pirouettes, puis elle fendait les vagues et s'élançait hors de l'eau en voltiges élégantes.

Flippie adorait chanter et danser. Malheureusement, si elle était une danseuse très gracieuse, sa voix était absolument catastrophique. Flippie chantait affreusement faux et, lorsqu'elle ouvrait sa bouche gigantesque, il en sortait des sons tonitruants et insupportables. Ces mugissements épouvantables résonnaient à travers l'océan, à des kilomètres à la ronde, terrorisant les poissons et toutes les créatures marines qui nichaient dans les rochers et les récifs. Et c'était encore pire lorsqu'il faisait beau, car alors la chaleur du soleil rendait Flippie plus joyeuse que jamais, ce qui l'incitait à chanter et à danser de plus belle. C'était si terrible que les habitants de l'océan en étaient tous venus à souhaiter que le ciel soit maussade et qu'il pleuve.

« Il faut faire quelque chose ! se lamenta Orélia, la méduse. Les rugissements de Flippie me tourneboulent complètement et mon cerveau est tout ébranlé. Je suis toute désorientée et je ne trouve même plus mon chemin ! »

« Eh bien, moi, je sais où je vais aller, dit Pacha, le homard. Aussi loin que possible. Je crois que ma tête va éclater si j'entends encore les horribles chants de Flippie. »

« Il faut que l'un d'entre nous aille interdire à Flippie de chanter », dit Céleste, la raie.

« Mais cela risque de la blesser », dit Orélia.

« Pas autant que sa voix ne nous blesse les oreilles ! » marmonna Pacha.

Céleste fut désignée pour aller, le lendemain, dire à Flippie qu'ils ne voulaient plus jamais l'entendre chanter. Orélia approuva. Flippie, entendant que les autres détestaient ses chants, fut bouleversée et se mit à pleurer à chaudes larmes.

« Je voulais juste m'amuser un peu ! sanglota-t-elle. Je ne me suis jamais rendu compte que je dérangeais les autres. »

« Là, là, dit Céleste, regrettant d'avoir été chargée de cette difficile mission auprès de la petite baleine. Tu peux continuer à danser, bien sûr. »

« Sans la musique, ce n'est pas la même chose, murmura tristement Flippie. Je ne pourrai pas suivre le rythme. » Et elle s'éloigna dans les profondeurs, disant qu'elle voulait rester seule quelque temps.

Flippie était allongée sur le fond sablonneux, attristée et s'apitoyant sur son sort, lorsqu'un son magnifique venu de loin à travers l'océan résonna à ses oreilles. On aurait dit quelqu'un qui chantait. Flippie aurait bien voulu savoir qui produisait de si jolies notes. D'un battement de queue, elle fendit l'eau et se dirigea dans la direction d'où provenaient les sons.

En s'approchant, Flippie entendit une voix douce chanter une belle mélodie. Arrivant près d'un rocher percé, elle aperçut sur le sable une petite pieuvre.

Oscillant et ondulant, la petite pieuvre chantait. Ses tentacules s'agitaient dans tous les sens, tandis qu'elle se déplaçait maladroitement. Puis, elle essaya de tournoyer sur

elle-même mais ses longues tentacules s'emmêlèrent et elle s'écroula sur le sable.

« Oh, la, la, dit Multipattes, la pieuvre. J'ai vraiment l'impression d'avoir huit pieds gauches ! »

Flippie regarda timidement à travers le rocher percé.

« Qu'essaies-tu de faire ? » demanda-t-elle.

La petite pieuvre sembla un peu embarrassée.

« J'essayais de danser, répondit-elle en rougissant. Mais je crois que je ne suis pas très douée. »

« Veux-tu que je t'apprenne, dit Flippie. Je suis une bonne danseuse. En échange, j'aimerais que, toi aussi, tu m'apprennes quelque chose ! »

Quelques semaines plus tard, Orélia, Pacha et Céleste bavardaient et constataient combien Flippie leur manquait, lorsqu'ils entendirent un son étrange et beau qui se propageait dans l'océan.

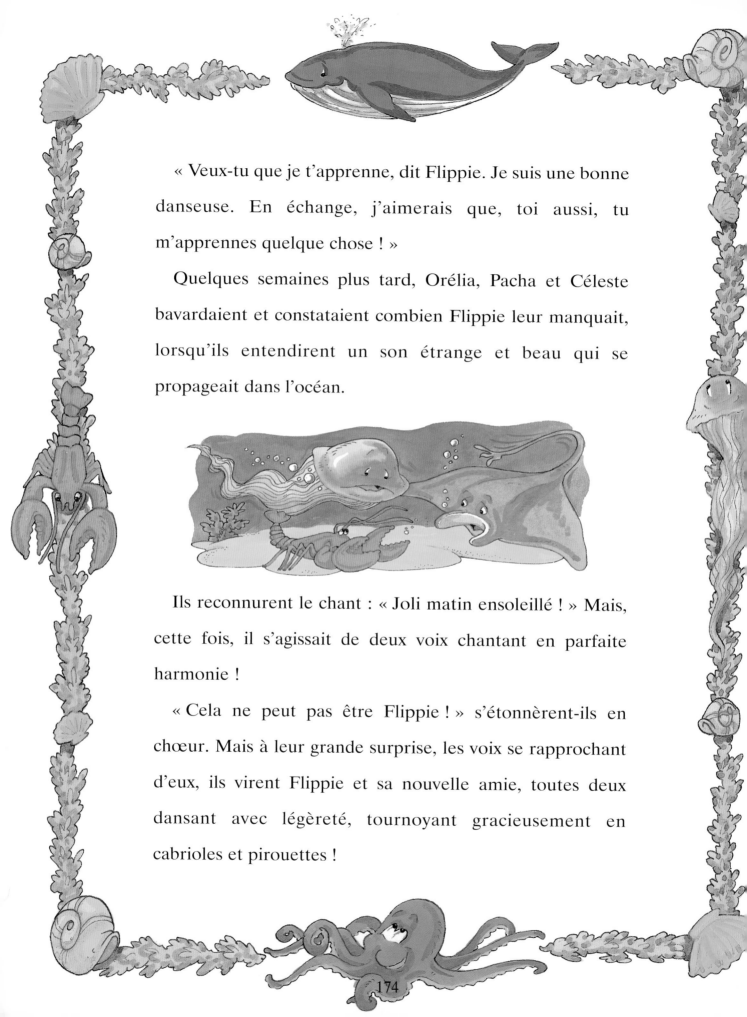

Ils reconnurent le chant : « Joli matin ensoleillé ! » Mais, cette fois, il s'agissait de deux voix chantant en parfaite harmonie !

« Cela ne peut pas être Flippie ! » s'étonnèrent-ils en chœur. Mais à leur grande surprise, les voix se rapprochant d'eux, ils virent Flippie et sa nouvelle amie, toutes deux dansant avec légèreté, tournoyant gracieusement en cabrioles et pirouettes !

La vieille Mère Richard

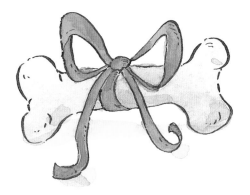

La vieille Mère Richard
Vint chercher dans le placard
Un os à donner à son pauvre chien,
Mais quand elle arriva devant
Elle vit qu'il était vide, malheureusement
Et le pauvre chien ne mangea rien.

Tom-Tom, un jour de Mardi gras

Tom-Tom, un jour de Mardi gras,

Vola un cochon et détala !

Le cochon fut mangé et Tom-Tom fut grondé.

Fâché, il courut dans la prairie se cacher.

Hip-hippo

Ohé, du bateau !
C'est moi l'hip-hippo
Hip-hippo hourra !
Dans la boue de mon bain,
Plitch, platch, je suis si bien
Comme un poisson dans l'eau
Je trouve ça très rigolo.

Ces grosses bulles, quelle merveille !

J'aime respirer par le nez

Me tortiller, me prélasser,

La boue entre les orteils

Et le croiriez-vous ?

Après tous ces glouglous,

Je sors bien parfumé de ma gadoue !

Cocorico !

Cocorico !

La princesse a perdu son soulier,

Le musicien a perdu son archet,

Que faut-il faire ?

Cocorico !

Devinez ce que la princesse fait,

Le musicien ne pouvant plus l'accompagner.

Elle danse nus pieds.

Cocorico !

La princesse a retrouvé son soulier

Et le musicien a retrouvé son archet.

Cocorico !

Grassouillet, le petit porcelet

Lundi, Grassouillet, le petit porcelet,
au marché, est allé.

Mardi, Grassouillet, le petit
porcelet, à la maison, est resté.

Tortiller…

chaque…

doigt de pied…

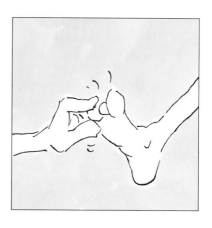

184

Mercredi, Grassouillet, le petit porcelet, un bifteck a mangé.

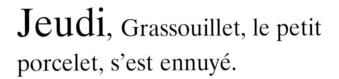

Jeudi, Grassouillet, le petit porcelet, s'est ennuyé.

Vendredi, Grassouillet, le petit porcelet, a crié toute la journée

« Oin-oin-oin ! »

l'un…

après l'autre.

Chatouiller !

« OIN-OIN-OIN »

Un ours trop gourmand

S'il y a bien une chose que les oursons aiment plus que tout au monde, ce sont les gâteaux – les gros gâteaux bien crémeux et sucrés, croustillants dehors et moelleux dedans. Un ourson ferait n'importe quoi pour un gâteau. Mais pour un petit ours nommé Clarence, les gâteaux étaient pratiquement son unique raison de vivre!

Paméla, la poupée, faisait régulièrement cuire dans le four les plus merveilleux gâteaux. Elle confectionnait des gros gâteaux et des petits, des gâteaux aux fruits ou à la crème, des pains au chocolat ou aux raisins, et encore des meringues et des éclairs ! Elle les partageait entre tous les jouets qui vivaient dans la salle de jeux et tous se régalaient. Pourtant aucun d'entre eux ne les aimait autant que Clarence.

« Si tu veux bien me donner ton gâteau, je te cirerai tes bottes ! » disait-il au soldat de plomb.

Et parfois, lorsque le soldat de plomb n'avait pas très faim, il acceptait. Il y avait toujours quelqu'un qui consentait à céder son gâteau à Clarence en échange d'une faveur ou d'un service. Il arrivait que Clarence mange cinq ou six gâteaux le même jour !

Aussi, on le voyait souvent occupé à laver les vêtements des poupées, à brosser Choupi le Chien ou à nettoyer la voiture des policiers. Il était même prêt à accepter que le clown lui jette des tartes à la crème au visage !

Tu le vois, Clarence n'était pas un ours paresseux, mais un ours glouton et, malgré toutes ses occupations, il était en train de devenir un petit ours obèse. Tous les gâteaux qu'il avait mangés produisaient leur effet, et les coutures de sa fourrure commençaient même à craquer !

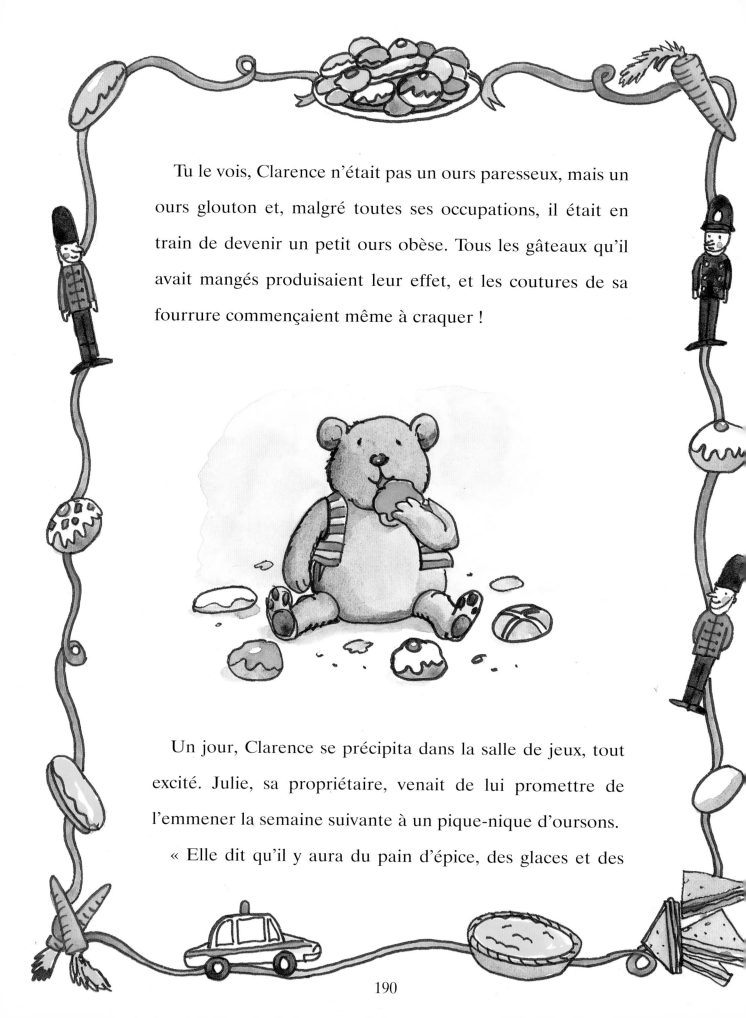

Un jour, Clarence se précipita dans la salle de jeux, tout excité. Julie, sa propriétaire, venait de lui promettre de l'emmener la semaine suivante à un pique-nique d'oursons.

« Elle dit qu'il y aura du pain d'épice, des glaces et des

cookies, et des monceaux de gâteaux de toutes sortes ! dit
Clarence à ses camarades en se frottant les mains. Je ne peux
plus attendre ! Toute cette excitation m'a donné faim. Je
crois que je vais manger un petit gâteau. » Et il sortit un gros
gâteau à la crème qu'il avait caché sous un coussin.

« Oh, Clarence ! dit Lapinot. Un de ces jours, tu vas tout
simplement éclater ! »

« Estime-toi heureux que je n'aime pas les carottes ! » dit
Clarence en souriant.

Cette semaine-là, Clarence fut plus occupé que jamais. Chaque fois qu'il pensait au fameux pique-nique, il commençait à avoir faim et devait absolument trouver quelqu'un qui lui cède son gâteau. Il mangeait gâteau après gâteau et n'écoutait pas Paméla quand elle le prévenait que les coutures de sa fourrure commençaient à se détendre dangereusement.

Le jour du pique-nique arriva enfin. Clarence, tout excité, riait et gesticulait en tout sens. Tout d'un coup, il ressentit une curieuse sensation de tiraillement au niveau de l'estomac. Il tenta de s'asseoir dans le lit mais, à sa grande stupeur, il constata qu'il ne pouvait plus bouger. En regardant son ventre, il découvrit que les coutures de sa fourrure avaient craqué et que le rembourrage s'échappait par le trou !

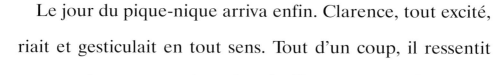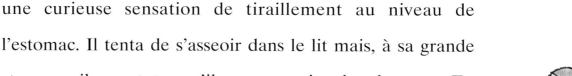

« Au secours ! cria-t-il. Je suis en train d'exploser ! »

Juste à ce moment-là, Julie se réveilla. « Oh, Clarence ! cria-t-elle en le voyant. Je ne peux pas t'emmener au pique-nique dans cet état-là ! »

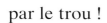

Julie montra Clarence à sa maman, qui décida qu'il était urgent de l'emmener à l'hôpital.

Clarence fut parti pendant une semaine entière, mais lorsqu'il revint, il était comme neuf. Un peu de rembourrage avait été retiré mais il était complètement recousu.

À l'hôpital, il avait eu tout le temps de réfléchir à sa gourmandise. Comme il aurait voulu n'avoir pas raté le pique-nique. Ses amis les ours lui avaient raconté que ce jour-là avait été le meilleur qu'ils aient jamais connu. À la place de Clarence, Julie avait emmené Lapinot.

« C'était affreux, bougonna Lapinot. Pas une carotte à l'horizon. Mais j'ai réussi à te rapporter un gâteau. » Et il sortit de sa poche un gros gâteau à la crème.

« Non, merci, Lapinot, dit Clarence. Bizarrement, je n'ai plus envie de gâteaux ! »

Bien sûr, Clarence ne renonça pas longtemps aux gâteaux, mais il se contenta d'en manger un par jour. Il continua à rendre service à ses camarades, mais il le fit désormais gratuitement !

Dix petits hommes

Dix petits hommes debout depuis hier,

Dix petits hommes ouvrent la barrière,

Dix petits hommes en rond se voient,

Lever ses dix doigts

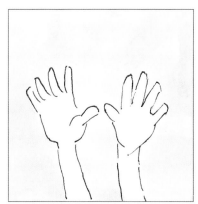

DIX PETITS HOMMES…

Faire pivoter ses mains

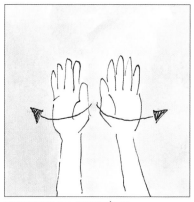

OUVRENT LA BARRIÈRE…

Mettre ses doigts en rond

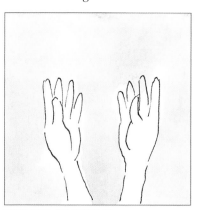

EN ROND SE VOIENT…

Dix petits hommes saluent le roi,

Dix petits hommes dansent sous la pluie,

Dix petits hommes s'enfuient.

Incliner ses doigts

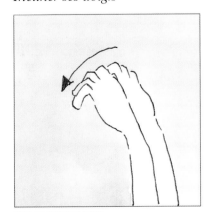

SALUENT LE ROI…

Faire danser ses doigts

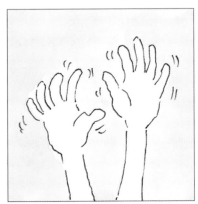

DANSENT SOUS LA PLUIE…

Cacher ses mains derrière son dos

… S'ENFUIENT

Le duc de la Poche-Percée

Indécis était le duc de la Poche-Percée,

Mais, mille hommes, il commandait.

Tout en haut de la colline, il les fit grimper.

Puis, quand au sommet, ils furent arrivés,

Tout en bas de la colline, il les fit marcher.

Puis, quand la plaine, ils eurent arpentée,

Tout en haut, il voulut remonter.

Mais les mille hommes étaient fatigués.

Le duc de la Poche-Percée

ne savait vraiment pas ce qu'il voulait.

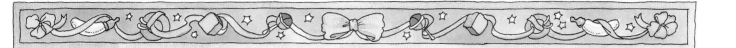

Dodo, l'enfant do

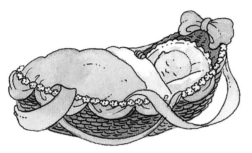

Dodo, l'enfant do,

L'enfant dormira bien vite,

Dodo, l'enfant do,

L'enfant dormira bientôt.

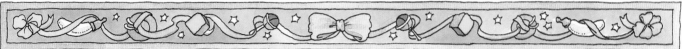

L'araignée Gipsy

L'araignée Gipsy monte à la gouttière,

Tiens, voilà la pluie,

Gipsy tombe par terre.

Mais le soleil a chassé la pluie !

L'araignée Gipsy monte à la gouttière.

Joindre l'index et le pouce opposé, en faisant pivoter ses poignets

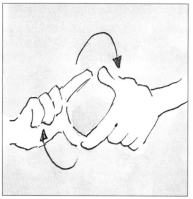

MONTE À LA GOUTTIÈRE...

Agiter les doigts en abaissant ses bras

VOILÀ LA PLUIE...

Dessiner un grand cercle avec ses bras et reprendre au début

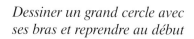

LE SOLEIL A CHASSÉ LA PLUIE...

Pauvre Zacharie

Je rêvais que le pauvre Zacharie
Tombait de mon lit
Et sentait sur sa tête
Une bosse comme une noisette !

Je poussai un grand cri,
Mon rêve était fini.
Je me rendormis
Et rêvai alors de sorbets aux fruits !

Élysée a disparu

J'ai perdu mon bel ourson, Élysée,
Partout, il m'accompagnait,
Mais, aujourd'hui, je ne sais pas où il est,
Où peut-il bien se cacher ?

J'ai regardé dans la salle à manger,
Derrière le canapé et sous le buffet,
J'ai regardé sous le lit,
Et même derrière le lambris !

J'ai regardé dans la baignoire,
Et derrière la rôtissoire,
Mais où peut bien être Élysée ?
Partout, je l'ai cherché !

Enfin, j'ai essayé la buanderie,
Et là, j'eus la surprise de ma vie.
Élysée était dans la machine à laver
Et, dans le tambour, il tournoyait!

Le pont de Londres

Le pont de Londres est en train de s'écrouler,

De s'écrouler, de s'écrouler,

Le pont de Londres est en train de s'écrouler,

Mon pauvre monsieur !

Réparons-le avec du bois et de l'argile,

Du bois et de l'argile, du bois et de l'argile,

Réparons-le avec du bois et de l'argile,

Mon pauvre monsieur !

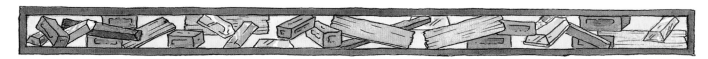

Le bois et l'argile ne tiendront pas,

Ne tiendront pas, ne tiendront pas,

Le bois et l'argile ne tiendront pas,

Mon pauvre monsieur !

Réparons-le avec des briques et du mortier,

Des briques et du mortier, des briques et du mortier,

Réparons-le avec des briques et du mortier,

Mon pauvre monsieur !

Les briques et le mortier ne tiendront pas,

Ne tiendront pas, ne tiendront pas,

Les briques et le mortier ne tiendront pas,

Mon pauvre monsieur !

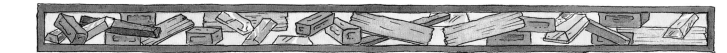

Réparons-le avec du fer et de l'acier,

Du fer et de l'acier, du fer et de l'acier,

Réparons-le avec du fer et de l'acier,

Mon pauvre monsieur !

Le fer et l'acier vont se plier,

Vont se plier, vont se plier,

Le fer et l'acier vont se plier,

Mon pauvre monsieur !

Réparons-le avec de l'or et de l'argent,

De l'or et de l'argent, de l'or et de l'argent,

Réparons-le avec de l'or et de l'argent,

Mon pauvre monsieur !

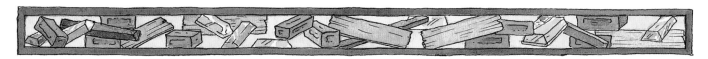

L'or et l'argent seront volés,

Seront volés, seront volés,

L'or et l'argent seront volés,

Mon pauvre monsieur !

La nuit, laissons un homme monter la garde,

Monter la garde, monter la garde,

La nuit, laissons un homme monter la garde,

Mon pauvre monsieur !

Il était une petite tortue

Il était une petite tortue,

Qui vivait dans une boîte.

Elle nageait dans les mares,

Et grimpait sur les rochers.

Elle voulut attraper un moustique,

Elle voulut attraper une puce.

Elle voulut attraper un poisson,

Elle voulut m'attraper, moi.

Mimer la tortue avec une main au-dessus de l'autre

Faire semblant de dessiner une boîte

Mimer la tortue qui nage dans les mares

Mimer les rochers en arrondissant la main

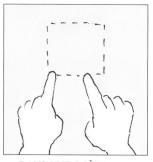

… PETITE TORTUE

… DANS UNE BOÎTE

… DANS LES MARES

… SUR LES ROCHERS

Elle attrapa le moustique,

Elle attrapa la puce.

Elle attrapa le poisson,

Mais... elle ne m'attrapa pas, moi !

Joindre le pouce et l'index quatre fois de suite

Taper dans ses mains trois fois de suite

Secouer la tête et pointer son menton avec le doigt

... ELLE VOULUT ATTRAPER

ELLE ATTRAPA

... NE M'ATTRAPA PAS !

La vache qui sautait par-dessus la lune

Boing, boing, boing ! Lapin Véloce sautait sur ses talons et bondissait à travers champs.

« Regardez comme je peux sauter haut ! » dit-il aux autres animaux de la ferme. Sa petite queue en pompon frétillait dans tous les sens.

« Très bien ! » dit Ulysse le Mouton, qui était facilement impressionné.

« Oui, très bien, dit Swift, le chien de troupeau. Mais pas aussi bien que moi. Je peux sauter par-dessus la barrière. »

Et c'est ce qu'il fit, il sauta par-dessus la barrière et fila dans le champ.

« Étonnant ! » dit Ulysse le Mouton.

« Oui, étonnant, dit Parsifal le Cheval, en secouant sa crinière. Mais pas aussi étonnant que moi. Je peux sauter par-dessus la haie. Regardez-moi ! » Et c'est ce qu'il fit, il galopa, puis s'élança dans les airs et franchit la haute haie.

« Incroyable ! » dit Ulysse le Mouton.

« Oui, incroyable ! dit Daisy, la vache, mâchouillant tranquillement une touffe d'herbe. Mais pas aussi incroyable que moi. Je peux sauter par-dessus la lune ! »

« Ah, on ne peut pas te croire, Daisy, dit Parsifal le Cheval. Personne ne peut sauter par-dessus la lune. Ça n'arrive que dans les contes de fées. »

« Eh bien, moi je peux le faire, dit Daisy, obstinée. Et je peux le prouver ! Vous allez pouvoir vérifier ! »

Les autres animaux étaient tous d'accord pour vérifier que Daisy pouvait sauter par-dessus la lune.

« Retrouvez-moi tous cette nuit, ici, dans ce champ, leur dit Daisy, quand la lune sera pleine et que les étoiles brilleront. »

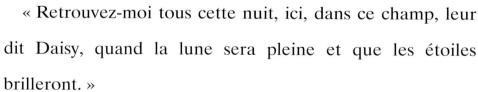

Ainsi à la nuit tombée, quand la lune fut haut dans le ciel, les animaux, tout excités, se retrouvèrent tous ensemble dans le champ. Tous les animaux de la ferme étaient venus, ayant entendu dire que Daisy la vache allait sauter par-dessus la lune. Ils étaient tous impatients de le voir de leurs propres yeux.

« Allons-y, Daisy, dit Swift, le chien de troupeau, tandis que les animaux piaffaient d'impatience. Es-tu prête à nous montrer comment tu sautes par-dessus la lune ou non ? »

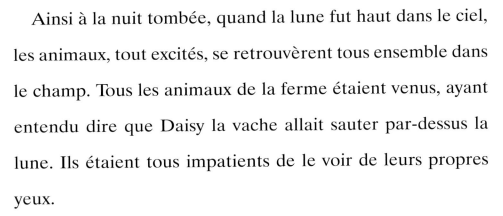

« Je l'ai fait ! s'écria Daisy. Vous n'allez même pas m'applaudir ? » Les animaux se regardaient, tous extrêmement troublés.

« Mais tu as juste franchi le ruisseau ! » dit Parsifal le Cheval, perplexe.

« Viens ici, tu vas voir », dit Daisy, toujours sur l'autre rive. Les animaux se rassemblèrent sur le bord de l'eau. Ils

regardèrent et virent la pleine lune se refléter dans l'onde chatoyante du ruisseau ! Les animaux éclatèrent de rire lorsqu'ils comprirent que Daisy les avait bien eus.

« Vous voyez ! dit Daisy. Je peux vraiment sauter par-dessus la lune ! » Et, pour le prouver encore une fois, elle sauta de nouveau au-dessus du ruisseau. Les animaux l'acclamèrent et l'applaudirent.

« C'était un habile stratagème ! » dit Swift.

« Époustouflant ! dit Ulysse le Mouton. Mais, quelqu'un pourrait-il m'expliquer de nouveau ? »

Deux petits hommes verts

Deux petits hommes verts
Ont fait le tour de la terre

Du haut de leur drôle d'engin
Ils n'ont pas beaucoup aimé les humains

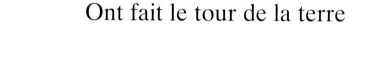

Alors ils ont fait marche arrière.

Lève et baisse les bras

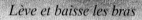

Soulever l'enfant doucement

Tourner la tête à gauche

Tourner la tête à droite

Cacher les yeux

Reprendre au début

Au grand magasin

Lever les bras au-dessus de la tête

Au grand magasin.

Bouger les mains en haut, puis en bas

Les ascenseurs

montent et descendent.

Ouvrir et fermer les bras en les balançant

Les portes s'ouvrent et se ferment.

Bouger les poings d'avant en arrière, et inversement

Les gens entrent et sortent.

Pousse-pousse le pouce

Pousse-pousse le pouce,

Pousse-pousse le pouce,

Où es-tu ?

Suis ici, suis ici.

Comment vas-tu ?

Alex l'index, etc,

Moqueur le majeur, etc.

Andy l'annulaire, etc.

Mini l'auriculaire, etc.

Serrer les poings, sortir les pouces et les remuer

Lever les index et les remuer

Lever les majeurs et les remuer

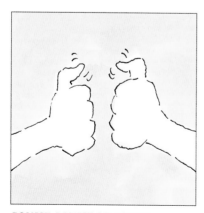

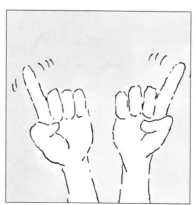

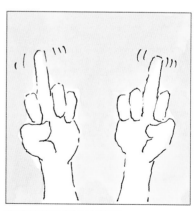

POUSSE-POUSSE LE POUCE…

ALEX L'INDEX…

MOQUEUR LE MAJEUR…

Tous les doigts !
Où êtes-vous ?
Sommes ici, sommes ici.
Comment allez-vous ?

Lever les annulaires et les remuer

Lever les petits doigts et les remuer

Lever tous les doigts et les remuer

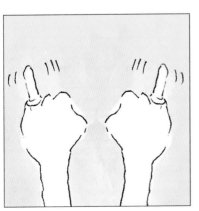

ANDY L'ANNULAIRE…

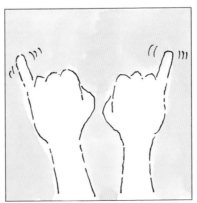

MINI L'AURICULAIRE…

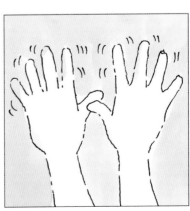

TOUS LES DOIGTS…

221

Le marchand de cakes dorés

Avez-vous vu le marchand de cakes dorés,

Le marchand de cakes dorés ?

Avez-vous vu le marchand de cakes dorés,

Il habite dans la rue des Potiers ?

Oui, j'ai vu le marchand de cakes dorés,

Le marchand de cakes dorés.

Oui, j'ai vu le marchand de cakes dorés,

Il habite dans la rue des Potiers.

Le roi Guilleret

Le roi Guilleret était un roi très gai.

Chaque jour, en fumant sa pipe, de la musique il voulait,

Et à tue-tête, il chantait.

Quand il avait fini de chanter, des blagues, il racontait,

À ses trois violonistes qui jouaient.

Hue ! Joli cheval

Hue ! Joli cheval,

Emmène-moi au bal,

J'entends tes sabots taper

Sur le chemin mouillé.

Ce soir, je vais danser,

Et le prince charmant trouver.

Hue ! Joli cheval,

Emmène-moi au bal.

*Faire sauter bébé
doucement
sur ses
genoux*

226

Une petite souris sourit

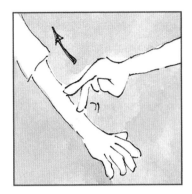

Faire monter ses doigts le long du bras

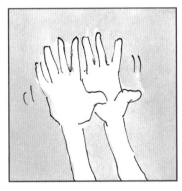

Taper des mains une fois

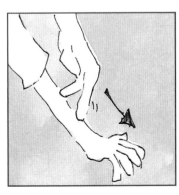

Faire descendre ses doigts le long du bras

Une petite souris sourit et grimpe, grimpe tout en haut de l'horloge.

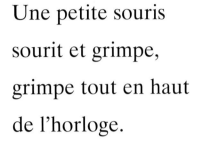

L'horloge sonne un coup,

La petite souris descend, descend tout en bas de l'horloge.

La petite souris sourit.

227

Les oursons des neiges

Pouce et Pimpouce, deux petits ours en peluche, étaient amis depuis toujours. Ils vivaient avec une petite fille nommée Émilie, qui les gardait sur son lit. Étendus sur les oreillers, ils pouvaient voir par la fenêtre et aimaient beaucoup voir le jardin changer au fil des saisons.

Un froid matin d'hiver, Émilie sauta de son lit, ouvrit les rideaux et poussa un cri de joie : « Oh ! de la neige ! »

Elle se précipita vers son armoire et commença à s'habiller. Pouce et Pimpouce, étonnés, la regardaient enfiler un tee-shirt, un pantalon, des chaussettes, une chemise, deux pull-overs, un gilet, un chapeau, une écharpe, des moufles et, enfin, son manteau ! Oh, la, la ! Que de vêtements !

« Il va faire très froid dehors, expliqua-t-elle aux deux oursons. Beaucoup trop froid pour vous deux ! Vous n'avez qu'à me regarder par la fenêtre, je vais fabriquer un

bonhomme de neige ! » Elle courut dans l'escalier et descendit dans le jardin.

« Trop froid, trop froid ! » dit Pimpouce en reniflant de dépit, quand elle fut partie. Qu'est-ce que ça veut dire, trop froid ? Nous sommes des ours, nous, donc, nous aimons le froid ! »

« En plus, notre manteau de fourrure nous tiendra chaud, dit Pouce. Et puis, qu'est-ce que c'est un bonhomme de neige ? »

« Je ne sais pas, dit Pimpouce. Regardons par la fenêtre et voyons si nous parvenons à le découvrir. »

Les petits ours observaient Émilie qui courait et sautait dans la neige.

Un éléphant sur une balançoire

Un éléphant sur une balançoire,

Ça n'existe pas, ça n'existe pas.

Le soleil qui brille dans le noir,

Ça n'existe pas, ça n'existe pas.

Une fourmi sur une balançoire…

Continuer la comptine…

Balancer bébé d'avant en arrière

238

Voici l'église

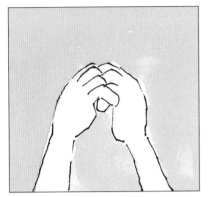

Entrelacer ses doigts

Voici l'église,

Voici le clocher.

Pointer ses index vers le haut

Ouvre les portes,

Ici, tout le monde est réuni.

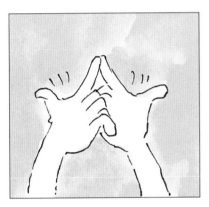

Sortir les pouces et les index

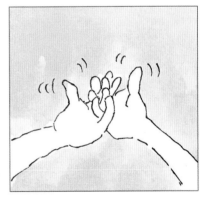

Retourner ses mains et remuer ses doigts

Voici le prêtre montant l'escalier,

Ici, il dit ses prières.

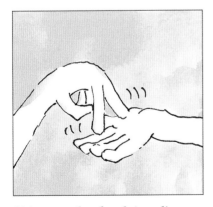

Faire marcher les doigts d'une main sur l'autre main

Placer ses mains paume contre paume

Le chat et la chouette

Un chat et une chouette voguaient sur la mer

Dans un superbe bateau vert.

Ils avaient emporté du miel et beaucoup d'argent,

Parés pour un voyage féerique.

Dans la clarté de la lune et du ciel scintillant,

La chouette devint romantique

Et, au son de sa guitare, se mit à chanter :

« Minou, mon amour ! Minou, mon amour !

Quel chat magnifique tu es !

Minou, mon amour ! Minou, mon amour ! »

Le chat répondit : « Le plus beau des oiseaux, c'est toi !

Et quelle voix charmante, tu as !

Marions-nous ! Nous avons déjà eu trop de patience.

Mais comment ferons-nous pour les alliances ? »

Ils voguèrent plus d'une année

Jusqu'aux Caraïbes et, dès leur arrivée,

Ils rencontrèrent un joli porcelet

Avec un anneau dans le nez,

Dans le nez, dans le nez,

Avec un anneau dans le nez,

« Cher porcelet, voudrais-tu, contre un peu de monnaie,

Nous vendre ton anneau ? » « D'accord », répondit le porcelet.

Ils le prirent et l'antilope, qui n'habitait pas loin,

Les maria le lendemain.

Ils firent un énorme et joyeux festin,

Et burent du thé au jasmin.

Main dans la main, au bord de la lagune,

Ils dansèrent au clair de la lune.

De la lune, de la lune,

Ils dansèrent au clair de la lune.

Louisette

Louisette a perdu sa pochette,
Juliette l'a retrouvée,
Dans la pochette, pas de monnaie,
Mais le ruban qui la fermait.

L'ombrelle de Cendrillon
Est toute mitée, qu'en dira-t-on ?
Quand il pleut, mironton,
Elle en a de gros frissons.

La lampe d'Aladin est bien rouillée,
Et ne brille plus comme elle devrait,
Fâchée de n'être plus astiquée,
Elle crache des ronds de fumée.

Tourne, tourne

Tourne, tourne et touche le sol,

Tourne, tourne et touche le sol,

Tourne, tourne et touche le sol,

Et tombe par terre.

Le bébé dans son berceau

Le bébé dans son berceau,
Dodo, dodo, dodo.

L'horloge sur le buffet,
Tic-tac, tic-tac.

La pluie sur la fenêtre,
Tip-tap-tip, tip-tap-tip,

Mais quand vient le soleil,
Nous tapons des mains !
Clac, clac, clac !

Arrondir les bras

Balancer son bras devant toi

Taper sa main avec un doigt

Taper dans ses mains

DODO

TIC-TAC

TIP-TAP-TIP

CLAC

Ohé du navire !

Par un beau jour d'été, trois petits garçons partirent pique-niquer sur le bord de la rivière. Ils emportèrent leurs affaires de baignade, quelques sandwiches et du fromage, et bien sûr leurs ours en peluche.

Quand ils arrivèrent, ils trouvèrent un petit bateau amarré à un arbre. Emportant leurs ours, les garçons montèrent à bord et jouèrent aux pirates. Chacun subit le supplice de la planche et, les yeux bandés, se retrouva à l'eau. Ils tombèrent tous et continuèrent à jouer et à nager dans la rivière. Ils se poursuivirent en longeant la berge et furent bientôt hors de la vue des ours.

Désormais, les trois ours étaient seuls à bord du bateau et ne se débrouillaient pas très bien pour naviguer. Oscar, un petit ours couleur de miel, était très ami avec Mabelle, qui avait de longs poils bruns, mais aucun des deux n'aimait Toby. Celui-ci était plus gros qu'eux et c'était une brute. Il passait son temps à gronder contre les autres et à leur expliquer ce qu'ils devaient faire.

Dès que les garçons eurent disparu, Toby sauta sur ses pieds. Le bateau tangua. Oscar et Mabelle lui demandèrent de s'asseoir.

« Je suis un marin courageux, s'écria Toby. J'ai navigué sur toutes les mers du monde et, aujourd'hui, je vais naviguer encore. » Il largua les amarres et éloigna le bateau de la rive. Le bateau fit une embardée.

« Allez, matelots. Remuez-vous ! cria Toby. Faites ce que je dis, sinon vous aurez à subir le supplice de la planche. » Maintenant qu'il était détaché, le petit bateau bleu commençait à dériver. Il vira doucement puis, empruntant le courant, il commença à prendre de la vitesse.

« Toby ! s'écria Oscar. Nous bougeons ! »

« Bien sûr que nous bougeons, mauviette ! gronda Toby. Nous sommes des pirates sans peur voguant en haute mer. »

Oscar et Mabelle, effrayés, se blottirent l'un contre l'autre tandis que le bateau descendait la rivière. Les champs et les maisons défilaient sous leurs yeux. « Au secours ! crièrent-ils. Toby, arrête ce bateau. » Mais Toby s'amusait beaucoup.

« Ha, ha, s'écria Toby. Ça, c'est la vie ! »

Oscar regarda par-dessus bord et regretta immédiatement de l'avoir fait. La vue du paysage défilant à toute allure lui donna le mal de mer.

« Regarde, Toby ! cria-t-il. Nous fonçons sur la berge. Redresse le bateau. »

Mais Toby n'en fit rien. La bateau heurta brutalement la rive et Toby tomba en avant. Le bateau pivota et se dirigea de nouveau vers le milieu de la rivière.

« Toby ! cria Mabelle. Sauve-nous ! »

Mais Toby, assis sur ses fesses, frottait une grosse bosse qu'il s'était faite à la tête.

« Je ne peux pas. En fait, je ne sais pas piloter un bateau », gémit-il faiblement. La tête dans les pattes, il se mit à pleurer. Les petits ours, tout apeurés, étaient ballottés d'un bord à l'autre tandis que le bateau zigzaguait sur la rivière. À un moment, la rivière devint plus large et ils commencèrent à entendre le cri des mouettes.

« Oh, Toby, s'écria Mabelle. Fais quelque chose, nous nous dirigeons vers la mer ! »

« Personne ne m'aime, pleurnicha Toby. Maintenant, nous allons faire naufrage, et vous m'aimerez encore moins ! »

Oscar n'écoutait plus. Il avait trouvé un cordage pendant de la voile. « Levons la voile et essayons de regagner le rivage », dit-il.

« Nous allons dériver vers la mer », gémit Toby, mais Oscar ignora la remarque et poursuivit. Le vent commença à gonfler la voile, et le petit bateau se mit en mouvement. Poussé par le vent, il traversa l'estuaire puis accosta enfin sur la plage.

« Bravo, Oscar, tu es un héros ! soupira Mabelle, en l'embrassant. Tu nous as sauvés ! »

Les ours furent alors stupéfaits de découvrir les trois petits garçons courant sur la plage — ils étaient allés chercher les garde-côtes et avaient donné l'alerte. Quand les enfants trouvèrent leurs ours sains et saufs, ce fut une débauche de câlins et d'embrassades. Depuis ce jour mémorable, Toby devint le plus gentil et le plus prudent des ours, et plus jamais il ne tyrannisa ses petits camarades.

Que font mes mains ?

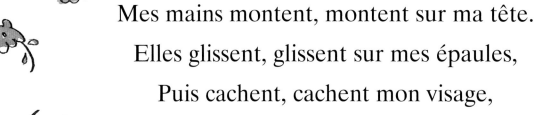

Mes mains montent, montent sur ma tête.

Elles glissent, glissent sur mes épaules,

Puis cachent, cachent mon visage,

Et tombent, tombent sur mes hanches.

Mettre ses mains sur sa tête

… sur ses épaules

… sur son visage

… sur ses hanches

Elles touchent, touchent mes orteils,

Puis s'élancent, s'élancent dans le ciel.

Et moi, je tape, tape trois fois dans mes mains,

Et je me repose en croisant les bras.

Toucher ses orteils

Lever les bras en l'air

Taper trois fois dans ses mains

Croiser les bras

257

Grand-père est couché

Grand-père est couché,

Il ronfle, évitez de le réveiller.

Hier soir, quand il s'est couché,

La tête, il s'est cognée,

Et, ce matin, il refuse de se lever.

Regardez son crâne bosselé.

Aujourd'hui

Aujourd'hui, Paul et moi, nous nous rendons,

Dans le grand champ, pour retrouver Ninon.

Des brassées de lavande, nous allons ramasser,

Pour confectionner de beaux et gros bouquets.

Dans la carriole, nous pourrons chanter,

Il ne manque que les chevaux pour nous emmener.

Le fermier est solitaire

Le fermier est solitaire,

Le fermier est solitaire,

ÈRE, ÈRE !

Le fermier est solitaire,

Le fermier veut une femme,

Le fermier veut une femme,

AME, AME !

Le fermier veut une femme.

La femme veut un enfant,

La femme veut un enfant,

AN, AN, AN !

La femme veut un enfant.

L'enfant veut une nourrice,

L'enfant veut une nourrice,

ISSE, ISSE !

L'enfant veut une nourrice,

La nourrice veut un chien,

La nourrice veut un chien,

UN, UN, UN !

La nourrice veut un chien.

Nous voulons tous caresser le chien,

Nous voulons tous caresser le chien,

IN, IN, IN !

Nous voulons tous caresser le chien.

Trois petits lutins

Un lutin malin tape dans ses mains,

Un lutin mutin touche ses genoux,

Un lutin coquin lève les bras,

Trois lutins divins s'envolent dans le ciel.

Taper des mains en rythme

Toucher ses genoux

Lever les bras

Agiter ses mains levées

LUTIN MALIN

LUTIN MUTIN

LUTIN COQUIN

... DANS LE CIEL

Cinq petits singes

Cinq petits singes sautaient sur le lit,

L'un tomba et la tête s'ouvrit.

Maman appela le docteur, et le docteur dit :

« Sauter sur le lit, aux petits singes est interdit ! »

Quatre petits singes...

Trois petits singes...

Deux petits singes...

Un petit singe...

Répéter ces gestes avec quatre doigts, puis trois, et ainsi de suite

Lever la main

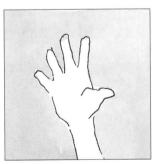

CINQ PETITS SINGES

Toucher sa tête

... LA TÊTE S'OUVRIT

Téléphoner

... APPELA LE DOCTEUR

Remuer son index

C'EST INTERDIT...

Dans la ferme
du vieux Père Bourru

Dans la ferme du vieux Père Bourru,

A...E...I...O...U

Il y a des vaches dodues,

A...E...I...O...U

Et ça fait Meuh ! Meuh ! par-ci,

Et Meuh ! Meuh ! par-là,

Meuh ! Meuh ! ici,

Meuh ! Meuh ! ici et là.

Dans la ferme du vieux Père Bourru,

A...E...I...O...U

Dans la ferme du vieux Père Bourru,

A...E...I...O...U

Il y a des canards au bec pointu,

A...E...I...O...U

Et ça fait Coin ! Coin ! par-ci,

Et Coin ! Coin ! par-là,

Inventer les couplets suivants avec d'autres animaux : le mouton qui fait Bêê ! Bêê ! le chat qui fait Miaou !
Miaou ! le chien qui fait Ouaf ! Ouaf ! etc.
On peut aussi jouer à dire cette comptine de plus en plus vite.

Une mamie à lunettes

Une mamie à lunettes, c'est ma mamie.

Ma mamie à chapeau

Tape dans ses mains, c'est rigolo,

Mains sur les genoux, elle se repose.

Dessiner des cercles autour de ses yeux

Mimer un chapeau

Taper dans ses mains

Poser ses mains sur ses genoux

Un papi à lunettes, c'est mon papi.

Mon papi à chapeau,

Les bras croisés,

Tout doux, il s'est endormi.

Dessiner des cercles autour de ses yeux

Mimer un chapeau

Croiser les bras

Faire semblant de dormir

Souriçotte

Rentrer son index dans son autre main fermée

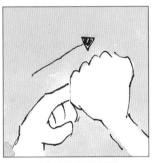

SOURIÇOTTE CAHOTE

Faire sortir son index de l'autre côté

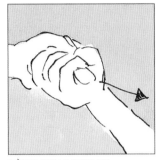

LÈVE SON MUSEAU

Faire trembler son doigt

DE FIÈVRE, ELLE TREMBLOTE

Faire sortir son doigt brusquement

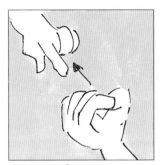

ATCHOUM !

Souriçotte, dans son trou, cahote.

Elle lève son museau qui la picote,

Et dans un mouchoir crachote.

De fièvre, elle tremblote.

Souriçotte est toute pâlotte.

« ATCHOUM ! »

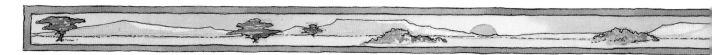

Lion Paresseux

Lion Paresseux sommeillait à l'ombre d'un arbre. Immobile dans l'épaisse chaleur du soleil, il agitait mollement sa queue pour chasser les mouches qui voletaient et bourdonnaient autour de lui.

Lion Paresseux n'aimait rien tant que dormir. S'il avait pu, il aurait dormi jour et nuit, ne se réveillant que de temps en temps pour manger.

« Hmm, se dit-il. Ça, c'est la vie. Ne rien faire, sauf se dorer au soleil et dormir. Idéal ! »

À ce moment-là, une hyène ricanante vint à passer.

« Debout, Lion Paresseux ! gloussa-t-elle. À moins que tu n'aies envie de prendre une douche ! Il va pleuvoir ! »

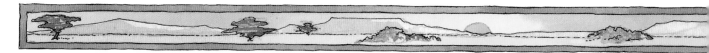

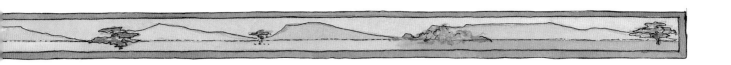

Lion Paresseux ouvrit un œil. « Stupide créature ! » dit-il en reniflant, tandis que la hyène s'éloignait, ricanant toujours. « C'était juste une blague pour me réveiller et me faire bouger ! » bougonna-t-il. Il referma son œil et se rendormit.

Peu de temps après, il sentit une petite tape sur son arrière-train.

« Debout, Lion Paresseux. Il va pleuvoir. » Une girafe, son long cou incliné, lui donnait de petits coups de museau. « Tu devrais songer à trouver un abri. La rivière risque de déborder ! »

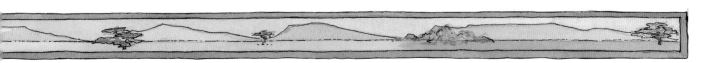

« Ne sois pas ridicule ! dit Lion Paresseux. Je vois que la hyène t'a rempli la tête de ses bêtises ! » et il referma les yeux. Quelques secondes après, il ronflait de nouveau.

Mais, à peine endormi, il sentit quelque chose lui tirer la moustache.

« Debout, Lion Paresseux ! » C'était une petite souris.

« Il va pleuvoir. Pourrais-tu nous emmener à l'abri, mes enfants et moi ? » demanda la souris.

« Oh, je suis bien trop occupé, dit Lion Paresseux. En plus, qu'avez-vous donc tous à parler de pluie ? Il fait beau, il y a du soleil ! » Et, sur ce, il referma les yeux et se rendormit.

Un moment plus tard, il fut réveillé par quelque chose qui lui tirait la queue. C'était un singe.

« Debout, Lion Paresseux ! Il va pleuvoir. Pourrais-tu m'aider à transporter mes bananes jusqu'aux rochers ? »

271

« Pourquoi tout le monde s'acharne-t-il à me réveiller ? demanda sèchement Lion Paresseux. Vous ne voyez donc pas que je suis occupé ? »

« Désolé, Lion Paresseux, mais tu ne sembles pas aussi occupé que moi, » dit le singe.

« Bien sûr que si ! gronda Lion Paresseux. Je suis extrêmement occupé à penser à ce que je vais faire au prochain qui me réveille ! » Et il adressa un regard méchant au singe avant de refermer les yeux et de se rendormir.

Après ça, plus aucun animal ne s'avisa de réveiller Lion Paresseux. Aussi, ils ne purent pas le prévenir que des nuages d'orage approchaient et que la pluie commençait à tomber.

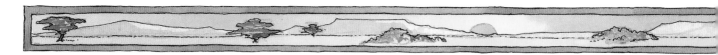

Ils se dépêchèrent seulement de s'abriter sous les rochers et dans des grottes pour se protéger de l'orage.

Toujours couché et en plein rêve, Lion Paresseux eut un frisson. Une grosse goutte de pluie lui tomba sur le nez. Puis une autre, et une autre. Lion Paresseux se retourna. « Oh, zut ! pensa-t-il. Il pleut. Bon, c'est sans doute un grain. Je vais dormir encore un peu. » Et il se rendormit.

Mais la pluie se mit à tomber de plus en plus fort. Bientôt, l'épaisse fourrure de Lion Paresseux fut trempée, et il commença à avoir froid et à être mal à l'aise. Mais il était trop paresseux pour bouger et se réfugier à l'abri des rochers. « Je dors juste cinq minutes encore ! » se dit-il.

Mais, le temps passant, la pluie était de plus en plus violente et la rivière grossissait. Puis, dans un coup de tonnerre assourdissant et un gigantesque éclair, la rivière sortit de son lit et inonda les plaines ! Soudain, Lion Paresseux se retrouva sous l'eau, se débattant pour garder la tête hors des flots déchaînés.

Depuis les rochers où ils s'étaient réfugiés, les autres animaux virent avec effroi Lion Paresseux sous l'eau, entraîné par la force du courant.

Puis soudain, sa grosse tête émergea et il reprit son souffle.

Lion Paresseux nagea de toutes ses forces en direction des rochers, sous les encouragements des autres animaux.

« Oh, que c'est dur ! » dit-il, haletant. Comme il aurait souhaité avoir écouté les autres et n'avoir pas été aussi paresseux.

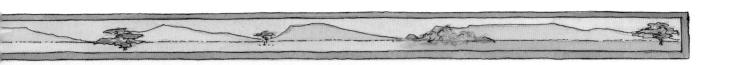

Enfin, trempé et épuisé, il réussit à atteindre les rochers.

Les autres animaux l'entourèrent, inquiets.

« Ça va, Lion Paresseux ? » demanda le singe.

« Je suis éreinté ! » dit Lion Paresseux d'une voix haletante.

Puis il ajouta : « Mais avec une bonne sieste il n'y paraîtra

plus ! »

J'ai vu un serpent serpentant

J'ai vu un serpent serpentant
Et, dans le gazon, ondulant.
J'ai trouvé ça embêtant.

Faire onduler ses mains

Faire des cercles autour de ses yeux

Il m'a regardé avec ses yeux
ouverts tout grand.

Je lui ai dit : « Quitte
ce jardin et va-t-en. »

Va-t-en !

Reprendre au début

« SSSSS »,
dit le serpent serpentant,
Et, dans le gazon, ondulant.

Renard est en retard

Voici la tanière du renard.

Renard, es-tu là ?

Renard est en retard,

Il n'est pas encore là.

Et quelques minutes plus tard,

Coucou ! C'est moi.

*Entrelacer ses doigts en laissant
un trou entre l'index et le majeur*

LA TANIÈRE DU RENARD

*Faire mettre le doigt de l'enfant
dans le trou*

RENARD EST EN RETARD

*Coincer le doigt de l'enfant
entre les siens*

COUCOU !

279

Titou, où étais-tu ?

Titou, où étais-tu ?

Je tâtais à tâtons sous le trône de tante Titine.

Titou, que tentais-tu ?

Je tentais d'attraper un rat tout gras que je prenais pour un tatou.

Dis donc, jeune effronté !

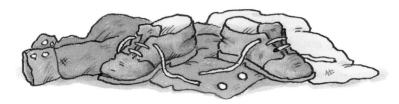

Dis donc, jeune effronté !

Pourquoi t'es-tu couché tout habillé ?

Quand je suis arrivé, j'ai ôté mon premier soulier,

Puis, la fée du sommeil m'a fait tomber.

As-tu déjà vu ?

As-tu déjà vu

Une étoile de mer vêtue d'une brassière ?

Un hippocampe coiffé d'une lampe ?

Un crabe perché sur un baobab ?

Une seiche voyageant en calèche ?

Un poisson-chat mangeant du chocolat ?

Un coquillage portant un tatouage ?

Eh bien, moi, je l'ai vu.

Atchoum !

Ma souris chérie aime les légumes,

Aujourd'hui, elle se mouche et s'enrhume.

Elle éternue, éternue,

Car du fromage, elle a aperçu.

Elle me dit : « Mais, ai-je la berlue ?

De mon allergie, tu étais prévenu.

Hors de ma vue, hors de ma vue ! »

Je crois que j'ai commis une bévue.

La capucine

Dansons la capucine

Y'a pas de pain chez nous,

Y'en a chez la voisine

Mais ce n'est pas pour nous.

YOU !!!

Pour un sou

Pour un sou, j'ai mangé un bol de riz au lait.

Pour deux sous, j'ai mangé une crème au café.

Pour trois sous, j'ai mangé des macarons sucrés.

Pour quatre sous...

Pour cinq sous...

Faire sauter l'enfant sur ses genoux et continuer avec quatre sous, cinq sous, etc.

Magali aime trop son lit

Magali, sors de ton lit,

Magali, sors de ton lit,

Oui ou non, Magali chérie,

Vas-tu sortir enfin du lit ?

Il est six heures passées, quitte ton oreiller,

Le soleil a pointé son nez, le soleil s'est levé.

Magali, sors de ton lit,

Magali, sors de ton lit,

Oui ou non, Magali chérie,

Vas-tu sortir enfin du lit ?

Il est sept heures passées, derrière tes rideaux,
Le soleil brille, le soleil est déjà haut.

Magali, sors de ton lit,
Magali, sors de ton lit,
Oui ou non, Magali chérie,
Vas-tu sortir enfin du lit ?

Il est huit heures passées, la cloche de l'école a sonné,
Et tu n'as toujours pas quitté ton lit douillet !

Mademoiselle la Lune

Mademoiselle la Lune, ce soir, sourit,

Et veille sur le sommeil des petits.

Elle a éteint les arcs-en-ciel

Et allumé les étoiles au firmament.

Si les enfants rêvent, c'est grâce à elle

Car, dans leurs oreilles,

Elle murmure des contes charmants.

Si, dans leurs songes, ils jouent à la marelle,

Sautent à la corde ou escaladent des murs géants,

C'est grâce à la lune, cette belle demoiselle.

Voici un beau gâteau

Voici un beau gâteau,
Un beau gâteau doré,
Voici un beau gâteau.
Un beau gâteau doré.

Bercer l'enfant

Faire sauter l'enfant doucement

Voici de bons bonbons,
De bons bonbons,
De toutes les couleurs,
Voici de bons bonbons.

Voici de belles bougies,
Voici de belles bougies,
Souffle-les,
Pff, PFF, PFF!

Souffler !

290

Petit Ange

Petit Ange a sa fourchette et son couteau,

Et sa table Petit Ange,

Et son miroir Petit Ange.

Petit Ange a son berceau,

Tout doux, tout doux, tout doux…

Entrelacer les doigts, paume de la main devant

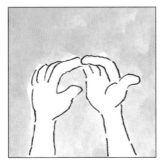

COUTEAU ET FOURCHETTE

Retourner les mains et simuler une table

TABLE

Joindre les deux index

MIROIR

Joindre les index et les auriculaires

BERCEAU

« À ce propos d'ailleurs, il serait temps qu'on en mette un nouveau », grommela-t-il. Ficelle continua à râler toute la matinée.

« S'il n'arrête pas de se plaindre, je vais lui fourrer mon chapeau dans la bouche », murmura le soldat dans l'oreille du clown, depuis l'étagère sur laquelle ils étaient assis.

« Si je n'y mets pas mes balles de jonglage avant ! » dit le clown. Tous les jouets éclatèrent de rire.

« Il est temps que nous lui donnions une leçon, dit Paméla la poupée. Que pourrions-nous faire pour qu'il arrête de rouspéter ? »

« Et si nous lui collions un morceau de sparadrap sur la bouche pendant qu'il dort ? » gazouilla la chouette, futée.

« C'est une excellente idée ! » dit Paméla, et tout le monde approuva.

Cette nuit-là, pendant que Ficelle dormait, Paméla prit un morceau de sparadrap dans la salle de bain et le colla solidement sur la bouche du ronchon. Tous les jouets étaient ravis – ils allaient enfin avoir la paix et être tranquilles !

Le lendemain matin, le réveil sonna et Cathy se rendit à la salle de bain. Ficelle ouvrit son œil et s'apprêtait à ronchonner parce que le réveil continuait à sonner, quand il se rendit compte qu'il ne pouvait pas ouvrir la bouche !

Il crispa, étira et tordit son visage autant qu'il le put mais il ne réussit pas à ouvrir la bouche. Puis il remarqua que tous les jouets l'observaient. Quand il se regarda dans le miroir, découvrir le sparadrap le rendit furieux ! Il l'arracha et se tourna vers ses camarades, très en colère.

« Qui a fait ça ? rugit-il. Quand je trouverai celui qui a fait ça, il va y avoir du grabuge ! Vous n'avez aucun respect pour un vieil ours. » Il allait et venait en tout sens. Son visage était devenu cramoisi et il avait l'air fou de rage. Les jouets commençaient à être un peu inquiets.

Puis, alors qu'il tempêtait de plus en plus, il se passa une drôle de chose. Sa voix commença à se casser. Il essaya de s'éclaircir la gorge mais cela ne servit à rien. Il était complètement aphone !

« Cela t'apprendra ! dit Paméla. Tout ce que tu sais faire, c'est ronchonner et rouspéter, et nous en avons assez de t'entendre. Nous t'avons mis du sparadrap sur la bouche pour te donner une leçon. Et maintenant tu as tellement bougonné que tu as perdu ta voix. »

Une grosse larme coula sur la joue de Ficelle. Il n'était pas si fort, au fond. Il ne s'était pas rendu compte qu'il ronchonnait tant et il en était vraiment désolé.

Paméla n'aimait pas voir Ficelle si triste. Tous les jouets se sentaient un peu coupables de ce qu'ils avaient fait.

« Je vais aller te chercher du miel dans la cuisine, dit Paméla. Cela apaisera ta gorge. Mais tu dois me promettre de ne pas recommencer à te plaindre. »

Quand Paméla eut donné une cuillerée de miel à Ficelle, il murmura : « Je suis désolé. Je vous promets que je vais essayer de ne plus me plaindre. Je ne m'étais pas rendu compte que j'étais devenu un vieux ours aussi bougon. »

Sur ce, tous les jouets embrassèrent Ficelle et Paméla lui donna encore du miel.

Depuis, Ficelle a vraiment essayé de ne plus bougonner. Et, quand il commence à le faire, il repense au morceau de sparadrap et s'arrête tout de suite, avant que quelqu'un ne l'ait entendu ! Et ses camarades les jouets font tout ce qu'ils peuvent pour prendre soin de lui et pour le rendre heureux.

Mon petit oiseau

Mon petit oiseau a pris sa volée !

Mon petit oiseau a pris sa volée !

A pris sa, à la volette,

A pris sa, à la volette,

A pris sa volée.

Joindre les pouces et faire onduler ses mains

MON PETIT OISEAU

Agiter ses mains...

A PRIS SA VOLÉE

et les élever ...

À LA VOLETTE

aussi haut que possible

A PRIS SA VOLÉE

Deux petits oiseaux

Coller un petit bout de papier sur chaque index

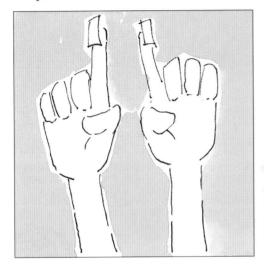

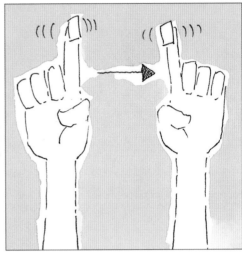

Lever les doigts et les faire bouger

Deux petits oiseaux

Assis sur un mur,

L'un s'appelait Kiki,

Et l'autre Coco.

Cacher un bras derrière le dos

Cacher l'autre bras et sortir le premier

Kiki s'envola !

Coco en fit autant !

Kiki revint,

Coco en fit autant.

Pour fabriquer un garçon

Pour fabriquer un petit garçon,

Prenez quelques limaçons,

Un escargot et deux cornichons,

Ajoutez des grenouilles et un peu de citron.

Voici un beau petit garçon.

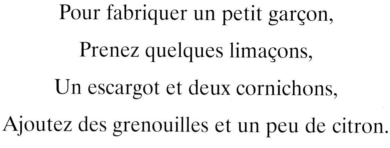

Pour fabriquer une petite fille,

Prenez quelques myrtilles,

Des fraises et de la camomille,

Ajoutez du sucre, du miel et de la vanille.

Voici une belle petite fille.

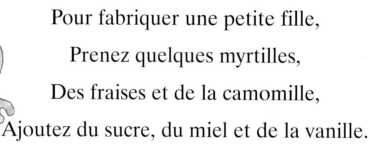

302

Je suis un pauvre petit chat

Une jolie petite fille est ma maîtresse,

Elle a de belles boucles blondes et parfois des tresses.

Elle est souvent douce et gentille,

Mais parfois, pour une peccadille,

Elle ne l'est vraiment pas.

Je suis un pauvre petit chat.

Papa est parti

Papa est parti,

Au milieu de la nuit.

Sur un joli bateau, il a embarqué.

Il vogue toutes voiles levées.

Quand il reviendra

Du poisson, Papa rapportera.

Quand il arrivera au port

Moi, je dormirai encore.

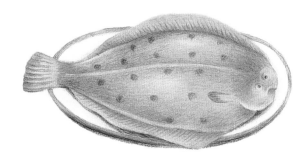

Monsieur l'ambassadeur

Monsieur l'ambassadeur était assis sur un mur,

Une bourrasque de vent le fit tomber sur le sol dur,

En mille morceaux, il s'est cassé,

Personne n'a jamais pu le réparer.

Les jolies dames vont à cheval

Les jolies dames vont à cheval,

Doucement, doucement.

Les beaux messieurs vont à cheval,

Sautillant, sautillant.

C'est le fermier sur son cheval,

Galopant, galopant.

Et le boucher sur son cheval,

Tout fringant, tout pimpant.

Et flop ! dans le fossé...

Rigolons, rigolant !

Faire sauter l'enfant de plus en plus vite à mesure que le rythme s'accélère, et le laisser glisser entre ses genoux au dernier vers...

Cinq canetons

Cinq canetons sur la mare nageaient,

Si loin qu'ils se retrouvèrent de l'autre côté.

Maman Canard cria : « Coin-coin ! Coin-coin ! »

En voici quatre, il en manque un.

Continuer avec quatre, trois, deux canetons…

Un caneton sur la mare nageait,

Si loin qu'il se retrouva de l'autre côté.

Maman Canard cria : « Coin-coin ! Coin-coin ! »

En voici cinq, tout finit bien.

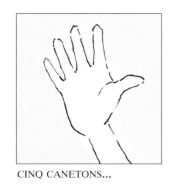

CINQ CANETONS…

SI LOIN

COIN-COIN !

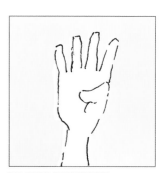

QUATRE CANETONS

Flip-Flap la grenouille

« Coâ ! Coâ ! Regardez-moi ! » coassa Flip-Flap, la grenouille sautillante, en bondissant dans des gerbes d'eau de nénuphar en nénuphar. « Je suis la grenouille la plus vive du monde ! Coâ ! Coâ ! »

« Coin-coin ! cancanait Mère Canard. Cette grenouille est vraiment une calamité. Elle ne regarde jamais où elle va et ne s'inquiète pas de savoir qui elle éclabousse. »

« C'est assez épouvantable, approuva Baron, le cygne. Et elle fait tant de bruit qu'il est même parfois impossible de s'entendre soi-même ! »

Mais Flip-Flap n'écoutait pas. Elle était bien trop occupée à bondir aussi haut qu'elle le pouvait sur les nénuphars.

« Venez, venez ! cria-t-elle aux petits canetons. Venez par ici, nous allons faire un concours de plongeon ! »

Les canetons étaient tout excités et remuaient la queue de joie en rejoignant Flip-Flap. Ils se mirent à tout éclabousser autour d'eux en s'ébattant et en plongeant dans la mare.

« Elle a vraiment une influence désastreuse sur nos petits, dit Mère Canard. Si seulement nous pouvions faire quelque chose. »

« Ce n'est sans doute que de la bonne humeur juvénile, dit Baron. Bientôt, elle grandira et se calmera. »

Mais ce ne fut pas le cas, bien au contraire, son agitation empirait. Elle était capable de réveiller tout le monde dès potron-minet en chantant à tue-tête de sa voix coassante :

« Voici le petit jour, c'est l'heure de jouer, hip, hip, hip, hourra ! » Et elle pouvait, dès l'aube, bondir en tout sens, faisant sortir les canards et les cygnes de leurs nids, tirant Lapinot de son terrier et hurlant dans la cachette des campagnols. Bien sûr, Flip-Flap se croyait une grenouille amicale et sympathique. Elle ne se rendait pas compte que plus personne ne la supportait.

« Je suis pourtant d'accord pour qu'on s'amuse un peu, dit le campagnol. Mais la jeune Flip-Flap va toujours trop loin. »

Puis un jour, Flip-Flap apparut, encore plus excitée que d'habitude.

« Écoutez tous, cria-t-elle. Un concours de saut va être organisé de l'autre côté de la mare. Toutes les grenouilles, à des kilomètres à la ronde, vont venir y participer. Mais je suis sûre de gagner parce que je suis la grenouille la plus agile du monde ! » Sur ce, elle sauta en l'air très haut, juste pour prouver qu'elle disait vrai.

Le jour du concours arriva et tout le monde se rassembla de l'autre côté de la mare pour assister au spectacle. Flip-Flap n'avait jamais vu autant de grenouilles rassemblées au même endroit.

« Attendez de voir comme je peux sauter haut ! » dit-elle bondissante et terriblement excitée.

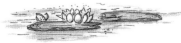

Mais, à la grande surprise de Flip-Flap, toutes les grenouilles savaient sauter haut et loin. Acclamées par la foule, elles sautaient gracieusement au-dessus des nénuphars.

Si elle voulait gagner, Flip-Flap allait devoir sauter plus haut et plus loin qu'elle ne l'avait jamais fait. Enfin, ce fut son tour. « Bonne chance ! » crièrent les canetons.

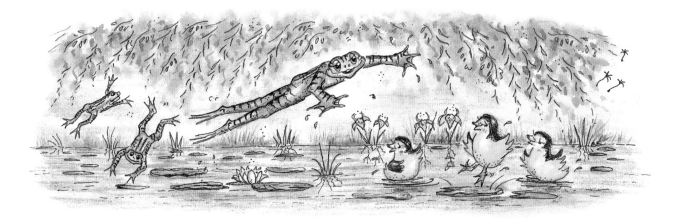

Flip-Flap prit place sur la ligne de départ, rassembla toutes ses forces, sauta très haut, fendant l'air, et passa la ligne d'arrivée, jusqu'à ce que – GULP ! Elle atterrit directement sur le brochet rusé qui attendait bouche grande ouverte. Comme d'habitude, Flip-Flap n'avait pas regardé dans quelle direction elle allait !

Le vilain brochet ne fit qu'une bouchée de Flip-Flap,
puis plongea et disparut sous l'eau. Tout le monde cherchait,
consterné – il n'y avait rien à faire. Flip-Flap avait disparu.

Quoi qu'il en soit, il n'y avait aucun doute. C'est Flip-Flap
qui avait sauté le plus haut et le plus loin.

« Je déclare Flip-Flap vainqueur », dit d'un air abattu
Globule, le crapaud, qui avait organisé le concours. Et tout le
monde rentra à la maison, dépité et triste.

Après cet épisode, l'ambiance fut beaucoup plus calme
pour tous les habitants de la mare.

Mais au lieu de se réjouir de cette paix retrouvée, ils regrettaient l'absence de Flip-Flap.

« C'était une petite grenouille joyeuse », dit Baron.

« Elle manque terriblement à mes petits, dit Mère Canard. Elle s'occuperait d'eux si elle était là. »

Mais dans le fond de la mare, le brochet se lamentait sur son sort. Il pensait avoir été très habile en attrapant cette grenouille, mais depuis il avait une terrible indigestion. En effet, Flip-Flap, même à l'intérieur de l'estomac du vilain poisson, passait encore son temps à bondir en tout sens ! Le brochet monta à la surface de l'eau et ouvrit grand la bouche pour aspirer une bouffée d'air frais. À ce moment-là, Flip-Flap en profita pour bondir à l'extérieur !

Tout le monde fut enchanté de la revoir et l'acclama. Elle fut déclarée vainqueur du concours de saut et on lui remit une médaille.

« C'est merveilleux, dit Flip-Flap. Mais j'ai retenu la leçon – désormais, je vais faire attention avant de sauter ! » et elle continua à sauter et à bondir avec les canetons, mais plus calmement.

Où allez-vous, jolie demoiselle ?

Où allez-vous, jolie demoiselle ?

Où allez-vous, jolie demoiselle ?

Je vais traire les vaches, Monsieur, dit-elle,

Monsieur, dit-elle, Monsieur, dit-elle,

Je vais traire les vaches, Monsieur, dit-elle.

Puis-je vous accompagner, jolie demoiselle ?

Puis-je vous accompagner, jolie demoiselle ?

Soyez le bienvenu, Monsieur, dit-elle,

Monsieur, dit-elle, Monsieur, dit-elle,

Soyez le bienvenu, Monsieur, dit-elle.

Quelle est votre richesse, jolie demoiselle ?

Quelle est votre richesse, jolie demoiselle ?

Mon visage est ma richesse, Monsieur, dit-elle,

Monsieur, dit-elle, Monsieur, dit-elle,

Mon visage est ma richesse, Monsieur, dit-elle.

Je peux donc vous épouser, jolie demoiselle

Je peux donc vous épouser, jolie demoiselle,

Personne ne vous l'a demandé, Monsieur, dit-elle,

Monsieur, dit-elle, Monsieur, dit-elle,

Personne ne vous l'a demandé, Monsieur, dit-elle.

Tout sale est mon minois

Tout sale est mon minois,

Tout sale est mon minois,

Je le brosse, le frotte et le nettoie,

Je le brosse, le frotte et le nettoie,

Tout sale est mon minois.

Mimer les actions.
Continuer avec les mains, les genoux et les pieds.

En rythme, tape dans tes mains

Tape dans tes mains, tape dans tes mains,

En rythme, tape dans tes mains.

Touche tes épaules, touche tes épaules,

En rythme, touche tes épaules.

Frappe tes genoux, frappe tes genoux,

En rythme, frappe tes genoux.

Secoue la tête, secoue la tête,

En rythme, secoue la tête.

Tape dans tes mains, tape dans tes mains,

Puis repose-toi.

Un petit homme biscornu

Il était un petit homme biscornu

Qui marchait sur une route biscornue,

Il passa sous un arbre biscornu,

Planté dans un jardin biscornu.

Il apportait un chat tout biscornu,

Qui avait pris une souris biscornue,

À son voisin très biscornu,

Dans sa maison biscornue.

L'ambassadeur de la lune

L'ambassadeur de la Lune,

Sur la Terre, était tombé.

À Morlaix, il voulait aller,

Mais se perdit. Quelle infortune !

Il s'adressa à deux lapins,

Qui lui indiquèrent le chemin.

Dors, petit bébé

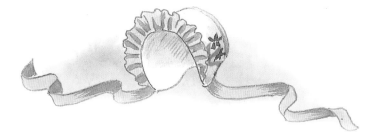

Dors petit bébé, dors dans ton berceau,

Quand le vent soufflera, le berceau balancera.

Ne crains rien, je veille sur toi,

Dors petit bébé, dors dans ton berceau.

Cinq petits soldats

Des cinq petits soldats du roi,
Au garde-à-vous, ils étaient trois,

Et deux ne l'étaient pas.
Quand le capitaine passa,
Que crois-tu qu'il arriva ?
Au garde-à-vous,
Ils étaient TOUS là.

Lever les cinq doigts

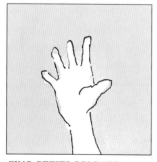

CINQ PETITS SOLDATS

Replier deux doigts

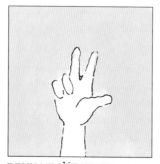

DEUX NE L'ÉTAIENT PAS

*Passer l'index de l'autre
main devant la première*

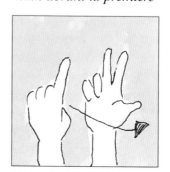

LE CAPITAINE PASSA

Dresser tous les doigts

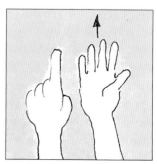

ILS ÉTAIENT TOUS LÀ

Voici le commandant

Voici le commandant,

Et ses deux soldats,

Voici un coq,

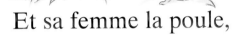

Et sa femme la poule,

Voici leurs poussins,

Ils se cachent ici,

Picoti,
Picoton,
Ceci est mon
menton

329

Sacrés petits ours !

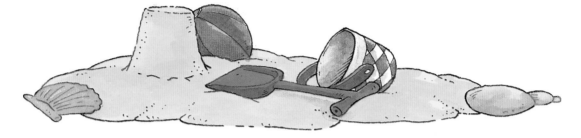

Par une belle journée d'été, les parents de Ben et de Basile dirent à leurs enfants de préparer leurs affaires de baignade pour aller à la plage.

« Youpi ! dit Ben. Pouvons-nous emporter nos ours ? »

« Du moment que vous les surveillez, dit Papa. Il n'est pas question que nous passions notre temps à les chercher si vous les perdez de nouveau ! »

Ben et Basile emportaient leurs ours partout mais ils les perdaient tout le temps et c'était alors, pour tout le monde, une interminable battue pour les retrouver. Mais la vérité, c'était que, lorsque personne ne les surveillait, ces vilains petits ours s'échappaient en quête de sensations fortes et d'aventure.

Ce ne serait pas différent aujourd'hui. Toute la famille arriva à la plage et déballa les affaires. Papa se mit à lire le journal et Maman sortit un livre. Aussitôt, Ben et Basile commencèrent à faire des pâtés de sable. Quand les vilains ours virent que personne ne les regardait, ils s'échappèrent en pouffant de rire, pour courir sur la plage.

« Allons explorer les environs, dit Billy, qui était le plus âgé. Je vois une grotte là-bas. » Il pointa du doigt un trou noir creusé dans les rochers proches de l'eau.

« Cet endroit a l'air un peu sombre et inquiétant », dit Bella.

« Courage, dit Billy. Tu es une ourse et tous les ours aiment les grottes sombres ! »

Les petits ours escaladèrent les rochers et entrèrent dans la grotte. Elle était très profonde et obscure. Bella aperçut un objet brillant sur le sol. Elle le ramassa et le montra à Billy.

« De l'or ! s'écria Billy, tout excité, en prenant la pièce dans la main de Bella. C'est peut-être une grotte de brigands ! Peut-être les brigands sont-ils dans les parages. Allons voir ! »

« Non ! dit Bella. Ils peuvent être dangereux. Allons-nous-en. » Elle tourna les talons et courut vers la sortie. Elle vit alors avec horreur que, pendant leur exploration, la mer était montée et avait isolé les rochers de la plage.

« Billy ! appela-t-elle. Viens vite, nous sommes coincés ! »
Pendant ce temps, Ben et Basile avaient fini de faire des pâtés de sable et s'étaient aperçus de l'absence des petits ours.

« Oh, non, gémit Papa. Pas encore ! »

Toute la famille entreprit de chercher le long de la plage, mais il n'y avait aucune trace des ours. « Peut-être sont-ils allés prendre un bain », dit Basile, la voix tremblante à cette idée.

Revenus à la grotte, les vilains petits ours aperçurent leurs propriétaires les cherchant partout. Ils sautèrent sur place en agitant les pattes. « Ce n'est pas la peine, dit Bella, ils ne peuvent pas nous voir. Nous sommes trop petits. »

« Ne t'inquiète pas », dit Billy, essayant de se montrer plus brave qu'il n'était.

À ce moment-là, deux hommes sortirent de derrière les rochers. Les ours se figèrent sur place – peut-être étaient-ils des brigands ! Ils tremblaient de peur lorsque les hommes les attrapèrent, descendirent des rochers et les jetèrent dans un petit bateau qu'ils n'avaient pas vu. Les ours tombèrent dans le fond du bateau et les hommes embarquèrent et commencèrent à ramer. Mais où les emmenaient-ils ?

Au bout d'un moment, le bateau s'immobilisa et les deux hommes sautèrent sur la plage. Ils attrapèrent les ours et les levèrent au-dessus de leur tête en criant : « Quelqu'un a-t-il perdu des ours ? »

Tout le monde sur la plage leva les yeux, et Ben et Basile coururent pour aller récupérer les ours.

« Merci, dit Papa. Nous avions cherché partout. »

« Nous les avons trouvés dans une grotte », dit l'un des hommes, pointant son doigt vers les rochers. « Vos enfants ont dû les abandonner là-bas. »

« Mais ce n'est pas possible, ils ont fait des pâtés de sable tout l'après-midi… » dit Papa, perplexe.

Personne ne sut jamais comment les vilains ours étaient allés dans la grotte ni d'où venait la petite pièce d'or qui se trouvait dans la poche de Billy. Mais depuis, Papa exige qu'ils restent à la maison. Les deux garnements ne se plaignent pas. Ils ont vécu assez d'aventures pour le moment. Et ils passent beaucoup de temps à jouer à cache-cache, leur jeu favori !

Je suis musicien

Je suis musicien,

Et je m'appelle Zinzolin.

Je viens de très loin,

Bien plus loin que Pékin.

J'ai joué du clavecin,

Mais j'ai appris d'un mandarin

Que le piano console

tous les chagrins.

Je suis musicien,

Et je m'appelle Zinzolin.

Je viens de très loin,

Bien plus loin que Pékin.

J'ai joué du violoncelle,

Mais j'ai appris à La Rochelle

Que le tambour séduit

les demoiselles.

Je suis musicien,

Et je m'appelle Zinzolin.

Je viens de très loin,

Bien plus loin que Pékin.

J'ai joué du hautbois.

Mais j'ai appris d'un Bavarrois,

Que la trompette réjouis

les villageois.

Je suis musicien,

Et je m'appelle Zinzolin.

Je viens de très loin,

Bien plus loin que Pékin.

Avec mes mains

Avec mes mains,

Que puis-je découvrir ?

Voici mon crâne,

Et dans mon crâne,

Mon cerveau,

Et dans mon cerveau,

Tous mes rêves.

C'est l'école qui me l'a appris.

Avec mes mains,

Que puis-je découvrir ?

Voici mes paupières,

Et sous mes paupières,

Mes yeux,

Et dans mes yeux,

De beaux paysages.

C'est l'école qui me l'a appris.

Avec mes mains,

que puis-je découvrir ?

Voici mon visage,

Et sur mon visage,

Mon nez,

Et dans mon nez,

Des odeurs de bonbon.

C'est l'école qui me l'a appris.

Avec mes mains,

que puis-je découvrir ?

Voici ma cage thoracique,

Et dans ma cage thoracique,

Mes poumons,

Et dans mes poumons,

L'air que je respire.

C'est l'école qui me l'a appris.

Martin Madame

Monsieur Martin Madame sur la mer a embarqué,

Des boucles d'argent sur ses souliers.

En revenant, il m'a épousée.

Madame Martine Martin Madame, je suis désormais.

Petit Jacques Cancoin

Petit Jacques Cancoin,

Est assis dans un coin,

Mangeant une tourte aux prunes.

Ah ! dit-il, En voilà une !

Toutes les prunes, il goûte,

Mais entière, il laisse la croûte.

Justin et Justine

Justin et Justine descendent la colline
Où ils ont rempli leur baquet d'eau.
Justin tombe, l'eau dégouline,
Et Justine valdingue sur le dos.

Justin et Justine descendent la colline
Roulant-boulant comme des bobines.
Doucement, ils iront la prochaine fois.
On se demande pourquoi.

La théière de ma mère

La théière de ma mère,

Est une théière particulière.

Ronde comme une montgolfière,

Elle ressemble à une aiguière

Et chauffe comme une chaudière.

Elle était dans le placard de grand-mère,

Qui était bijoutière.

Grand-mère l'a offerte à ma mère,

Car cette théière vraiment particulière

Se moquait des cafetières.

Purée de pois cassés

Purée de pois cassés chauffée,

Purée de pois cassés glacée,

Purée de pois cassés fouettée,

Purée de pois cassés.

Certains l'aiment chauffée,

Certains l'aiment glacée,

Certains l'aiment fouettée,

La purée de pois cassés.

La chanson de quat' sous

C'est une chanson de quat' sous,

Pour un joli soufflé doré

Où un malin cuisinier

Cacha quelques merles filous.

Au moment de servir le pâté

Les oiseaux se mirent à chanter,

N'était-ce pas un plat de choix

Digne d'un très grand roi ?

Alors, extrêmement perplexe, Monsieur Lapin rentra chez lui.

« On dirait que tout le monde sait qui est le voleur, mais personne ne veut rien dire ! » dit Monsieur Lapin à sa femme.

« Pas tout le monde, chéri, dit-elle. Moi, je ne sais pas. Tout ce que je sais, c'est que demain c'est l'anniversaire de nos enfants et que nous devons leur faire une surprise. » Dépités et intrigués, ils allèrent se coucher, déterminés à trouver la clé du mystère le lendemain matin.

Le lendemain, les petits lapins se rendirent en courant dans la cuisine, où leurs parents avaient préparé le petit déjeuner.

« Bon anniversaire à tout le monde ! » cria Flocon.

« Joyeux anniversaire ! » s'écrièrent les autres petits lapins.

« Ce n'est pas grand-chose mais je voulais offrir une surprise à chacun de vous ! poursuivit Flocon. J'espère que tu ne m'en voudras pas, Papa. » Sur ce, Flocon sortit une botte de belles carottes appétissantes entourée d'un joli nœud, et il en offrit une à chacun de ses frères et sœurs.

« Hé ! s'écria Moustache, j'ai eu la même idée ! » et il sortit une autre botte de carottes.

« Moi aussi ! » dit Câline.

« Moi aussi ! » dit Cannelle.

« Moi aussi ! » dit Muscade.

Il y eut bientôt un monceau de belles carottes sur la table de la cuisine.

« Voilà donc ce qui est arrivé à mes carottes ! s'écria Monsieur Lapin, stupéfait. Je croyais qu'on me les avait volées ! » Et quand il raconta l'histoire ils se mirent à rire aux larmes. Puis Madame Lapin enfila son tablier et mit tout le monde à la porte.

« Laissez-moi les carottes, dit-elle. J'ai moi aussi une surprise d'anniversaire en réserve ! »

Ainsi le mystère était résolu. Il s'avéra que Lièvre Gourmand avait vu les petits lapins les uns après les autres se faufiler et ramasser les carottes quand ils pensaient que personne ne pouvait les voir. Lièvre Gourmand savait que c'était leur anniversaire et devinait ce qu'ils étaient en train de faire. Il l'avait dit à ses camarades de la forêt et tout le monde avait trouvé ça très drôle.

Monsieur Lapin avait honte de s'être mis en colère, alors que chacun gardait juste le secret. Pour se faire pardonner sa mauvaise humeur, il invita tout le monde l'après-midi même pour un thé spécial anniversaire, ce qui fut une délicieuse surprise pour les petits lapins.

Et bien sûr, le moment le plus apprécié de la journée fut l'arrivée de Madame Lapin sortant de la cuisine avec, dans les bras… un énorme gâteau aux carottes !

Le vent du nord

Le vent du nord,
Souffle encore.
Le petit rouge-gorge, gelé,
Doit au plus vite s'abriter.
Pauvre rouge-gorge.

Il devra quitter sa branche,
Se réfugier dans la grange,
Et enfouir sa tête mouillée
Sous son aile frigorifiée.
Pauvre rouge-gorge.

Le soleil
a chassé la pluie

Le soleil a chassé la pluie,

Rangez vos parapluies.

Le petit rouge-gorge sourit,

Au ciel qui désormais bleuit.

Sèche mes plumes, Monsieur Soleil,

Et allume des arcs-en-ciel !

Un, deux, trois

Un, deux, trois,

J'ai pêché un poisson-chat.

Quatre, cinq, six,

Dans la rivière, je l'ai remis.

Pourquoi as-tu fait ça ?

Parce qu'il m'a mordu le doigt !

Quel doigt a-t-il pris ?

Celui-ci, le tout petit.

Le lion
et la licorne

Un lion et une licorne

Se battaient pour la couronne.

Le lion obligea la licorne

À quitter la cité qu'il revendiquait.

Certains, conquis par son unique corne,

Donnèrent à la licorne un peu de lait,

D'autres lui apportèrent du pain

Et l'accompagnèrent très loin.

Patti, pataud

Patti, pataud,

Qu'il est lent, qu'il est gros,

Patti, pataud,

Qu'il est lourdaud.

Remue la queue,

Une, deux, une, deux,

L'éléphanteau

Deux enfants sur son dos.

Patti, pataud,

Qu'il est lent, qu'il est gros.

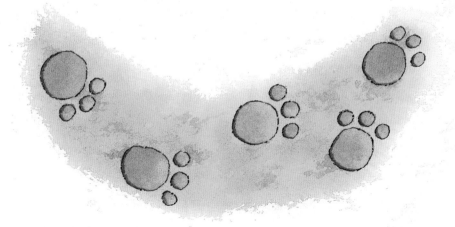

Petit mouton

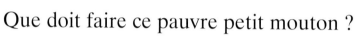

Petit mouton ne peut pas s'endormir,

Il ne peut empêcher ses paupières de s'ouvrir !

Il tourne, vire et fait des bonds.

Que doit faire ce pauvre petit mouton ?

Une vieille chouette futée,

Vint à passer et dit d'un ton pincé :

« Stupide mouton, tu es un godichon,

Pour dormir, compte donc les moutons ! »

« Sept, quatre, treize, dix-sept,

Je me suis trompé, je dois recommencer... »

Jusqu'au matin, il compta et resta éveillé,

Mais il ne savait toujours pas compter!

Le chant
de la girafe

Il est merveilleux d'avoir un long cou élancé,

Il peut voir partout car il est haut perché.

Je peux les feuilles des cimes attraper,

Et dans le ciel avec les oiseaux bavarder.

Il est merveilleux d'avoir un long cou élancé,

À des kilomètres d'ici, je peux observer

Pour savoir où mes amis sont allés,

Et où le meilleur repas ils ont trouvé.

Il est merveilleux d'avoir un long cou élancé,

Je ne dois cependant pas jubiler,

Car ce fut, un jour, une calamité,

Quand une angine m'a terrassée !

Petit berger

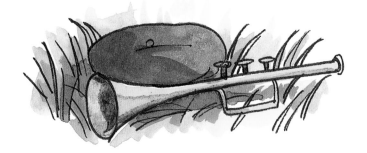

Petit berger, où es-tu allé ?

Les vaches piétinent le maïs et les moutons le blé.

Le croiriez-vous qu'il soit si fatigué,

Que, dans le champ, il soit couché ?

Qui ira le réveiller ?

Sûrement pas moi, je le ferais pleurer.

Un cavalier dans la cité

Un cavalier dans la cité est arrivé,

Sur un cheval blanc, il était monté.

Il a levé son chapeau à plume et l'a fait tomber.

Tout le monde, de lui, s'est alors moqué.

Le chagrin de Vieil Ours

« Boo hoo ! Je veux rentrer à la maison ! »

Alors qu'une petite fée nommée Cybelle voletait, en se bouchant le nez, au-dessus d'une décharge à ordures, elle entendit un son parfaitement reconnaissable provenant d'un tas de détritus très malodorant.

« Cela ressemble bien à des pleurs d'ours, se dit-elle. Je ferais bien d'y aller et de voir si je peux être utile. »

Elle descendit donc pour jeter un coup d'œil et, là, sur un tas d'épluchures de pommes de terre et de peaux de bananes, était assis un ours très âgé et semblant désespéré. Cybelle s'assit et lui tint la patte pendant qu'il lui racontait ce qui lui était arrivé :

« La petite fille à qui j'appartiens, Mathilde, a été obligée de ranger sa chambre. Elle est très désordonnée mais elle est gentille et douce, dit Vieil Ours en reniflant. Elle m'a jeté par erreur avec une vieille couverture – elle ne s'est pas rendu compte que j'étais en train de dormir à l'intérieur.

Puis des hommes dans un gros camion sale sont arrivés et ont vidé la poubelle jetant les détritus ici et moi avec. Mais je veux rentrer chez moi ! » Et Vieil Ours fondit de nouveau en larmes.

« Là, là, dit Cybelle. Je vais t'aider à rentrer chez toi. Mais d'abord, j'ai besoin que tu me donnes deux larmes. » Elle ouvrit le couvercle d'un petit bocal et recueillit deux grosses larmes salées qui coulaient sur les joues du vieil ours.

« Pourquoi as-tu besoin de ces larmes ? » demanda Vieil Ours, un peu surpris.

« Juste un petit tour de magie ! dit Cybelle. Maintenant, attends-moi ici et je te promets de revenir très vite. » Et elle disparut d'un petit coup de baguette magique.

Vieil Ours s'enroula dans la couverture et resta assis, tentant d'être courageux et de ne pas pleurer. Il resta ainsi toute la nuit. Il avait froid, se sentait seul et avait peur. Comme il aurait voulu déjà être rentré au chaud dans sa maison douillette.

Pendant ce temps, Cybelle était très occupée. Elle voletait de-ci de-là dans tout le voisinage, jusqu'au moment où elle entendit des sanglots s'échappant d'une fenêtre ouverte. Elle descendit et se posa sur le rebord de la fenêtre et regarda à l'intérieur de la maison. Une petite fille était allongée sur son lit, sa maman assise près d'elle.

« Je veux mon ours ! » sanglotait la petite fille.

« Mais Mathilde, si tu n'étais pas aussi désordonnée, tu ne perdrais pas toujours quelque chose », lui répondit gentiment sa maman.

« Mais j'ai rangé ma chambre aujourd'hui ! » dit Mathilde.

« Bon, essaie de dormir maintenant, dit sa maman en l'embrassant, et nous chercherons Vieil Ours demain matin. »

Cybelle observa la pauvre Mathilde sanglotant sur son oreiller jusqu'au moment où, enfin, celle-ci s'endormit. Cybelle descendit alors du rebord de la fenêtre, sortit son petit bocal et versa les deux larmes de Vieil Ours sur les paupières fermées de Mathilde. Il y eut comme un petit scintillement d'étoiles et le tour de magie commença à opérer. Mathilde se mit à rêver. Elle voyait un vieux pneu, un

journal, des boîtes de conserve, des écorces d'orange, une couverture. Mais… c'était sa couverture et, là, enroulé à l'intérieur, il y avait un ours, avec de grosses larmes qui coulaient sur ses joues ! Vieil Ours était à la décharge à ordures !

Le lendemain matin, Mathilde se réveilla en sursaut et se rappela son rêve. Elle courut en bas dans la cuisine où sa maman préparait le petit déjeuner et elle lui raconta tout.

« Il faut que nous allions à la décharge ! Nous devons sauver Vieil Ours ! » s'écria Mathilde.

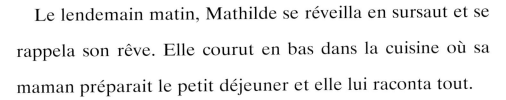

Maman essaya de lui expliquer que ce n'était qu'un rêve mais, Mathilde ne voulant rien entendre, elle décida de se rendre à la décharge.

Elles arrivèrent juste au moment où une grosse machine commençait à ramasser les détritus et à les verser dans un broyeur. Et là, suspendu au bord de la pelle de la machine, il y avait Vieil Ours !

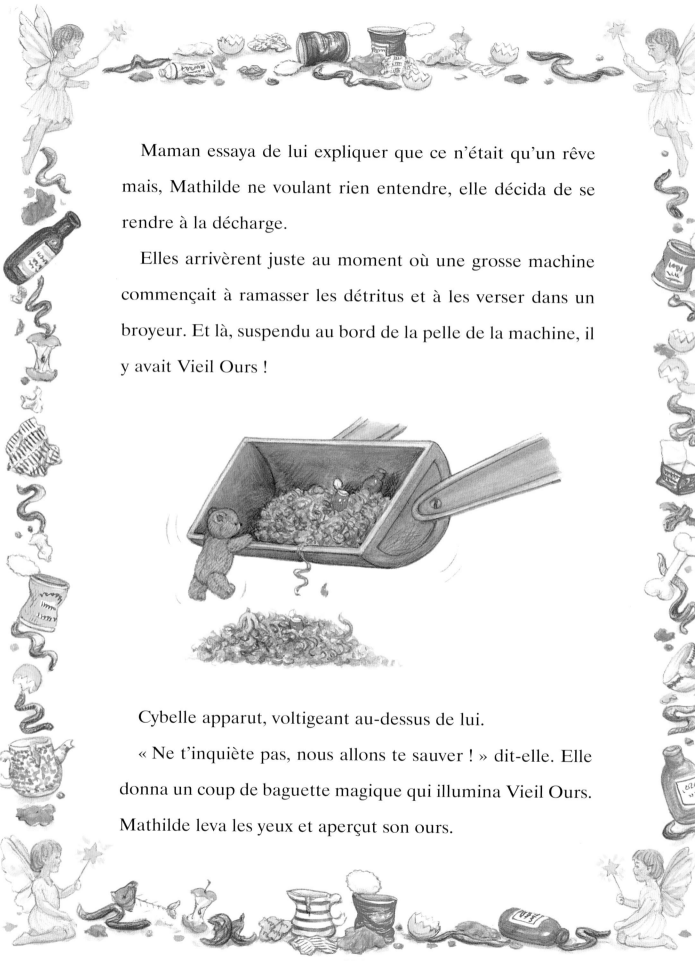

Cybelle apparut, voltigeant au-dessus de lui.

« Ne t'inquiète pas, nous allons te sauver ! » dit-elle. Elle donna un coup de baguette magique qui illumina Vieil Ours. Mathilde leva les yeux et aperçut son ours.

« Il est là ! s'écria-t-elle dans tous ses états, en pointant du doigt vers Vieil Ours. Il va être écrasé ! Maman, fais quelque chose, vite ! » Maman s'élança vers l'homme qui conduisait la machine en agitant les bras dans tous les sens.

Il arrêta la machine juste à temps.

Vieil Ours et Mathilde furent très vite réunis. Ils pleurèrent, non de chagrin cette fois-ci, mais de joie. Et, depuis cette aventure, la chambre de Mathilde est la chambre de petite fille la mieux rangée qu'il soit.

Marie, Marie, c'est l'heure de l'école

Marie, Marie, c'est l'heure de l'école,
Chante le gros tournesol.
Marie, Marie, il faut y aller maintenant,
Sonnent les clochettes d'argent.

Par un beau jour d'été

Par un beau jour d'été,

Dans mon panier jaune et vert,

J'ai mis une lettre de mon grand-père,

Et sur la route, elle est tombée.

Par malheur, je ne me suis pas aperçue

Que je l'avais perdue.

Une petite fille l'a prise

Et dans sa poche l'a mise.

Ma poule noire

Ma poule noire,

Ne veut plus me voir.

Ces derniers jours,

Elle ne m'a pas dit bonjour.

Elle est fâchée,

Je crois que je l'ai vexée !

Dans les champs

Dans les champs, il pousse du blé,

Dans les champs, il pousse de l'orge,

Quelqu'un sait-il comment ?

D'abord, le fermier sème des graines,

Puis il prend ses aises,

Tape des pieds et tape des mains,

Puis il tourne autour du champ.

Ding, dong

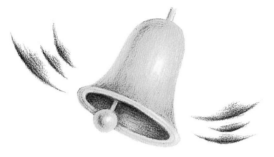

Ding, dong, ding, dong,

Néro est dans le puits !

Qui l'a mis ici ?

C'est le petit Denis.

Qui l'a repêché ?

C'est le petit Didier.

Quel vilain garçon

Celui qui a tenté de noyer ce chaton,

Qui n'est jamais méchant,

Et tue les souris pour plaire à Maman.

Mystères et boule de gomme

Faire danser son pouce

Connaissez-vous cet homme,

Qui danse sur la colline,

Se tortille et dandine ?

Mystères et boule de gomme !

Connaissez-vous cette dame,

Qui danse et fredonne,

Et sur la musique s'enflamme ?

Mystères et boule de gomme !

Connaissez-vous cette fille,

Qui danse avec ce gentilhomme,

Virevolte et sautille ?

Mystères et boule de gomme !

Connaissez-vous ce mouton,

Qui cabriole et s'époumone,

Et dans l'herbe fait des bonds,

Mystères et boule de gomme !

Connaissez-vous ce chien,

Qui caracole et bouillonne,

Et hurle sur le chemin ?

Mystères et boule de gomme !

383

FIN

Illustrations de :
Georgie Birkett, Stephanie Boey, Mario Capaldi, Dorothy Clark,
Kate Davies, Maggie Downer, Frank Endersby, Serena Feneziani,
Andrew Geeson, Piers Harper, Elaine Keary, Angela Kincaid, Jane Molineaux,
Claire Mumford, Rikki O'Neill, Pauline Siewart, Jessica Stockham, Linda Worrell.